THE OLD TESTAMENT NAMES OF GOD

A PERSPECTIVE

Wipf & Stock
PUBLISHERS
Eugene, Oregon

Wipf and Stock Publishers
199 W 8th Ave, Suite 3
Eugene, OR 97401

The Old Testament Names of God
By Lockyear, W. H.

ISBN: 1-57910-281-6
Publication date 9/30/1999

"And those who know Thy name

will put their trust in Thee

For Thou, O LORD, has not

forsaken those who seek Thee."

Psalm 9:10
(NAS)

CONTENTS

ACKNOWLEDGEMENTS

Many thanks and much appreciation to those behind the scenes who provided the support that made this book possible:

Bill, Sue and Beth for proofing early punctuation and spelling drafts.

Fred Emery for endless hours editing the several drafts.

Dr. Don Hagner for providing many words of encouragement and recommendations regarding the way to proceed.

Robbie Jones-Cook for patience beyond the call of duty in typing the final draft and ensuing corrections.

"Jinny" for great patience with her author husband. "It's taking forever."

INTRODUCTION

The documented study and detailing of the names of God is an individualistic endeavor with an approach suited to the writer's needs, desires and intents. An individual trained in theology proceeds in one manner. An member of the laity may well go another way. Neither approach is the more correct but each of the two documented points of view or perspectives contribute to the other and so are a blessing to all.

In the Perspective at hand, an individual with training as an engineer searches for names of God in the Old Testament Scriptures. As the search begins, it appears that a rather limited and finite number of names exist. These can be verified and cataloged and the search seemed complete. However, according to the applications of good engineering practices, it was early on realized there is much more to be done. A search of the literature, a thorough comparison of selected Scripture versions with one serving as a commentary on another, and detailed documentation of the findings has produced a unique compilation of facts from which have been extracted a significant inventory of the names of God in the OT.

Are all the names listed? No, no, no! Any effort to create such a list soon indicates that the listing must be conducted in phases. There is a quick list phase, mostly available from memory. It varies in length and thoroughness depending on the writer's familiarity with the Old Testament. Then there is a phase with a much more extensive register of names available from careful and detailed study, comparison of Scripture version materials and special preparation of details in cataloging. But this is not the end. There is a third phase of listings that will result from extended consideration of the literature, interpretation of English translations from the basic

Greek and Hebrew languages and even attention to such details as punctuation and word capitalization practices of the translators and editors.

The listings in this Perspective are detailed but are not exhaustive. It is fully realized that there are yet undiscovered appellations of deity to be found, verified and cataloged.

With a grasp of the possible trilogy of such a compilation arrangement of the names of God, the uniqueness of this Perspective is to be understood. It intends to include appellations from the simplest observation listings, but it also provides room for names yet to be discovered and verified.

FORWARD

“And they that know thy name will put their trust in thee: for thou, LORD, has not forsaken them that seek thee.” (Psa. 9:10.) “I will say of the LORD, He is my refuge and my fortress: my God; in him will I trust.” (Psa. 9:12.)

These and many other passages can be called upon to demonstrate the importance of divine names. They reveal to us vital truth about our relationship to God as One whose name we know and in whom we trust. And the question is asked, why study God’s name at all? Because, if we are to know Him better and ever trust Him more, we need to understand Him by His names.

These names, above every name, come in a marvelous variety. There is the generic appellation, Elohim, which corresponds to the English word God. Then there is the special name El that speaks of the great might and power of God. And there is His personal identity, Yahweh, which is translated into the English word LORD. These identifiers reveal something of His characteristics, nature and quality. Then, there are the large quantity of names that reveal something of His works and attributes.

Accepting the existence in Scripture of this massive quantity of words that reveal something of His character, we are also aware that even all of His appellations and definitions only begin to identify this One we call God, whom we are to trust. Verification of their applications as names needs to be established by their use in the Scriptures. Some names will be applied on many occasions. Other names will be used just a few times or will even be unique to a single passage and we want to know them all. We want to remember them, we want to study them, we want to itemize them for others to consider. To achieve this we will accept the challenge to locate and verify as many names as possible. We will write them and their support data down in a manner that will produce a repository of information called a perspective.

Now, we could simply prepare a mental list of the verified names. However, be aware of two considerations. First, we need to write down the names, for as someone has said, "if we can't write it, do we really know it?" Secondly, a listing by one individual is only that particular person's thinking. This effort is a perspective of one person's thoughts. Other perspectives are also needed in order to form a fuller picture of the names of God.

Thinking further about a perspective, it can be a simple list with no supporting detail; or it can be a collection of information, literature, research summaries, various Bible version comparisons, as well as a consideration of the application of similar materials from others. And from this perspective of detailed information, the desired end product, a summary list of names is produced.

A perspective, then, is a compilation of information. It must be arranged in a manner that allows it to assimilate additional data, with proper credits, to other contributors. Likewise, the perspective must be documented so that the collected material can be easily applied by others. Finally, remember—a perspective is really never finished. It always stands ready to accept new thinking additional facts, and corrections of old ideas demonstrated to be incorrect.

Along these lines of thought, this Manuscript or Perspective has been produced. Let us examine the internal requirements and utility of this document. First, it is to be limited to the names of God found in the Old Testament. All references and support materials are to be derived from or sustained by the Books of Genesis through Malachi.

Secondly, The King James Version[1] is used as the basic scripture for several reasons. This version has been accepted as, and bears the identification of, the AV (Authorized Version). The AV enjoys the test of time. The writings of many old masters and authors of yesteryear apply the AV as their primary referencing documentation. Of course the choice of the KJV as the basic study scripture does not limit the use of other Bible versions. The version of scripture which best meets the study needs of an individual should certainly be applied. Indeed, it is most advisable to compare versions, allowing one to serve as a commentary on another. The magnificent, more modern versions of scripture, including the NIV, NKJV, JER, TLB, BECK and many others have been used as strong supporting documentation in this detailed study.

There is another factor of importance as we consider use of the AV as the basic documentation. About the turn of the century, James Strong produced a concordance with a unique word identifier or numbering system (the Strong Reference Numbers = SRN). Each word in the Hebrew bible has been assigned a number. This numbering system provides the means to find Hebrew words and the equivalent English word quickly and accurately. It is common to identify either or both Hebrew and English words with this system allowing rapid reference to any given word without benefit of appreciable knowledge of the Hebrew language. This system is frequently used in this Perspective. When a word is identified by this method, it is referred to as being SRN identified or as a SRN term or word. Rapid application of the SRN system is made feasible by the use of a modified Macintosh IISi computer and "THE WORD processor"

[1] *THE HOLY BIBLE containing THE OLD AND NEW TESTAMENTS*, Authorized Version, Oxford University Press, New York © 1909, 1917. © renewed 1937, 1945 by Oxford University Press, New York.

software program.[2] In this system the Hebrew/English SRN identifiers are instantly located by the computer and displayed, as requested, for any word in the KJV.[3]

Regarding the abbreviations of the names of Bible Books: The applied computer software is designed to use a 3-digit system for book abbreviations. For example, Genesis is coded GEN., Deuteronomy is DEU., 1 Kings is 1KI. This method of abbreviation is followed in this manuscript using small letters. For example, Genesis is coded Gen., Deuteronomy is Deu., 1 Kings is 1Ki. (See attached table of Book Abbreviations).

Now consider the planned data to be produced by this Perspective. We, of course, will identify the located names of God. A discussion or argument is provided as to why the word—or compound of words—of particular interest is a name. Careful attention is given to the name locations(s). In many instances, multiple passages apply the name. This information is supplemented with appropriate passage comparison in various versions. The particular aspect of God's name that is highlighted or emphasized as well as the special human need that is met by it is discussed.

The gathered information has been assembled in manuscript form. Pertinent facts, applied impressions and concepts and unusual passages containing the names are all a part of this manuscript. In some cases, certain paramount side issues are presented. These are discussed when they have particular bearing on the located names. For instance, the possessive case is given special consideration, since the genitive is so prevalent in the Old Testament (i.e., The God of Abraham, The spirit of God and The spirit of Israel). Then the application of metaphors

---

[2] The WORD processor *Family of Products*, Version 5, Bible Research Systems, Austin, TX, Copyright 1982, 1990.
[3] The WORD processor Family of Products continues to be expanded, currently containing several Bible versions as well as the SRN system appllied to the NIV.

represented by the phrase "The LORD is my Shepherd" is carefully scrutinized.

Significant study effort is given to proper name (noun) capitalization and punctuation, as these communication mechanics affect the discovery or separation of the names of God in the KJV or other various scripture versions.

Before we conclude this thinking about the test contents and preparation, let us add a few comments about the Appendices, their purpose and relationship to the main text.

During the preparation of the text material, it became obvious that some information would be more advantageously presented in an appendix format rather than burdening the main text with extra detail, perhaps of limited interest to all readers. This material includes the explanation of the methods applied in the verification of some names. Also, the inclusion of comparison tables and extended justification arguments for certain names.

Since Appendices inclusion is only deemed necessary with certain names, not every chapter requires appendix representation. Also, in any given chapter some names need appropriate appendix support, while others do not. To lessen the Appendix identification confusion, the inclusion of appendix material (or not) is indicated on each Chapter Title Page where all names with appendix information support are marked with a star (*).

Then, in conclusion, a name is an appellation, title, identifier or epithet. This name may be a word or phrase (compound name) by which a person is known or called. The name points out some quality considered characteristic or descriptive of the person or thing. In regard to a name, Unger[4] writes,

---

[4] Merrill F. Unger, *The New Unger's Bible Dictionary*, R.K. Harrison editor, Moody Press, Chicago, Update Edition 1988, p. 903.

In Hebrew a name is sometimes used to signify the collected attributes or characteristics of the object named. The expression "name of God" indicates the entire administration of God by which He reveals Himself and His attributes to men; the glory and power of God displayed in nature (Psa. 8:1); God's revelation of Himself to His people (Zec. 10:12); and when God announces His mighty presence it is said, "Thy name is near" (Psa. 75:1).

Bible Book Abbreviations

Genesis	Gen.	Proverbs	Pro.
Exodus	Exo.	Ecclesiastics	Ecc.
Leviticus	Lev.	Song of Solomon	Son.
Numbers	Num.	Isaiah	Isa.
Deuteronomy	Deu.	Jeremiah	Jer.
Joshua	Jos.	Lamentations	Lam.
Judges	Jdg.	Ezekiel	Eze.
Ruth	Rth.	Daniel	Dan.
1 Samuel	1Sa.	Hosea	Hos.
2 Samuel	2Sa.	Joel	Joe.
1 Kings	1Ki.	Amos	Amo.
2 Kings	2Ki.	Obadiah	Oba.
1 Chronicles	1Ch.	Jonah	Jon.
2 Chronicles	2Ch.	Micah	Mic.
Ezra	Ezr.	Nahum	Nah.
Nehemiah	Neh.	Habakkuk	Hab.
Esther	Est.	Zephaniah	Zep.
Job	Job	Haggai	Hag.
Psalms	Psa.	Zechariah	Zec.
		Malachi	Mal.

The Old Testament Names of God

A Perspective

Chapter 1

Introduction To God

The very title of this book suggests that God has more than one name and appellation. To confirm this, turn to the first page of the Old Testament in an English Bible—to be more specific, a copy of the King James Version of the Scripture. Here we find, first of all, the word God; in fact in the first chapter of Genesis the term God appears at least once in all but five verses, while in six verses the word God appears twice. In the 31 verses of the chapter the word God is displayed 32 times. So, we ask, who is being called God? But something more, we find in Genesis 2:4 the compound name, the LORD God, and this term is used exclusively for the remainder of Chapter 2 and on into Chapter 3, where at verse 1 both this compound name and the unaugmented designation God appear in the same passage. Then these two names continue to appear, sometimes the compound and sometimes the word God used alone. After this, in Genesis 4:1, another variation appears, in that the title LORD takes over.

So far we have little information as to the nature, attributes and ways of the Persons bearing these designations. We are well aware from other sources of information that these names are all used to refer to the same deity, who is depicted here as our Creator, our Covenant maker, our Sovereign Judge, and our Redeemer. But how do these names relate to each other? What do the names mean or, more importantly, where did the names come from? Certainly it is well for us to investigate the many aspects of these names, because, as we will learn soon enough, there are an abundance of designations for God in the Bible. Each name reveals some aspect of the character of God and His dealings with mankind. In this study we will begin by considering the appellations that correctly are referred to as names. Then we will proceed to terms that are properly called titles rather than names, but always keeping in mind the fact that names and titles are very similar and that many times they get intermingled and confused in their application and usage.

Looking More Closely at the Name of God:

We have already referred to the first chapter of Genesis, where Scripture opens with the statement, "In the beginning God..." This word God is translated from the Hebrew term '^{e}lohim, meaning god in the general sense. '^{e}lohim, particularly in the singular, is also sometimes used to indicate men (Exo. 7:1), angels (Gen. 31:11), or heathen gods (Gen. 31:30). Normally the plural form '^{e}lohim is specifically used, as in Genesis 1, to refer to the Supreme Being.[1] That is, the Hebrew word '^{e}lohim has the standard ending of all masculine nouns in the plural. Modifying verbs and adjectives in each context may be singular even though this noun is plural. God=Elohim is a distinct term identifying or separating from others this Awesome One who makes Himself known by His great acts and works. Etymologically it contains within it the idea of creative and governing power, omnipotence and sovereignty. He has absolute authority as the Creator and Ruler of the universe. Elohim has the power and right to make covenants and as such stands in a covenant-relationship to His people. It is

---

[1] Demonstration of the plural tense of Elohim occurs consistently in the OT. For examples see Gen. 1. 36:7; Deu. 32:39; Isa. 45:5; Psa. 7:9, 57:2.

Elohim who keeps covenant (1Ki. 8:23) who is the foundation of His creatures' hope in all generations.[2] It is not the intent here to lay out a full description of God, for all the attributes of all the names and titles of this manuscript only begin to describe Him. And yet, even with His characteristics and ways so elaborate beyond our comprehension, we often times refer to Him simply by the generic or general name God with minimum attention being given to whom we are addressing. Indeed this divine name, although not the most frequent in Scripture, appears more than 2500 times in the Old Testament.

There are two other Hebrew terms also used to indicate god in the generic sense. These are the words El(Heb. 'el) and Eloah(Heb.'eloah). El=God is frequently used, especially where the great might and powerful nature of God is a distinctive (for example Num. 23:22 or Isa. 9:6). El either applied alone and meaning the One True God of Israel or in compound with other qualifying names such as in El Shaddai (God Almighty) or El Elyon (God Most High)—or even applied to angels(Psa. 89:6) or men(Eze. 32:21)—occurs some 227 times in the Old Testament. It should be noted that this name is in the singular. Eloah=God—some argue Eloah is the singular of 'elohim—is the least often used of the three general terms. It occurs 57 times in the OT It is found mostly in the book of Job in the dialogues between Job and Eliphaz and in Elihu's monologue. The word is also sparsely found in Deuteronomy, Chronicles, Psalms, Proverbs, Isaiah, Daniel, and Habakkuk.

---

[2] For example, Elohim made covenants with Noah (Gen. 6:13, 18 and Gen. 9:9), with all Flesh upon the Earth (Gen. 9:17), with Abram (Abraham) (Gen. 17:1-8), with Isaac (Gen. 26:24), with Jacob (Gen. 28:13, 14) with Moses (Exo. 6:2, 3, 4, 7, 8; Deu. 7:9) with David Psa. 111:5).

Now-Consider Another Word For God, Yahweh:

One encyclopedia[3] details the name Yahweh in this manner:

> In addition to the general names and qualifying names, God also bears a qualifying name that is His OT name par excellence, that characterizes Him as the living God of revelation and reconciliation in a particular way, and that thus comes to have the nature of a proper name. This is the name Yahweh…, which consists basically of the consonants YHWH.

Some English Bibles[4] transliterate His name Yahweh directly. Other English Bibles present the name Yahweh in the hybrid form Jehovah.[5] But most of our English Bibles translate Yahweh by the word LORD (all capital letters) to distinguish it from another English word of concern, Lord. Modern Christian literature in English has employed a hybrid word, Jehovah, which is a flawed rendering of Yahweh. But application of this hybrid word can be confusing. It is recommended that the transliteration Yahweh or the translation LORD be substituted where possible for the hybrid form. This practice is followed in this book. The Tetragrammaton YHWH or, with added vowel sounds, Yahweh, translated LORD, is by far the most frequent name of

---

[3] See *The International Standard Bible Encyclopedia*, Vol. 2; p. 497.

[4] The Jerusalem Bible

[5] The English form "Jehovah" arose by a latinized combination of the four consonants (YHWH) with the vowel points that the Masoretes used to show that they meant the reader to say " 'Adonai" when reading the Tetragrammaton. That is, they left the consonants for "Yahweh" in the text but put with them the vowels for " 'Adonai"-^{a},o,a. Though the older English versions sometimes used this hybrid form with compound names (such as Jehovah-Jireh [Gen. 22:14]), usually the divine name has been rendered "the LORD." The International Standard Bible Encyclopedia, Vol. 2; p. 507.

deity in the Old Testament, occurring 6823 times either alone or in a compound expression.

One writer[6] points out that, "in the name Yahweh (Jehovah) the personality of the Supreme is distinctly expressed. It is everywhere a proper name denoting the person of God, and Him only."

> For example, "the Jews may say 'The Elohim', the true God, in opposition to all the false gods; but he never says 'The Yahweh' for Yahweh is the sacred personal name of the true God. The Jew says again and again, 'My God' or 'My Elohim', but never 'My Yahweh', for when he says my God he means Yahweh. He speaks of the God (Elohim) of Israel but never the Yahweh of Israel, for there is no other Yahweh. He speaks of the living God, but never of the living Yahweh, for he cannot conceive of Yahweh as other than living."

When God wishes to make a special revelation of Himself, He used the name Yahweh, for as Yahweh He is especially the God of revelation to creatures who can apprehend and appreciate the Infinite—the becoming One. Elohim is the general name of God concerned with the creation and preservation of the world, that is, His works. As Yahweh, He is the God of revelation in the expression of Himself in His essential moral and spiritual attributes. For example, the marvelous passage of Exo. 34:5-7 reveals

---

[6] Stone, Nathan J. *Names of God.* Chicago: Moody Press, 1944. p. 20.

something of what is contained in that wonderful name. "And Yahweh descended in the cloud...and proclaimed Yahweh by name. And Yahweh passed by before him, and proclaimed, Yahweh, Yahweh, El, merciful and gracious, slow to anger, and abundant in lovingkindness and truth; keeping mercy for thousands, forgiving iniquity and transgression, and sin...."

To Make This Trio Of Primary Names Complete, Consider Adonai

The Hebrew words 'adon and 'adoni are respectively translated lord, and my lord, master and my master, husband, sir if applied to men. The latter word is changed to 'adonây when deity, the lord par excellence, is indicated, in the case of deity, the English word Lord is spelled with an initial capital letter, the other letters remaining as usual. The word 'adon is commonly applied to men out of respect for the person (Gen. 18:12, 40:1 and many others). Its application to God clearly implies dignity and dominion (Psa. 2:4; Isa. 7:7). Adonai, Lord, occurs frequently in the Old Testament (277 occurrences). As a substitute for the tetragrammaton YHWH the special form of the title, the Lord, occurs more than 6000 times.

Regarding the relationship of the Tetragrammaton YHWH and the word 'adonây: so holy and sacred was the name Yahweh to Israel that they feared to pronounce it. Perhaps that fear was based on Moses' injunction that they should not profane that name; the penalty was death imposed for blasphemy of the name (Lev. 24:16). To this day the name Yahweh is never vocalized in the synagogue or uttered by the people, the word 'adonây being the spoken substitute. Indeed, the original pronunciation of the name we call Yahweh, regarded as too sacred to be uttered, has been lost to this day. It is said by orthodox Jewry that one of the signs of true Messiahship will be the ability to pronounce this Name and convince Israel it is done correctly.

Think Now, How Are We Going To Sort These Names?

After some short time studying these names of God, it becomes readily apparent that some method of categorization of the vast amount of information must be developed if one is ever to track the tremendous detail available. How might this be done?

Scofield[7] in his notes arranges the names of deity in groups designated The Primary Names, The Compound Names with El=God and The Compound Names with Yahweh=LORD. Nine names are ordered among these three groups this way. There are three names listed in each group.

On the other hand, Andrew Jukes[8] leans toward arranging the names of deity in different categories pertaining to God's nature or His relationship to things or people as follows:

God's Nature	God's Relationship to Things or Persons
Elohim (Unchanging Love)	Adonai
Yahweh (Righteousness/Truth)	El Olam

---

[7] The Holy Bible, Scofield Reference Notes entitled Summary of the OT revelation of Deity, p. 983. C. 1909, 1917, Oxford University Press, New York; and The Holy Bible, New KJV Reference Notes entitled Deity (OT)-its revelation, Summary: p 1110, C 1967, Oxford University Press, New York, N.Y.

[8] Andrew Jukes, *The Names of God in Holy Scripture.* Forward by Charles R. Wood. Grand Rapids, Michigan, 1991. p. 109-110.

God's Nature	God's Relationship to Things or Persons
El Shaddai (Giver of Self for Others)	Yahweh Sabaoth
El Elyon (Most High yet He is of a kindred nature)	

It would be understood from the Jukes writings that the included names are only the ones he has considered to the date of his listing. He does not hint of other names that are yet to be considered. Therefore, the lists allow for other names under the two categories. Jukes simply does not consider them (for instance; El Hai, El Roi and others). On the other hand, Scofield places some limit on the names by his triad system. This is a detail to be considered. What shall be done with the other names?

In this study a modified application of the Scofield groupings is employed. Adherence to the so-called Primary names, because of their frequency of appearance in the Old Testament, is retained. However, the compound name groupings relating to both El and Yahweh are enlarged and modified as necessary to accommodate additional compounds. A selection of the Elohim compound names is also provided. These changes are discussed as they appear in the manuscript.

Look At The Names Of God With El=God

The literature[9] suggests that there are only three or four compound names with El=God. However, in excess of 34 compounds of this nature have been located. The

---

[9] Scofield, p. 983.

location process (and its limitations) applied in our search for the El=God compounds are explained in Appendix 1 of this document, where Table A.1.3 displays the 34 Compound Names with El. Table A.1.5, shown here and also in the Appendix, displays all the El compound names appearing 4 times or more in the OT. These are referred to as the "Prominent El Compound Names".

Table A.1.5

Prominent El Compound Names Appearing at least 4 Times in The OT

English Name	Hebrew Name	References
Almighty God	El Shaddai	Gen. 17:1; 28:3; 35:11; 43:14; 48:3; Exo. 6:3; Eze.10:5
Great God	El Gadowl	Deu. 10:17; Neh. 1:5; Job 36:26; Psa. 77:13; 95:3; Jer. 32:18; Dan. 9:4
Jealous God	El Quanna	Exo. 20:5; 34:14; Deu. 4:24; 5:9; 6:15; Jos. 24:19; Nah. 1:2
Mighty God	El Gibbor	Deu. 7:21; Neh. 9:32; Job 36:5; Psa. 50:1; Isa. 9:6; 10:21; Jer. 32:18
Most High God	El Elyon	Gen. 14:18, 19, 20, 22; Psa. 78:35; Isa. 45:15
Living God	El Hai	Jos. 3:10; Psa. 42:2; 84:2; Hos. 1:10
Terrible (Awesome) God	El Yare	Deu. 7:21; 10:17; Neh. 1:5; 9:32

Consider First The Name Almighty God:

God Almighty (Hebrew 'el-Shadday) appears in the Old Testament according to Strong's Concordance, only 7 times; however, the name Almighty, referred to God, appears 47 times. The El here is expressing the idea of God with might and power, exaltation and elevation, the Supreme Being. But look now at the other portion of this name, Shadday. The literature indicates that the root meaning of the word shadday is at variance. Some scholars argue that shadday is simply translated almighty, possibly producing the aforementioned concordance count. Stone[10] suggests that some scholars believe that a root meaning of "strong, powerful," or "to do violence," particularly to violate the laws of nature or the ordinary course of nature, is more accurate. But still other scholars more correctly feel that the derivation of shadday is from a different word altogether a word that appears 14 times in the Old Testament. This is the Hebrew word shad, translated "breast." Indeed it is interesting to note that both Nathan Stone[11] and Andrew Jukes[12] agree that shadday primarily means breasted, or more exactly a woman's breast, yielding the idea of one who nourishes, supplies and satisfies. Jukes[13] goes on to say that it probably is mothers who best understand this meaning. A baby is crying. Nothing can quiet the child. But the breast can. Indeed, the breast can give fresh life and nourishment. Stone comments,[14] "It is God as El who helps, but it is God as Shaddai who abundantly blesses with all manner of blessings of the breast." Jukes says,[15] "It is El Shaddai, the Pourer-forth, who pours Himself out for His creatures; who gives them His life-blood; and who sheds forth His spirit..."

---

[10] Stone, Nathan J. *Names of God*, Chicago: Moody Press, 1944. p. 33-35.
[11] Ibid. 10, p. 35.
[12] Andrew Jukes, *The Names of God in Holy Scripture*. Forward by Charles R. Wood. Grand Rapids, Michigan, 1991. p. 66-67.
[13] Ibid. 12, p. 67.
[14] Ibid. 10, p. 34.
[15] Ibid. 12, p. 69.

Nathan Stone sums it all up this way:[16] the name of God is seen to be the power or shedder-forth of blessings, the all-sufficient and the all bountiful One, for only an all-powerful One could be all sufficient and all bountiful.

> He is Almighty, because He is able to carry out His purposes and plans to their fullest and most glorious and triumphant completion. He is able to triumph over every obstacle and over all opposition; that is, He is sufficient for all these things. He is able to subdue all things to Himself. But the word able applied to God refers more than anything else to what He wants to be and do for man. So He is able to save to the uttermost. And He is able to do exceedingly abundantly above all that we ask or think. From all this it is felt that the name El Shaddai or God Almighty is much better understood as that El who is sufficient and all bountiful, the source of all blessing and fullness and fruitfulness.

On the other hand, Jukes reminds the reader that he has observed that the thought of fruitfulness is present wherever El Shaddai is spoken of. When Isaac sends Jacob away to Padan-aram to seek a wife, it is El Shaddai that he calls upon, saying, "God Almighty bless thee, and make thee fruitful and multiply thee, that thou mayest be a multitude of people." (Gen. 28:3).

We also read of Jacob, "And God said unto him, 'I am God Almighty: be fruitful and multiply; a nation and a company of nations shall be of thee and kings shall come

---

[16] Ibid. 10, p. 36.

out of thee' " (Gen. 35:11). It is to God Almighty that this same Jacob looks to save his children when he hears that Simeon is detained in Egypt and that his beloved Benjamin is required to go there (Gen. 43:14). And in his blessing upon his sons it is under this name, "Almighty," that he blesses Joseph with "blessings of the breasts and of the womb." (Gen. 49:25). The name is ever linked with fruit and fruitfulness, even in cases where it is the loss of fruit and fruitfulness, even in cases where it is the loss of fruit that is lamented. Thus Naomi twice speaks of her sons' death as "affliction from the Almighty." (Rth. 1:20-21).[17]

Andrew Jukes summarizes his El Shaddai discussion in this manner: "It is 'El Shaddai,' 'God Almighty' who works His will in His elect by giving Himself to them, that they may give themselves to Him and then by Him be blessed to others, in and by that circumcision or self-Judgment, which makes them vessels, through which He can minister His own fullness."[18]

Consider The Second Prominent EL Compound Name, Great God:

Great God (Hebrew, 'el gadol). According to the *BDB Hebrew and English Lexicon*, the word gadowl or its derivatives is used in the compound name Great God, where God=El, in only 2 verses in the OT. This is remarkable, since the English word "great", translated from 44 different Hebrew words, appears 673 times in the OT. These 44 Hebrew words are used to indicate excellent in qualitative comparisons such

---

[17] Ibid. 12, p. 73-74.
[18] Ibid. 12, p. 81.

as great (in any sense) or exceeding (as in surpassing), and, most often, they are used as the comparative of "much". Quantity can also be expressed such as great in numbers, abundance and size. In this study, however, attention is focused on the compound name formed by adding the single Hebrew word gadol to the divine name El. As stated, there are only 2 verse applications with this name. If the limitation of El=God is broadened to also include Elohim=God, the number of compound names of course increases. We will encounter the Elohim compounds later in this chapter. Or if some leniency is exercised with definitions of words like "great" and "mighty", the count will vary, since these two words are occasionally interchanged. For example, compare Deu. 7:21 and Deu. 10:17. In the first verse the English word "mighty" is translated from the Hebrew word gadol. In the second verse the English word "great" is translated from the same Hebrew word.

In any case, the intent in this compound name is to couple the two words great and God together in order to amplify and enhance the description of the magnitude of the greatness of God. Not only is He known by the simpler name El, which in itself means power and strength, but He is the "exceedingly great and mighty power and strength."

Now Look at the Third Prominent Name, Jealous God:

Jealous El (Heb. 'el quanna') appears in the OT Scriptures according to Strong's Concordance only 7 times. A related expression occurs in the writings of Nahum, where this prophet says that God (El) is jealous (Nah. 1:2). In five of the other 6 cases (those appearing in Exo. 20:5; 34:14; Deu. 4:24; 5:9; 6:15) the particular writer is relating to the covenant given by God to the people wherein the people are instructed or reminded to obey the law that demanded that the people have no other gods than Yahweh. In the case of the occurrence in Jos. 24:19, that great leader was presenting his last charge to Israel before his death. He too reminds the people that they must fear and serve the LORD and put away all heathen gods that they or their father have previously worshipped, because the LORD is a jealous and holy God; He will not tolerate transgressions, especially idolatry.

Scripture tells us that His very name is Jealous (Exo. 34:14). Like every other name of God, this one is revealed to meet a specific need of the creature, namely, the constant battle against idolatry. It was limited to the special case relating to the giving of the Covenant, particularly the first commandment. However, application continues today because of idolatry among His people.

Consider the Fourth Prominent Name, Mighty God:

Mighty God: Some degree of attention must be given to the phrase Mighty God, for programming the computer.[19] Simply to identify the verses that contain the English phrase, Mighty God, falls short of providing necessary information as to whether the particular phrase is a compound name of God where God=El. The computer indicates that there are nine verses that contain the English translation Mighty God. Three of

---

[19] Mac IISi Computer with "THE WORD processor" system of software, Bible Research Systems, Austin, TX. CR 1990.

these passages[20] contain Hebrew idioms that are translated into the English expression Mighty God in the KJV, but in other more modern translations (such as NIV and NEB) these idioms are translated into "mighty One." Another four[21] in the group of nine are translated with the English expression mighty God, where the Hebrew terms gadol or gibbor, meaning mighty, are combined with El to formulate the expression mighty God. The eighth expression (SRN 6697) applies the Hebrew idiomatic word tsur with El to form the expression Rock, referring to the mighty God in the more modern versions. But in the KJV the idiom is translated mighty God.

These eight expressions, translated into the English Mighty God (=El) are all appropriately considered names of God(=El).

The ninth Hebrew phrase translated into the English compound Mighty God is a special case. Consider the passage Psa. 50:1: the word 'el is applied as an adjective modifying the word God (Elohim) and we have literally "God, God." The word 'el is not applied here as an El name as in the other eight compounds above and is not considered a compound name of God(=El).

There is another factor critical to a study of the compound names of God that should be observed here. The idioms producing the compound names mighty God(=El) in the KJV (outlined in footnote 20) produce mighty One or Rock in many of the modern Scripture versions. On the other hand the very same idiomatic Hebrew words in the

---

[20] Hebrew idiomatic expressions for Mighty God, Gen. 49:24; and Psa. 132:2, 5.
[21] Hebrew expressions for mighty God, Deu. 7:21; Isa. 9:6; Isa. 10:21; Jer. 32:18.

KJV, in the group of verses outlined in footnote[22], are translated mighty One in the KJV. So it will make some considerable difference which version is used in name study. A summary table of these terms is provided in Chapter 13.5.

Consider the Fifth Prominent Name, Most High God:

The name El Elyon (Heb. 'el 'elyon) appears in the Old Testament Scripture, according to Strong's Concordance, as Most High God(=El) only 5 times; however, Most High referring to God but not explicitly in an El compound name appears 33 times. It is the El compound Prominent Names we are seeking to verify and understand as to meaning, so only the five passages containing this compound are of interest here. The El is expressing the idea of God's might, power, exaltation and elevation, and that He is the Supreme Being.

As the Most High God, He is referred to as the Possessor or Creator of heaven and earth (Gen. 14:19, 22). Jukes[23] indicates the word 'elyon is also sometimes applied to things and persons. When this occurs, the special and distinctive sense of the word is maintained; that is, the thing or person spoken of, is the highest in the order of like natures in the series. For instance, the uppermost basket in a tier of baskets (Gen. 40:17), the nation high above all nations (Deu. 26:19) or the king higher than the other kings (Psa. 89:27). The application of Elyon or Most High to God reveals that though He is the Highest, there are others below Him, endowed by Him with like nature, and

---

[22] Hebrew expressions for Mighty One, Isa. 1:24; 30:29; 49:26; 60:16.

[23] Andrew Jukes, *The Names of God in Holy Scripture*, p. 88.

therefore in someway related to Him. Since He is the Elyon in the order, He has the power to rule and turn the members as He wills, should they be disobedient or seek to exalt themselves against Him.

> ...and He doeth according to His will, in the armies of heaven, and among the inhabitants of the earth: and none can stay His hand, or say unto Him, What doest thou? *His* dominion is an everlasting dominion, and His kingdom is from generation to generation: (Dan. 4:35 and 34).

Questions arise regarding the ones below Him with like natures. Who are they? First, let us list angels as "sons of God" (Psa. 89:6 and Job 38:7) with a nature descending from Him. (Job 1:6.) But there are others, who for a little while are lower than the angels, who are also children of the Most High. (See Psa. 8:4-6.) Men are called "gods" and children of the Most High in Psa. 82:6. Scripture plainly reveals that man was created in the image of God. (Gen. 1:27.)

Indeed man is a son of Most High—a fallen son, nevertheless a son; and because he is a son, never to be forsaken by Him from whom He came. There is surely peril in this high truth, yet there is also rich blessing. The Most High cannot deny Himself, so, even if we forget our relationship to Him, He can and surely will overthrow and overturn and overcome us, until He has again His place in us for our blessing. For He is the "God of gods and Lord of lords."(Psa. 136:2-3).

The Melchizedek experience with Abram introduced, for the first time the name El Elyon (Gen. 14:18). But in every Scripture passage where the name occurs, its special import is the same. It reveals the relationship of God to all. Even to the world outside the election, where people either cannot or will not judge themselves, the Most High even through Judgment will carry out in them His own purposes. Every reference to the name repeats this teaching.

Now Consider the Sixth Prominent Name, The Living God:

The Living God (Hebrew 'el chay) appears in the Old Testament Scriptures, according to Strong's Concordance, 15 times in 9 books. Four of these times, the word God in the compound name is translated from the Hebrew term 'el. This establishes the El compound name but also limits the prominence to the four applications. Nine times, the word God in the compound is translated from the Hebrew 'elohim, and twice the compound expression uses Eloah, translated into the English word God. (The El chay compound variations and their locations are listed in Table 1.) It should also be mentioned that the word chay, translated living, is not only applied as an epithet of God, but the word chay is also used as an adjective characterizing man, animals, and even vegetation. Sometimes the word is applied to fresh or running waters and groups of people.

Table 1.1

Strong's Concordance of the Name, Living God

Reference	Living (SRN)*	Deity (SRN)*	Deity Name
Deu. 5:26	Living (2416)	God (430)	Elohim
Jos. 3:10	Living (2416)	God (410)	El
1Sa. 17:26	Living (2416)	God (430)	Elohim
1Sa. 17:36	Living (2416)	God (430)	Elohim
2Ki. 19:4	Living (2416)	God (430)	Elohim
2Ki. 19:16	Living (2416)	God (430)	Elohim
Psa. 42:2	Living (2416)	God (410)	El
Psa. 84:2	Living (2416)	God (410)	El
Isa. 37:4	Living (2416)	God (430)	Elohim
Isa. 37:17	Living (2416)	God (430)	Elohim
Jer. 10:10	Living (2416)	God (430)	Elohim
Jer. 23:36	Living (2416)	God (430)	Elohim
Dan. 6:20	Living (2416)	God (426)	Eloah
Dan. 6:26	Living (2416)	God (426)	Eloah
Hos. 1:10	Living (2416)	God (410)	El

*SRN-abbreviation for Strong's Reference Number (See Chapter 2, p. 29)

El	4x
Elohim	9x
Elah	2x

Total	15

Lastly, Consider the Prominent Name, Terrible (awesome)

Terrible El ('el yare) is a compound name of God wherein the word terrible refers to the profound respect or wonder inspired by the greatness, superiority and grandeur of God. The word terrible also contains an aspect of reverence mingled with love. In our language today we simply say God is "awesome." Further suggestions of the meaning of the word terrible are provided when it is noticed in the El=God verses that the epithetical name terrible (awesome) is accompanied in every case with the word great or mighty.

The computer indicates there are 51 verses in the OT where 'el yare is translated into the English word "terrible". In ten of these verses, the word terrible is used in an epithetical compound name for God where the deity portion of the compound is either El, Elohim or Yahweh. Because we are only concerned with El compounds at this time, we sort out of the ten possible candidates the five that are classed as El compound names. The five are: Deu. 7:21; 10:17; Neh. 1:5; 9:32; and Dan. 9:4.

Now Look at the Elohim=God names:

The approach used to locate the El=God names has been straight-forward. All 227 El possibilities were first examined. Then the 34 compounds were identified exclusive of the personal pronoun names, and finally the Prominent Compounds, those appearing four or more times in the OT, were displayed. A similar approach to the Elohim compound names is beyond the scope of this study, since there are some 2500 passages containing the word Elohim. Not all verses containing the word Elohim apply to God, since a few applications of elohim referring to other than the One True God of Israel occur. Personal pronouns with Elohim also are in the 2500 compound mix.

Two approaches have been applied to identify some of the Elohim compounds. Table 1.2, entitled El / Elohim Compound Name Similarities, displays a group of compound names common to both El and Elohim. This information was derived using El compounds as a guide. Table 1.2 also displays two interesting examples of verse phraseology wherein two phrases in the same verse (Psa. 118:28 and Isa. 46:9) contain identical modifiers of the word God, with the initial phrase translating the word God from El and the second from Elohim.

Secondly the outline of Elohim names provided in the *Theological Wordbook*[24] have been included here for consideration by the reader. The writers of the *Wordbook* make it plain that the occurrences of the term 'elohim are far too numerous to treat in entirety. These descriptive words and epithets really serve as compound name titles and indicate some of the various titles by which God's people came to know Him.

The compound Elohim Names in the *Wordbook* are presented in text form. We will place some of them in table form (Table 1.3) for more rapid observation.

---

[24] R. Laird Harris, Editor, *Theological Wordbook of the Old Testament*, Vol. 1, Moody Press, Chicago, 1980, p. 45-46.

Table 1.2

El / Elohim Compound Name Similarities

EL Compound	Reference	Elohim Compound	Reference
God that is above	Job 31:28	God above all gods	2Ch. 2:5
The everlasting God	Gen. 21:33	The everlasting God	Isa. 40:28
the glory of God	Psa. 19:1	the glory of God	Pro. 25:2
the goodness of God	Psa. 52:1	God is good (to Israel)	Psa. 73:1
a great God	Deu. 10:17	the great God	Neh. 8:6
God of heaven	Psa. 136:26	God of heaven	Gen. 24:3,7
most high God	Gen. 14:18	most high God	Psa. 78:56
God that is holy	Isa. 5:16	holy God	Jos. 24:19
a just (righteous) God	Isa. 45:21	righteous(just) God	Psa. 7:9
the living God (4x)	Jos. 3:10	the living God (9x)	Deu. 5:26
a mighty God	Deu. 7:21	the (mighty 410) God	Psa. 50:1
spirit of God	Job 33:4	Spirit of God (12x)	Gen. 1:2
God of the spirits--	Num. 16:22	God of the spirits--	Num. 27:16
God of truth	Deu. 32:14	God of truth (2x)	Isa. 65:16
Thou art my God 410	Psa. 118:28	Thou art my God(430)	Psa. 118:28
I am God(410)	Isa. 46:9	I am God(430)	Isa. 46:9

Table 1.3

Elohim Compound Names in the OT
(A partial listing from the *Theological Wordbook of the OT*)

Reference	Compound Name	Reference	Compound Name
Isa. 45:18	God, Former of the Earth	Jer. 10:10	Living God
Jon. 1:9	God of Heaven Who Made the Sea & Dry Land	Deu. 5:26	Living God Speaking Out of the Midst of the Fire
Isa. 54:5	"The God of the Whole Earth"	1Sa. 6:20	this Holy Lord God
1Ki. 20:28	God of the Hills	Jer. 23:23	God of Nearness
Jer. 32:27	God of All Flesh	Psa. 57:2	God Most High
Isa. 37:16	God of All the kingdoms of the Earth	Isa. 65:16	God of Truth (2x)
Neh. 2:4, 20	God of Heaven	Isa. 30:18	God of Justice
Gen. 24:7	Yahweh God of Heaven	Isa. 40:28	Everlasting God
2Ch. 20:6	God in the Heaven	Deu. 10:17	God is God of gods
Gen. 24:3	the Lord God of the Heaven and the God of the Earth; the LORD, the God of heaven, and the God of the earth		

Tables 1.2 and 1.3 illustrate the abundance of the Elohim compounds in the OT There are dozens of the more simple compound phrases, like God of Heaven, or Everlasting God. There are also many titles pertaining to the Savior God. Included are those in which God is linked to individuals whom He has called. Examples include "Their God" (Gen. 17:8), "The God of Abraham" (Gen. 26:24) and "The God of Abraham...and the God of Isaac" (Gen. 28:13). The *Workbook* indicates there are more than one-hundred such titles in the OT Similarly, there are many titles linking God to the whole or some portion of Israel. For example, "God of the Armies of Israel"(1Sa. 17:45) and "God of Jerusalem" (2Ch. 32:19).

Finally, Consider the Yahweh(=God) Compound Names:

The above discussion of the compound names relating to El (God) and Elohim (God) include the names that have been located and identified knowing full well there are yet others undetected. However, upon approaching the Yahweh (Jehovah) compound names, a somewhat different situation exists in that a distinction needs to be made between certain of the compounds. This is to set apart the redemptive-relationship-compound-names from the other names having to do more with the nature attributes of Yahweh. This is accomplished by placing in separate chapters the discussions of Jehovah-Jirah and the other seven Jehovah compound names particularly relating to Yahweh's (Jehovah's) relationship to man wherein every need of man from his lost state to the end have been met by God. The compounds having to do with the nature and character of the LORD are also treated in a separate chapter of this manuscript.

The Old Testament Names of God

A Perspective

Chapter 2

Contents

Applications

In Chapter 1 we examined the general or generic names of God, El and Elohim, in some detail. An understanding of some of the attributes of God are observable in the epithets and modifiers of the generic names. El has certain characteristics different from those of Elohim; they are two distinct names, but there is One God. We also touched on the names Yahweh (LORD) and Adonai (Lord). Now we will look in more detail at the applications of these names and their relationships to each other.

We will find it beneficial to keep in mind the attributes of El and Elohim that were discussed in Chapter 1 as we look at the applications of these names. It can be seen that either name appears alone in a multiple of uses. For instance, El stands alone in Gen. 14:18,19, 20 and 22. Here He is described as the Supreme, most high God. Or again we see Him as the mighty God in Isaiah 9:6. The name El (=God) alone and with epithetical enhancement is very common in the OT.

Looking at the name Elohim, we can cite many applications where God is referred to in stand alone fashion. See, for example, the many classic references to Elohim the Creator throughout Genesis 1 or the multiple appearances of the word Elohim in Exo. 3:6. These and many other verses contain references to Elohim. Of course the name Elohim is not without enhancement. For instance, Jeremiah 10:10 calls Him not only God but the "living" God. Psalm 7:11 speaks of God (=Elohim) as the judge. Joshua refers to Elohim as a holy God (=Elohim), (Jos. 24:19).

Not only do these examples illustrate stand alone names, but frequently we find both names adjacent to each other in the same verse. For instance, consider adjoining names like, "...the Lord thy God (= Elohim), He is God (=Elohim), the faithful God (=El)" (Deu. 7:9). Again we find "...O LORD God (=Elohim) of heaven, the great and terrible God (=El)..." (Neh. 1:5). Adjoining phrases referring to Elohim and El in the same verse are common. Look at Gen. 35:11, "And God (=Elohim) said unto him, I am God (=El) Almighty..." or Deu. 4:24, "For the LORD thy God (=Elohim) is a consuming fire, even a jealous God (=El)." So it can be seen that the two names frequently complement each other or are close together in the same verse. Indeed, out of the more than 2500 times the name Elohim appears in the OT; 42 times the name El will also appear at least once in the same Elohim passage.

The third basic generic Hebrew term for the true God of Israel, 'eloah, is not as prevalent as 'el and 'elohim, but should be remembered. Eloah is usually applied to Israel's God but the word also appears in connection with false gods (2 Ch. 32:15; Dan 11:37). This name is not known to occur in combination with other divine names; however, it does appear in compound names like "...the God (=Eloah) of Jacob; (Psa. 114:7) or "God (=Eloah) of forces" (Dan. 11:38). Actually, the Daniel passage contains the name Eloah twice. The name is also found in a couplet with the noun rock (Psa. 18:31). There Eloah appears to be synonymous with Elohim and can be used synonymously with the name Yahweh.

We also have been introduced to the names of Yahweh (LORD) and Adonai (Lord). What of the interrelationship of these names?

Yahweh, the proper noun, is the only personal name of Israel's God. There are many compound names with Yahweh, but the name Yahweh alone is the self-appointed identifier of the only true God. The orthodox Jew will not write the name Yahweh, substituting the appellations 'adōnāy or 'elohim. The word 'adōnay is also used as a royal title or a plural of majesty, excellence or intensity; therefore it is important to distinguish between the word usage when it appears as the name of the Lord, and when it is used as the title of plurality. The terms 'adōn, and 'adōnāy are distinguished from one another in their translation into English stylistically as LORD and Lord, respectively (Psa. 97:5 and Isa. 1:24). We recall one other point: in the postpatriarchal literature the name of El is clearly interchangeable with Yahweh.

In summary, all of these names can be translated into the English name God, but since the English fails to differentiate among them, their English separation is very difficult. This is illustrated in Table 2.1 and in the application examples.

Table 2.1

The English Word God

Hebrew	Meaning	Translated English	SRN *	Reference
'el	great, power, mighty strength the True God of Israel, used of a false deity, singular in form	God of Israel god (generic name)	410	Gen. 14:18 Gen. 36:11 Exo. 34:14
'elohim	the Supreme God (always plural in form) also used of false gods, angels, men	God of Israel gods (generic name)	430	Gen. 1:1 Deu. 10:17 etc.
'eloah	a deity, the True God, idea of might, strength, singular in form	God god (generic name)	433	Psa. 114:7 Dan. 11:37
'adōn	sovereign, lord, master, owner husband, angels, courteous form of address (Sir)	lord, Lord LORD	113	Psa. 97:5 Gen. 18:2
'adōnāy	proper name of God only; (always plural in form)	God my Lord	136	Isa. 1:24 Hab. 3:19
'adōnay	royal title (to be carefully distinguished from divine title	my lords	113	1Sa. 29:8
YHWH	Tetragrammaton, usually vocalized Yahweh. It is a proper noun as the personal name of Israel's God	God the LORD	3069	Gen. 2:4, etc.

*SRN Strong's Reference Number
All the original Hebrew words are treated in their alphabetical Hebrew order, and are numbered regularly from the first to the last, each being known throughout by its appropriate number.

Examples of the Usage of these Words in the Scripture:

1. Consider the name El (used as a stand along name):

> Num. 12:13 reads: "And Moses cried unto the LORD (SRN 3068), saying, heal her now, O God (SRN 410), I beseech thee."

If we substitute for the above SRN indicators the appropriate names of God and expand the meanings of these names, we have the following:

Moses cried unto Yahweh (*the personal name of Israel's true God)* saying, heal her now, O El *(addressing the great and mighty One of Israel with His generic name)* I beseech thee.

> Num. 23:8 reads: "How shall I curse, whom God (SRN 410) hath not cursed? or how shall I defy, whom the LORD (SRN 3068) hath not defied?"

Again if we substitute for the SRN indicators the appropriate names of God and expand the meanings of these names, we have the following:

How shall I curse, whom El *(identifying the great and mighty One of Israel with His generic name)* hath not cursed? Or how shall I defy, whom Yahweh *(Identifying the true God of Israel by his personal name)* hath not defied?

2. Now Consider the Name El: (used in a compound name):

> Gen. 28:3 reads: "And God (SRN 410) Almighty bless thee, and make thee fruitful, and multiple thee, that thou mayest be a multitude of people."

Performing the same substitutions and expansions as before, we have:

And El Shadday *(not just God but emphatically Almighty God)* bless thee, and make thee fruitful, and multiply thee, that thou mayest be a multitude of people.

> Gen. 14:22 reads: "And Abram said to the king of Sodom, I have lift up mine hand unto the LORD (SRN 3068), the most high (SRN 5945) God (SRN 410), the possessor (SRN 7069) of heaven and earth."

Performing the substitutions and expansions we have:

And Abram said to the king of Sodom, I have lifted up mind hand unto Yahweh *(identifying the true God of Israel by His personal name)*, El Elyon, *(against not just God but the most high God, the Supreme One)*.

Then the writer, desiring to further elevate El (if this be possible), adds the descriptive phrase or epithet Qoneh shamayim va'aretz *(the possessor of heaven and earth)*. Certainly El with Elyon forms a compound name. Likewise, the total phrase, El the possessor of heaven and earth, can be considered a compound.

3. In similar manner consider Elohim as a stand alone name:

> Gen. 1:4 reads: "And God (SRN 430) saw the light, that it was good: and God (SRN 430) divided the light from the darkness."

Now, performing the usual substitutions and expansions we have:

And Elohim *(God is identified by His generic name, Elohim, which is plural in form, suggesting the trinity, yet One in creative purpose)* saw the light, that it was good: and God *(the Supreme Creator known by the generic name Elohim)* divided the light from the darkness.

Twice God is referred to by His generic name Elohim. Elohim saw the light and Elohim divided the light, two independent actions, each applying the stand alone name Elohim.

4. Now consider the name Elohim in compound:

> Gen. 24:7 reads: "The LORD (SRN 3068) God (SRN 430) of heaven, which took me from my father's house, and from the land of my kindred, and which spake unto me, and that sware unto me, saying, Unto thy seed will I give this land; he shall send his angel before thee, and thou shalt take a wife unto my son from thence."

The usual substitutions and expansions will be made, but first consider comments about this peculiar yet very frequently[25] appearing compound name, "LORD God." We have been told that the name Yahweh, translated into the English word LORD, is a proper noun, being the personal name of the true God of Israel. But we also need to know that this name carries with it the idea of a God with attributes including love, truth and righteousness. Yahweh hates evil and judges wickedness and iniquities wherever they are found, yet He loves the sinner. He is just and holy, pursuing man until His creature is brought to Himself in salvation.

Briefly reviewing the name Elohim, who describes Himself as the great "I AM," we remember that His attributes also include love. Having a covenant relationship with

---

[25] The compound name LORD God appears 519 times in the OT

his creatures, He cares for and works on behalf of His fallen creation. He overcomes all hindrances and His will prevails, whatever the obstacle, never to forsake His own.

Now, substituting these ideas in the basic verse we have:

Yahweh *(the savior, the One who loves truth and righteousness, hates sin but loves the sinner) and Elohim the Creator, (the One who establishes His covenant with His creatures and prevails to overcome all hindrances, Who will never leave His creatures nor forsake them, indeed, the very God of the heavens)* which took me from my father's house and from the land of my kindred, and which spake unto me, and that swear unto me saying, 'Unto they seed will I give this land;' he shall send his angel before thee, and thou shalt take a wife unto my son from thence.

Notice that we have the dual name here in this compound. We can read it was Yahweh Elohim of the heavens or Yahweh, Elohim of the heavens, that performed the listed actions.[26] Surely the meaning is very similar, but the compound name structure between the two is different. The compound name may be, "The LORD, the God of heaven," or "the Lord God of heaven."

5. Now let us proceed to the appearance of Yahweh, El and Elohim together in a single verse:

Deu. 10:17 reads: "For the LORD (SRN 3068) your God (SRN 430) is God (SRN 430) of gods (SRN 430), and Lord (SRN 113) of lords (SRN

[26] In a survey of nine Scripture versions, it was observed that six are written with a break between the words The LORD and the phrase, the God of heaven. The other three versions read continuously, The LORD God of heaven.

> 113), a great God (SRN 410), a mighty, and a terrible, which regardeth not persons, nor taketh reward."

This verse presents interesting word studies, because at first count, there are no less than six designations of deity: Yahweh, Elohim (twice), El, Adonai and heathen gods. Yet the verse uses only four different Hebrew divine appellations or SRN terms.

First, let us perform the Hebrew substitutions for the English words addressing deity:

> For Yahweh your Elohim is Elohim of elohims, and Adonay of 'adons, a great El, a mighty, and a terrible, which regardeth not persons, or taketh reward.

Four times the English word God or gods appears, but with three different meanings. First, we have the divine identification followed by two superlatives: *Yahweh your Elohim is Elohim of elohims (or Yahweh the savior, the One who loves truth and righteousness, your Creator, who will never leave His creatures nor forsake them. He is the Supreme One above all other elohims or gods) and '<u>adonay</u> of '<u>adons</u>.* And again in the next phrase, "*a great and mighty El", we have the generic word for God, El.* So we have Elohim, elohims and El, all spoken of as God or gods, but certainly with varying significance.

6. As a final example, consider:

Deu. 4:24 reads: "For the LORD (SRN 3068) thy God (SRN 430) is a consuming fire, even a jealous God (SRN 410)."

If we substitute for the above SRN indicators the appropriate names of God and expand the meanings of these names we have the following: For *Yahweh (the name of Israel's true God), Elohim (the Supreme One the Creator)* is a consuming fire, even a jealous *El (the great and mighty One of Israel, the Creator referred to by His generic name.)*

This chapter illustrates some of the difficulties to be expected during in-depth Biblical word study. Our English usage falls short of Hebrew so many times when it comes to speaking of God. When someone says, "O God," who is being addressed? God=El, or God=Elohim, or god (=some false deity). Sometimes it may make little difference, but when we remember the meanings behind El, Elohim and 'el we become aware of the significance of what is being said.

In the following chapters we will find many problems with word definition, but the study is well worth any effort, because "The knowledge of God is more essential for the Christian, and indeed for all the world, than the knowledge of anything else, yes, of all things together."[27]

---

[27] Names of God, Nathan Stone, Moody Press, Chicago, p. 7.

The Old Testament Names of God

A Perspective

Chapter 3

Contents

In Genesis 1:26 God said, "Let us make man in our image, after our likeness..." It was Elohim who spoke and acted, creating the crowning creation of all the creatures He had made. N. Stone reminds us that the name Elohim displays a connotation of creative and governing power, of omnipotence and sovereignty. And truly, in the referenced verse as well as in the other verses of Genesis 1, we see that it is Elohim who by His mighty power creates the vast universe, who speaks and it is done, who brings into being what was not, and by whose word the worlds were framed so that things which are seen were not made of things which do appear. By these very facts He is constituted possessor and ruler of heaven and earth, whose presence cannot be confined by space, and whose power does not need man's aid, for through His great will and power all things and nations have their very being[28].

It is obvious from the Scripture account that after Elohim made man it was His intent to deal with his crowning creation in a very special manner. When He begins to do so he is identified by a different name. In Genesis 2:4 He is called LORD God, Yahweh Elohim[29]. Yahweh is the name which God uses to reveal Himself in His special relationship to man. In this identity God, as Yahweh, begins to communicate to His creation His attributes of holiness, hatred and Judgment of sin, and His love for and redemption of sinners through His appropriate sacrificial plan.

---

[28] Stone, Nathan J. (*Names of God*) Chicago: Moody Press, 1944, p.12

[29] The reader is reminded that in this text the Hebrew name Yahweh, or the LORD, is applied in lieu of the hybrid word Jehovah.

Yahweh, then, is distinctly the appellation of God associated with redemption. In this redemptive relationship to man Yahweh has many compound names referring to redemption names that reveal Him as meeting every need of man from the initial redemptive act to the time when man is at home with God in eternity. It is the intent here to examine these Yahweh-compound names seeking to obtain insight as to their meaning and significance as they make clear the redemptive relationship of God to man.

Some say that there are seven and some argue that there are eight Yahweh-compound names. The difference appears to depend on the manner in which the name Yahweh-jireh is counted. In this study the compound with jireh discloses the primary relationship of Yahweh with His people, wherein redemption for the lost soul via a substitute blood offering is provided by God. Without this redemptive act the promised relationships would be impossible and would never be realized. There would be no redeemed people of God. Therefore, Yahweh's redemptive act is the major or primary basis of the other seven Yahweh-relationships that follow.

All eight names are arranged in the Old Testament Scriptures in a fixed order to show spiritual purpose and progression and yet to meet man's specific need at the time. However, the names also typify the life needs of every christian. Indeed, all these OT demonstrated relationships are totally transferable to the New Testament in and through the life of our Lord Jesus Christ. The names portray the Lord Jesus and are typical statements of His life, teachings and actions.

The Yahweh-Compounds: Where did they come from?

Yahweh–jireh: (God will Provide): It has previously been stated that in this study the Yahweh-jireh compound name will be considered, not as one of the "magnificent" seven, but rather as a unique name, standing by itself. It resulted from one of the most moving and significant incidents in all the Scriptures, for in this event God, as Yahweh, accomplished redemption through a blood sacrifice that He provided.

The story occurs in Genesis 22. Abram, later to be renamed Abraham, had passed through a series of strenuous events involving his call out of Ur of the Chaldees, with the attendant promise that Abram would be the father of a great nation and that his name would be made great (Gen. 12:2). The direct communication of this promise was repeated a second time after Abram, following Yahweh's call, arrived in the land of Canaan (Gen. 12:7). Abram must have had trouble understanding the promise of great posterity, for at 75 years of age—well beyond the age of child bearing—he still had no heirs; nevertheless he believed God that someway it would happen.

Then God gives Abram (Abraham) a third review of the promise when He again tells Abram that his seed will be as the dust of the earth, "so that if a man can number the dust of the earth, then shall thy seed also be numbered" (Gen. 13:16).

And yet once more the LORD appears to Abram concerning the promise of great posterity (Gen. 15:4-5) Abram still didn't understand, but he believed God that it would all happen, and Scripture tells us that his belief was counted to him for righteousness (Gen. 15:6).

We can remember that Abram's faith got a little weak and that he took matters into his own hands and fathered Ishmael by Hagar, just to help God along with the posterity promise (Gen. 16:4). Apparently Abram thought that a son by this servant maid was better than no son at all, for in spite of the promises from Yahweh, Sarah, his wife before the LORD bore him no children.

Well, Abram got to be 99 years old and still saw only promises from God but no successor. And when Abram was 99, once more God, as El Shaddai (God Almighty), reiterates the covenant promise and changes Abram's name to Abraham (Gen. 17:1-5).

Then it happened, even as the LORD had said! Abraham is 100 years old when his wife, now called Sarah instead of Sarai, bears him a son, to be named Isaac, making possible the fulfilling of the long standing promises of great posterity for Abraham. So many years and so many reiterations of the promises, and now it could all come true Abraham could just sit back and wait for God to fulfill the tremendous promises of a great and mighty family, because he had a son to carry his name.

But Yahweh had something more for Abraham to learn, something more for him to do, something more for His servant to be a part of, in order that Abraham might provide a type-picture of redemption not to be duplicated elsewhere in Scripture.

We read that the LORD appeared again to Abraham with the astounding command to offer up Isaac as a sacrifice, a burnt-offering. Yes! Even his only and well beloved son Isaac. Ever since Abraham was in Ur of the Caldees, he had waited for fulfillment of the posterity promises. No doubt it was a disappointment beyond description to Abraham. But through the years, not only had Abraham received revelation after revelation of the posterity promises, he had also learned to trust God. Abraham didn't know how, but some way Elohim would keep His word concerning a family for Abraham that would indeed to be great in numbers, and this family would be mothered by Sarah.

Abraham, we are told in the Genesis 22 account, follows every detail of God's command. It is only at the last second that the LORD acts to stay Abraham's hand from slaying Isaac. Scripture tells us that Abraham lifted up his eyes, and looked, and behold, behind him a ram caught in a thicket by his horns: and Abraham went and took the ram, and offered him up for a burnt-offering in lieu of Isaac. (Gen. 22:13) God had delivered Isaac by providing a substitute offering which paid the price with its blood. "And Abraham called the name of that place Yahweh-jireh; as it is said to this day, In the mount of the LORD it shall be seen." (Gen. 22:14)

Regarding the word jireh, N. Stone tells us that the word is simply a transliteration of a Hebrew word which appears many times throughout the Scriptures. Only its unusual significance here, its connection with this remarkable event and its union with the title Yahweh, has brought it down to us as part of the compound name Yahweh-jireh[30].

---

[30] Stone, Nathan J., *Names of God,* Chicago: Moody Press, 1944, p. 60

Jireh is a form of the verb "to see." However, both English words "see" and "provide" are used to translate the one Hebrew word. This seems odd, but remember that with God to see is also to foresee. God knows from the beginning to the end. He foresees everything. Another word for seeing is vision, and with God foreseeing is prevision. God, having prevision of man's sin, fall and need, makes provision for that need. God's prevision is necessarily followed by provision, for He certainly will provide for that need which His foreseeing shows Him to exist. With God, prevision and provision are one and the same thing. All this is certainly expressed in the term Yahweh-jireh; and it is quite correct and in its proper sense to translate this name of God, Yahweh-jireh, God will Provide.

It is appropriate to capture here one further notation from N. Stone. The name Yahweh-jireh is most significant, looking back, for it is a commemoration of a great deliverance. It is a constant reminder of the wonderful grace of Yahweh who performed this deliverance of Isaac through the provision of a substitute.

A further significance of this name of God lies in the expectation of something yet to come. God provided then and He will provide in the future deliverance from death. The naming of the place Yahweh-jireh was meant to proclaim of this very thing, "as it shall be provided."

The mount (mount Moriah), through the years, has been of tremendous significance. On this place the site of the Temple, the center of Israel's worship and sacrificial system was established (2Ch. 3:1). It was also here, in David's time, that

God in His mercy stayed the hand of avenging justice when David offered the sacrifice of substitution.

But the paramount significance of the mount is that it was the site of Calvary and the scene of that grand and terrible sacrifice of God's only begotten and well beloved Son, who was put under Judgment for sin and became our Substitute. Perhaps Abraham understood better than we realize the wonder of Yahweh's provision for man's redemption when he said: "In the mount of Yahweh, He will appear."

Yahweh-jireh, The LORD will Provide. Surely it can be seen that without the redemption typified by his name when Jesus paid the supreme price for the sins of the world we have nothing. In the past, the present and the future, everything depends on the fact that the LORD will provide (redemption), and the other Yahweh compound names follow in order because of Yahweh-jireh[31].

Yahweh-rophe: (The LORD that Heals). The name Yahweh-rophe means the LORD that heals. It is the first of the seven compound relationship names of Yahweh after the stand-alone name Yahweh-jireh. First there is salvation through a substitute, and then there is healing.

The circumstances surrounding the name are detailed in Exodus 15:22-26. After crossing the Red Sea, Moses had led the Children of Israel three days into the

---

[31] Ibid. p. 60-66

wilderness of Shur. They were without water. It was hot and dry. The people were thirsty, and they bitterly grumbled against Moses. When on the third day they came to the desert spring of Marah, they could not drink because the waters were bitter.

Then Yahweh showed Moses a certain tree, which, when thrown into the waters, turned them from bitterness to sweetness, so that there was water for all to drink. Because of that the grumbling was turned to praise as their confidence in Yahweh and Moses was renewed. There the LORD made a statute and an ordinance for the people. He said. "if thou wilt diligently hearken to the voice of the LORD thy God, and wilt do that which is right in His sight, and wilt give ear to His commandments, and keep all His statutes, I will put none of these diseases upon thee, which I have brought upon the Egyptians: for I am the LORD that healeth thee" (Exo. 15:26)—I am the Lord that healeth, Yahweh–rophe.

Notice that with the promise of healing there was also given the condition of their obedience. Yahweh established a conditional relationship with this people—no more free rides. Yahweh-jireh had unconditionally provided a substitute offering in the case of Isaac, but now the people have a responsibility. Typically, salvation was free, but for healing the people had to turn from their sin. He pledged healing on the condition of obedience.

All humanity is in need of healing. In our own lives so many can state from first hand experience that a physician's services are required all too often because we are physically sick. Diseases seem to abound everywhere in varying degrees of magnitude throughout the world. There can be no doubt that the world is in serious need of Yahweh–rophe.

Yes, all humanity is in need of healing, physically, but even more so in the moral and spiritual realm. Isaiah said of the people's spiritual condition, "...the whole head is sick, and the whole heart faint. From the sole of the foot even unto the head there is no soundness in it; but wounds, and bruises, and putrefying sores: they have not been closed, neither bound up, neither mollified with ointment." (Isa. 1:5-6) N. Stone puts it this way, "the moral and spiritual sickness of mankind is an open, running sore." Jeremiah said that the heart of man is desperately wicked—morally wrong, sick.

The tree cast into the waters at Marah is a type of the tree on which hung the Yahweh of the New Testament, even Jesus. He is the only remedy for mankind's ills: he alone can sweeten the bitterness of human experience through the forgiveness of sin and the sanctifying of life.

Yahweh-rophe who heals in the Old Testament is the Jesus who heals in the New. As with Yahweh of the Old, so with Jesus: physical healing was only incidental to His chief object, the healing of the souls of men. Indeed, what Yahweh was to Israel at Marah the Lord Jesus is to all who will receive and obey Him, the Great Physician.[32]

<u>Yahweh-nissi: (The LORD Our Banner)</u>. The name Yahweh-nissi means Yahweh our banner. It is the second of the seven compound relationship names of

---

[32] Ibid. p 70-75

Yahweh after the stand-alone name, Yahweh-jireh. The account establishing this name is recorded in Exo. 17:8-15.

The Children of Israel had encountered their first battle after leaving Egypt. It was at Rephidim against Amalek. Moses instructed Joshua to select some men and go out and fight the enemy, while he would stand on the top of the hill with the rod of Elohim in his hand.

Joshua did as Moses instructed him to do and fought with Amalek. When Moses held up his hands with the rod of God, Israel prevailed in the battle. But when Moses let down his hands with the rod of God, Amalek prevailed. So arrangements were made to seat Moses on a stone, for he was tired, and his associates, Aaron and Hur, held his hands up till the days end. Scripture tells us that Joshua greatly discomfited Amalek, for the Israelites won the battle. Then Moses built an alter and called the name of it Yahweh-nissi, the LORD our Banner.

N. Stone comments on this event are interesting. He suggests that it should be noted that in all the victory or defeat, with the hands up or down, it was not the hands that were important but the fact that the hands contained the rod of God. It was that rod, that wonder working rod, that had brought the terrible plagues upon Egypt and which had opened a path of deliverance for Israel across the Red Sea. It was the rod of God's mighty hand and outstretched arm. Indeed it was this rod, as the Banner of Yahweh, which brought the victory. And God's people saw unquestionably that upon

God alone depends the victory. There could be no doubt that under His raised banner, victory was always assured.

Israel's experience of that battle is analogous to our own spiritual warfare. Amalek represents the forces of this world order which stand opposed to Yahweh in all ages. The characteristics of this order are well known to the Christian: the lust of flesh, the lust of the eyes, and the pride of life. "...The LORD hath sworn that the LORD will have war with Amalek from generation to generation." (Exo. 17:16)

This battle goes on in the life of the Christian continually; the indwelling Spirit wages continual conflict with the flesh, for these two are contrary the one to the other. However, like the people in the fight on that day long ago when Moses held up the rod of Yahweh, the Banner, we cannot wage successful warfare in our own strength alone. We cannot win the conflict in the power of itself. There is strength only under the mighty Banner of Yahweh. The army of Joshua learned this. Let us be careful to note and to apply the truth to our own personal battle, both within and without the body.[33]

<u>Yahweh-qadash: (The LORD Sanctifies)</u>. The name Yahweh-qadash means the LORD who sanctifies. It is the third of the seven compound relationship names of Yahweh after the stand-alone name, Yahweh-jireh. The account establishing this name is recorded in Leviticus 20:8. The Children of Israel had traveled on from Rephidim into the wilderness of Sinai and camped before the Mount. God gave there the Law and

[33] Ibid. p. 87-91

established the Sabbath as a sign between Yahweh and Israel that these people were to be sanctified. They were to be a separated (or set apart) people unto the LORD. And Elohim said, "...My sabbath ye shall keep: for it is a sign between Me and you throughout your generations; that ye may know that I am the LORD that doth sanctify you." (Exo. 31:13) God was speaking of a sign, the sabbath, between Himself and His separated people. But when were they sanctified. And in order to be sanctified what was required?

N. Stone comments that the people of God must be holy (or sanctified) in practice as well as separated in position. The one is meaningless without the other. This sanctifying or separating of the people is, on the part of Yahweh, a covenant act, but the practice of holiness in His people is the working out of that act for themselves. "...I am Yahweh which sanctify you." But, we read in the preceding verse, "Sanctify yourselves therefore, and be ye holy." (Lev. 20:7-8) God or Elohim has endowed man with a free will and He calls upon him to seek holiness. God commands His people to be holy but He will not force then to be so. He placed within Israel, on the basis of redemption, the power to be holy, and provided them with every incentive to holiness, but man must of his own free will exercise that provision and power. Yahweh would have man's free and willing separation and holiness, otherwise it is no holiness at all, for without free will it loses its moral character.[34] Therefore, if man does not elect to be

---

[34] Ibid. p. 104

holy or sanctified to God from the inside, God will not sanctify that one from the outside only. The LORD said, "And ye shall keep My statutes, and do them: I am the LORD which Sanctifies you," or "and ye shall keep My statutes, and do them: I am Yahweh-qadash." But to be sanctified, man must do his part, and without a sanctified people there is no need for the sabbath at all.

Yahweh-shalom: (The LORD is peace). The name Yahweh-shalom means the LORD is peace. It is the fourth of the compound relationship names of Yahweh after the stand-alone name, Yahweh-jireh. The account establishing this name is recorded in Jdg. 6:22-24.

It was more than 200 years since the LORD had revealed Himself to His people as Yahweh-qadash. During this time, the people had corrupted themselves with idol worship and other disgusting practices, and for this reason they lost their purity, peace, prosperity and liberty. The nation was attracted to the grossly materialistic gods of the heathens around them.

N. Stone summarizes the declining spiritual conditions and the call of Gideon this way: Every apostasy brought punishment and more misery, a chastening of the LORD to awaken them to their spiritual calling. Repentance brought deliverance through the leadership of judges raised up of God. It was a period of alternating prosperity and adversity, of sinning and repenting, of slavery and deliverance. These people would grievously sin and be brought very low. Then in their difficulties they would remember Yahweh their God and cry out to Him for deliverance. Yahweh would hear them and raise up a deliverer for them. After serving the LORD for a time, Israel would turn away again, and the whole process would be repeated.[35]

It was in the midst of this process that Gideon comes on the scene. The Children of Israel had done evil in the sight of the LORD (Jdg. 6:1), and as a result their enemies, the Midianites, prevailed over them, causing great suffering. Gideon's call came to him in the midst of this distress directly from the angel of the LORD (Jdg. 6:11). This may best be understood as a theophany; that is, an appearance of God Himself to Gideon. Gideon had a difficult time understanding and believing that the LORD had really visited and talked to him. When he was convinced he was greatly frightened, for had not Yahweh said to Moses, "...there shall no man see me and live"? (Exo. 33:20) "And the LORD said unto him, Peace be unto thee; fear not; thou shalt not die" (Jdg. 6:23). God assured Gideon that he was not going to die. The message of the angelic visitor was validated, and Gideon would prove to be a "mighty man of valour" even as the angel of the LORD had said.

Then Gideon built an altar there unto the LORD and called it Yahweh-shalom (Jdg. 6:24). He built the altar not for sacrifice but to commemorate God's message wherein Yahweh gave him peace in a time of great turmoil. Shalom is simply the Hebrew word for peace.

Yahweh-tsidkenu: (The LORD our Righteousness). The name Yahweh-tsidkenu means the LORD our righteousness. It is the fifth of the seven compound relationship

---

[35] Ibid. p. 111

names of the LORD after the stand-alone name, Yahweh-jireh. The account establishing this name occurs in Jeremiah 23:6.

The ten northern tribes of Israel had already long since gone into Assyrian captivity, and now the southern kingdom was well on its way to a similar fate among the Babylonians. Prophet after prophet had been sent by God with continual warnings for the people to repent and obey the LORD, but they paid little, if any, attention. So the fate predicted for an apostate nation in the later portion of Deuteronomy 28 was inevitable. Into this unhappy scene comes the prophet Jeremiah, commissioned to proclaim the message that Judah would be destroyed by a foe or an evil from the north (Jer. 1:14). John Graybill makes an interesting observation here. His Commentary on Jeremiah indicates that Jeremiah's message, coming to men whose desperate nationalism was all they had to cling to, was completely rejected. Jeremiah was regarded as a meddler and a traitor, and the people, nobles, and kings, alternately, tried to put him to death.[36]

Jeremiah clearly envisioned the imminent grave difficulties for his nation, and he saw also the only solution—submission of Judah to the Babylonian invaders. What an amazing proposal it was for his day, for it was in striking contrast to the apparent conditions all around him. Therefore, it is no wonder that the people of Judah didn't believe the prophet concerning their nation. But Jeremiah predicted far more, for he

---

[36] Graybill, John F., "*Jeremiah*," *The Wycliffe Bible Commentary*, Chicago: Moody

saw that at an appointed time the LORD will raise up unto David a Branch of Righteousness. A King shall reign and prosper, executing Judgment and righteous in the earth. In his days Judah will be saved, and Israel will dwell safely; and this is His name by which He will be called: The LORD our righteousness, Yahweh-tsidkenu (Jer. 23:5-6).

Today so many people of our world still don't understand the great prophecies of Jeremiah that remain to be fulfilled concerning the King who will reign, prosper, and execute Judgment and righteousness in the earth. His name will be called the Lord our righteousness.

Yahweh-rohi (The LORD our Shepherd). Rohi (Heb. ro'eh, SRN 7462) is the participle form of the root ra'ah. SRN 7462 occurs more than 140 times in the AV of the OT with the initial occurrence in Gen. 4:2 where it is translated "keeper." But in Gen. 29:7 the same Hebrew word is translated into the English word "feed." Further investigation shows that this SRN word is translated into 29 different English words with the word shepherd among them. The question at hand is, is the expression Yahweh ro'eh a verifiable name of God?

Let us examine the translation of the word ro'eh in Psa 23:1 where the term is used in a metaphor to represent the LORD as my shepherd. Gen. 49:24 has a powerful application of ro'eh where God is referred to as the Shepherd, the stone of Israel. Psalm 80:1 also addresses God as Shepherd of Israel. Then, consider one final example applying the word ro'eh as shepherd. Isa. 40:11 tells us that the LORD shall feed His flock like a shepherd.

With this background, consider the Eze. 34:11-16 passage. We find the LORD portrayed as One searching out His sheep (v11). He is portrayed again as the shepherd seeking the scattered sheep (v12). The LORD will bring them and feed them (v13). The sheep, obviously tended by the Shepherd, will be brought to good pasture and fed (v 14). The Lord GOD says He will feed His flock and will cause them to lie down (v 15). Then finally the Lord GOD as Shepherd will seek the lost, bring those driven away, bind up the broken and strengthen the sick.

Truly His Shepherding attributes, presented in so many OT passages, are brought together in this Ezekiel passage to sum up the LORD as Shepherd of His sheep. Indeed, He is the LORD the Shepherd, our Yahweh-ro'eh.

Some students maintain the better known LORD's prayer of Psa. 23 is a superior presentation of Yahweh-Rohi. This may well be true for an individual's intimate and personal relationship with the Shepherd, but to include all God's people we need to consider the Ezekiel passages. Yahweh in that day, will be the Great Shepherd, the Yahweh-Rohi of all His people.

Yahweh-shammah (The LORD is Present). The name Yahweh-shammah means the LORD is there or the LORD is present. It is the seventh and last in the series of compound relationship names of Yahweh after the stand-alone name, Yahweh-jireh. The account establishing this name is recorded in Eze. 48:35.

Ezekiel began his prophecies at a time when the nation Judah was at its lowest ebb, both spiritually and nationally, in their history. The ten northern tribes had gone into Assyrian captivity. Judah was also in exile in the land of Babylon. Ezekiel was in captivity himself in that land of great contrast. K. Yates writes that on the one hand there was the great city of Babylon, which some say was the most beautiful city in the world. Palaces, gardens, temples, and great fortifications made the city an outstanding show place of the east. On the other hand the Jewish people, with their temple gone, national life gone, and very little opportunity for business interests, presented a pitiable picture. But, they still had not fully learned from all the suffering they had experienced. These people had greatly transgressed against the LORD, and He refers to them as a rebellious house and nation, as impudent children, stiff-hearted, scorpions. (Eze. 2:3-6)

It was to these lonely and sad exiles that Ezekiel was called by God to preach, and preach he did, his mission being to destroy false hopes for an early return to Jerusalem. His mission also included several additional tasks. He was to interpret to the people the meaning and purpose of the exile. He was to gather and preserve the teachings of historians, prophets, and psalmists, and he was to organize new forms for the worship and life in the restored community. He was also to stimulate new hope for the future of Israel. [37]

N. Stone tells us that this part of Ezekiel's mission brought hope and consolation,

---

[37] Yates, Kyle, M., *Preaching From the Prophets,* Nashville, Broadman Press, 1942, p. 176-177

for the prophet predicts the restoration of land and people in a measure far beyond anything these people had ever experienced in the past or could imagine in the future. The pledge of all this is the name Yahweh-shammah, Yahweh is there.

The LORD who had departed from the old Temple, which was desecrated by the abominations of His people and destroyed by His Judgments (Eze. 10:18-19; 11:22-24), will return by the same way into a new and glorious city and temple (Eze. 43:1-7), which will be purged of all the old abominations and oppressions and characterized by righteousness, justice and holiness. The condition of God's continued presence among them will be their faithfulness to a covenant by which they promise to be a holy people to this holy God. It is true that the people have demonstrated again and again that they were unable to keep such a covenant; but in that day they will abide under the shadow of Yahweh in that new city, and the name of that city shall be Yahweh-shannah, the LORD IS there.[38]

Table Summary:

The great redemptive dealings of God with man began when man first sinned and God initiated actions to rescue this greatest of all His creation masterpieces. Man, made in the image of God Himself, was fearfully and wonderfully constructed. Even though so like his Creator, man had a great flaw, innate sin: and because of this sin,

---

[38] Stone, Nathan J., *Names of God,* Chicago: Moody Press, 1944, p. 151-152

man deserved to die or be destroyed. This was simply because of God's holiness and His hatred of sin.

But God, who is fully love, elected to provide a Redeemer to save man from the penalty of sin. This action produced the first great Yahweh Compound Name, Yahweh-jireh. That Name describes the greatest of the relationships of God, as Yahweh, toward man, for in the hour of man's tremendous need, God, to be remembered as Yahweh-jireh, provided a Redeemer.

So wonderful and unique is this Name that it stands apart from the other descriptive relationships of Yahweh to man. Without it, the other relationships could not exist, since there would be no people of God. It all starts with redemption; then Yahweh meets all the other needs of His people.

The stand-alone compound name Yahweh-jireh together with the other magnificent seven have been considered with special attention to their origins and the reasons for the establishment of each of them. Let us now review these compounds in Table form with emphasis on the relationships of these names to each other.

Table 3.1

The Yahweh Relationship Compound Names

Name	Man's Need That God Met	Progression
Yahweh-jireh	Sacrificial redemption from Sin	Stand-alone
Yahweh-rophe	Healing physically & spiritually	#1 *142
Yahweh-nissi	Banner providing victory	#2 *146
Yahweh-qadash	Sanctification with obedience	#3 *231
Yahweh-shalom	Peace with God	#4 *403
Yahweh-tsidkenu	Righteousness	#5 *1029
Yahweh-ro'eh	Shepherd provides care/guidance	#6 *1117
Yahweh-shammah	Preservation by His Presence	#7 *1140

*Reese Chronological Bible page numbers (see page 59)

Comments on Table 3.1

Column one lists the Yahweh compound names. Next follows the column entitled, "Man's Need That God Met." In each of the situations where the LORD revealed a new and different self-identity, it was done at a time when man was in a great need for that particular characteristic of God.

The third column presents observations of unusual interest. Listed are the seven compound names showing that they occur in a certain progression or order. That is, the location and arrangement of the names do not just happen randomly. Like all else in the Bible, their arrangement is set by the Holy Spirit so that all things fit together in the Word properly. Let us consider this detail carefully.

To begin with, it can easily be seen that the disposition of the names simply provides descriptions of the actions of God at different and very special times in the history of the peoples of Israel.

But there is more, for the order of the names, taken as a group, portrays the LORD's preparation of redemption through a blood sacrifice and then His provision for all the needs of man from the point of this new redeemed condition, to the completion of man's earthly estate and his promotion into his sojourn in the heavenlies. Since the Scriptures frequently discuss these conditions of man, or more specifically, these needs of God's people, it is to be expected that these redemptive relationships continually appear in the sacred writings. Sometimes this happens directly and can easily be observed. For instance in Psa. 103:2-3 we read, "Bless the LORD, O my soul...Who healeth all my diseases." This can also be read, "Bless the LORD, for He is the LORD that heals." At other times the relationship in the text must be more carefully sought out and identified. For example, healing is implied in Exo. 15:26, care and guidance or shepherding in Gen. 24:1, and righteousness as presented in Psa. 71:19. The entire set of seven relationships appear as one in at least two places, Psa. 23 and Exo. 6:6-8. These will be discussed at length at a later time.

Now just an observation regarding the assemblage of the names. There are seven Yahweh compound names in the group. Seven is the great number of spiritual perfection. Bullinger comments on the number seven, this number which occupies so large a place in the works, and especially, in the Word of God must be inspired by the Holy Spirit as having very special significance. The mere fact that there are seven names is enough to broadly flag the name assemblage as of great importance.[39]

Look again at the chronologically established order of the names. All were produced to reveal Yahweh's special relationship to His people. Certain of the events occurred in such a manner as to clearly identify the location of the name in the Scripture by means of the associated text. There are three of these, Yahweh-rapha (Exo. 15:26), Yahweh-qadash (Lev. 20:8), and Yahweh-shammah (Eze. 48:35). Three other Names are located for us simply by transliteration of the original Hebrew. These are Yahweh-jireh (Gen. 22:14), Yahweh-nissi (Exo. 17:15) and Yahweh-shalom (Jdg. 6:24). Yahweh-tsidkenu is set by scholarly agreement (Jer. 23:1).

Some have maintained that Yahweh-ro'eh is supported by Psa. 23. Others argue that this name is located in Eze. 34:15. Now the Ezekiel passage is addressed to the people, as are all other of the names, whereas Psa. 23 is personal, individualistic

---

[39] Bullinger, E.W. *Number in Scripture* Grand Rapids: Kregel Publications, 1973, p.178

and in the first person. Therefore, for ro'eh to be consistent with the other names, it must be located in the Ezekiel passage with the Psalm passage as secondary support. These positions and their location arguments are shown in Table 3.2 for convenience.

It has been mentioned earlier that Table 3.1 presents a column entitled Progression. At this point, it is appropriate to comment on this column. The AV of Scripture has been used throughout this study. It is fully realized that chronology is not a strong point in this version. However, the importance of chronology is a factor of considerable significance. Therefore, the Reese Chronological Bible, King James Version[40] has been used to assist in establishing the order and progression of relating passages. The page numbers in the referenced column apply to the Reese Bible.

Before we move on, it is fitting that a summation review of Table 3.1 be presented, remembering that they are a catalogue of the Lord's relationships to man wherein every need of man from his lost state to the end have been met by God.

Yahweh-jireh revealed the LORD as the One who provides the Sacrificial Lamb for our redemption. Yahweh-rophe revealed Him as the Healer of the illnesses and sorrows of life. In Yahweh-nissi, He is seen as the Standard of our Victory in the conflicts of life. As Yahweh-qadash He sets His people apart for His possession and to His holy service. As Yahweh-shalom, He is the God of our Peace. As Yahweh-tsidkenu, He is the Righteousness of His people, the only basis of their justification and

---

[40] Reese, E., *The Reese Chronological Bible,* Minneapolis, Bethany Fellowship, Inc., 1980

acceptance. Yahweh-ro'eh reveals the LORD as the Shepherd of all His people. Finally, Yahweh-shammah reveals Him as the God who is presently indwelling the believer in this life and providing pleasures forever more in His presence in the life to come.

Table 3.2

The Yahweh Compound Name Locations

The Name	Location Argument
Yahweh-jireh	Direct transliteration of the Name (Gen. 22:14)
Yahweh-rophe	Established by the text (Exo. 15:26)
Yahweh-nissi	Direct transliteration of the Name (Exo. 17:15)
Yahweh-qadash	Name is established by the text (Lev. 20:8)
Yahweh-shalom	Direct transliteration of the Name (Jdg. 6:24)
Yahweh-tsidkenu	The Name is established by the text (Jer. 23:6)
Yahweh-ro'eh	Name is established by the text (Eze. 34:15)
Yahweh-shammah	Name is established by the text (Eze. 48:35)

The Old Testament Names of God

A Perspective

Chapter 4

Contents

There is a wonderful and significant order in the compound names of Yahweh as they appear in the Scriptures. Their appearance may at first seem in random order or determined only by an ancient need of Israel at some special point in time. However, there was never a haphazard or casual arrangement. Undoubtedly God's people of long ago, who experienced the particular revelation of Yahweh that met their great need, believed that the action of God at that time was just the right one. But the Holy Spirit had the problem events and their Yahweh revealing solutions all planned so that not only the Israelite people would be blessed but also all believers down through the ages. Now we can look back at the spiritual progression in God's revelation and understand and rejoice at what God has done.

In the previous chapter, the blessings of the LORD's revelations to Israel over a considerable period of time were considered. Not only were problem solutions provided to the people—God's action also produced a series of Yahweh compound names. Now we will examine examples of these names and the Yahweh revealing actions as they relate to each other rather than as single, independent events.

The "I Wills" of Redemption

Moses, even while the Israelites were in Egyptian bondage, told these captives some wonderful truths that are recognizable to us as the magnificent seven revelations. God told Moses that although He had appeared to Abraham, Isaac and Jacob as God Almighty, He was about to reveal Himself by His personal name, Yahweh. And He was going to redeem His people and adopt them as His own, deliver them from bondage and lead them to the promised land.

Then Yahweh presents to Moses the great "I Wills" of redemption that are recorded in Exodus 6:6-8. Verse 9 tells us "Moses spake unto the children of Israel: but they hearkened not unto Moses for anguish of spirit and for cruel bondage." The children of Israel didn't grasp the immediate and close-in significance of what Yahweh was saying, let along any comprehension of the meaning for the future. The immediate application of the promises was their deliverance from cruel Egyptian bondage, healing from their pain and suffering, and victory over bondage. The future application dealt with sanctification, real peace, righteousness and eternal care and guidance from Yahweh. Since the LORD was speaking His relationship to the believer, what is the association of God's covenant "I Wills" to the believers spiritual progression detailed in the Yahweh compound names sequence? Let us examine the connections between these relationships presented in Table 4.1

Table 4.1

The "I Wills" of Redemption

The Compound Name	Speaks of	The related "I Will"
Yahweh-jireh (Redemption-Gen. 22:14)	Redemption and Deliverance from sin	Delivers from the burden of sin. (Exo. 6:6)
Yahweh-rophe (Healing-Exo. 15:26)	Spiritual and Physical Healing	Rescues from bondage (Exo. 6:6)
Yahweh-nissi (Victory under the banner of God-Exo. 17:15)	Victory provision beneath the mighty arm of God	Reclaim the believer with the mighty arm of the LORD. (Exo. 6:6)
Yahweh 'qadash (Sanctify-Lev. 20:8)	The setting apart or consecration as holy	Make believers, people of God (Exo. 6:7)
Yahweh-shalom (Peace-Jdg. 6:24)	Peace of God	Peace with God (Exo. 6:7)
Yahweh-tsidkenu (Righteousness-Jer. 23:6)	The LORD our righteousness	Yahweh everywhere righteous (implied from Psa. 129:4)
Yahweh-ro'eh (Shepherd-Eze. 34:15	Shepherd provides care and guidance	The Shepherd leader (Exo. 6:8)
Yahweh-shammah (Preservation-Eze. 48:35)	The eternal Presence of God	The believers heritage (Exo. 6:8)

First, are there seven or eight Yahweh compound names? There are seven interrelated names plus the stand-alone name (Yahweh-jireh). The argument for this division is simply this: without the action typically represented by (Yahweh-jireh), namely, redemption, there would be no restored people of God, and the other Yahweh names would lose their significance and interrelationship importance. The other seven names relate to each other in this fashion: First comes redemption, then healing from sin's control can take place (Yahweh-rophe). The redemption of healing will result in many battles between the flesh and the spiritual life of the believer, but under the banner or in the banner of God (Yahweh-nissi), victory over sin occurs. The believer now can be sanctified or set apart, (Yahweh-qadash) to accomplish the spiritual tasks at hand. Perfect peace, that is, peace with God (Yahweh-shalom), can now occur in the life of the believer. (Yahweh-tsidkenu) can either speak in righteousness from the right path that the believer should walk. Or the righteousness of Yahweh imparted to the believer progresses with spiritual growth. (Yahweh-ro'eh) typically speaks of the relationship that the believer receives as Yahweh, the Good Shepherd, provides the care and guidance that eventually leads the believer into heaven and the eternal presence of God (Yahweh-shammah).

The redemption "I wills" provide an interesting and controversial study of the Yahweh relationship names, aligning the sequence of faith, progress, or growth of the believer. In each case we ask, is this portion of Scripture unique or are there other passages that also outline the progress of the Christian's progression in the faith?

The Restoration of Israel

Let me call attention to that passage in Ezekiel 34:11-31, often referred to as the Restoration of Israel, that also deals with another sequence of "I Wills" or promises from God to the believer. Because of the subject matter and the I wills, perhaps it can be assumed immediately that the believer's spiritual growth is to again be the underlying subject. Consider Table 4.2 detailing the typical Yahweh relationship names found in the Ezekiel passage.

Table 4.2

The "I Wills" of Ezekiel 34:11-31

Verse	Scripture Text	Yahweh-name and Assigned Number	
11	"I will both search my sheep and seek them out" (Redemption)	Yahweh-jireh	S.A.
12	"...will deliver them out of all places where they have been scattered in the cloudy and dark day" (Healing)	Yahweh-rophe	1
13	"and will bring them out from the people, and gather them from the countries..." (Victory under the banner)	Yahweh-nissi	2
13	"...and I will bring them to their own land" (Consecration)	Yahweh-qadash	3
14	"...I will feed them in a good pasture... in a good fold...in a fat pasture upon the mountains of Israel" (Peace)	Yahweh-shalom	4
15	"...saith the Lord God." It is the LORD with His Righteousness speaking (cf Psa. 129:4, Jer. 23:6; 33:16).	Yahweh-tsidkenu	5
15	"I will feed my flock and cause them to lie down" (Care and Guidance)	Yahweh-ro'eh	6
30	"and they shall know that I the LORD their God am with them...are my people" saith the Lord GOD (Presence)	Yahweh-shammah	7

The information of Table 4.2 is similar to that already discussed in the "I wills" of the Exodus 6-8 passage. Column 1 identifies the Scripture verse detailing the text under consideration. In column 2 is an excerpt of that verse. Then column 3 lists the typical Yahweh-names and the spiritual growth order beginning with the Stand-Alone name Yahweh-jireh and progressing down the Assigned Number sequence.

As this text is considered, it is interesting to observe that there are some 22 "I will" promises pertaining to the Good Shepherd and His sheep. For example, again and again the Shepherd seeks His flock (vs. 11,12,16). And the Shepherd will feed His sheep (vs. 13,14,15,23). It appears that there are more than enough "I will" promises to produce two complete sets of typical Yahweh-names, the second set being detailed in Table 4.3. Certainly there is room for argument and controversy here, but the passage surely stirs special interest as to why there is this very significant quantity of promises of the Shepherd to His people.

Table 4.3

Additional Promises in Ezekiel 34:11-31

Verse	Scripture Text	Yahweh-name and Assigned Number	
16	" I will seek that which was lost and bring again that which was driven away"	Yahweh-jireh	S.A.
16	"and will bind up that which was broken and will strengthen the sick"	Yahweh-rophe	1
16	"but I will destroy the fat and the strong..."	Yahweh-nissi	2
20	"...Behold, I even I, will judge between the fat cattle and between the lean cattle"	Yahweh-qadash	3
22	"Therefore will I save my flock, and they shall no more be a prey..."	Yahweh-shalom	4
	It is the LORD with His Righteousness speaking (Jer. 23:6)	Yahweh-tsidkenu	5
23	"And I will set up one shepherd over them, and he shall feed them..."	care and feeding	6
31	"And ye my flock, the flock of my pasture, are men, and I am your God, saith the LORD God"	Yahweh-shammah	7

Now let us consider a familiar passage that contains all the Yahweh names but in an unusual and different sequence to that studied.

The Twenty Third Psalm

In this Psalm, Yahweh the LORD is directly addressed or indicated by a pronoun thirteen times in the six verses. The author (and by extension the reader) of the Psalm is referred to by the first person personal pronoun seventeen times. The Psalm is very personal, closely coupling the LORD and His actions and blessings to "me", one of His sheep.

Besides these superficial observations there is much more here. Examination of this Psalm indicates the presence of all the Yahweh relationship names but not in the sequence usually followed by a believer from his salvation until he is safe in heaven. Indeed, although the magnificent names are all present, the order is in variance to that of the great " I Wills" shown in Table 4.1, which details the order produced by the original events.[41] So let us now pursue resolution of this apparent anomaly in the sequencing. Why does it occur?

[41] See Chapter 3 for details concerning the establishment of the Yahweh-names.

First, what is the sequence of events in the Psalm? E. W. Bullinger[42] summarizes the order of appearance of the Yahweh-names to be as shown in Table 4.4. Detailed in the table are the verse of reference in the Psalm (column 1), an identification of the considered Scripture Text (column 2), and the typical Yahweh-name together with the Assigned Number or Identifier (column 3) relating the particular name to the originating sequence and circumstance discussed in Chapter 3.

Special attention to the occurring order of the Yahweh names in column 3 indicates the initial name is Yahweh-jireh representing Redemption. The Psalm appears to indeed present this thinking with the statement "I shall not want" anything physically or spiritually including redemption. But then, instead of Yahweh-rophe (Identifier 1), the name Yahweh-shalom (Identifier 4) appears represented by the text "He maketh me to lie down...He leadeth me beside still waters." And, then follows Identifiers 1,5,7,2,3 and 6.. This sequencing is anomalous if the progress of a believer's life style is being described.

---

[42] Bullinger, E.W., *Figures of Speech Used in the Bible,* Grand Rapids: Baker Book House, reprinted 1993, p. 737.

Table 4.4

The 23rd Psalm

Yahweh-Relationship Names and their Sequence

E. W. Bullinger

Verse	Scripture Text	Yahweh-name and Assigned Number	
1	"I shall not want" anything	Yahweh-jireh	S.A.
2	"He maketh me to lie down…He leadeth me beside still waters"	Yahweh-shalom	4
3	"He restoreth my soul"	Yahweh-rophe	1
3	"He leadeth me in the paths of righteousness" He is my righteousness	Yahweh-tzidkenu	5
4	"Thou art with me" the LORD is there	Yahweh-shammah	7
5	"Thou preparest a table before me in the presence of mine enemies"	Yahweh-nissi	2
5	"Thou anointest my head with oil"	Yahweh-qadash	3
6	"Surely" all these blessings are for time and eternity	Yahweh-ro'eh	6

However, the 23rd Psalm is not describing the believer's progress. Rather, this Psalm is an exclamation and description of the actions of Yahweh as He provides pastoral care for His believer sheep. The relationship of Yahweh to the sheep is one in which the LORD begins as the Shepherd and the sheep begin and remain sheep. No spiritual growth is observed in the sheep, but there is a discussion of and praise for the pastoral care of Yahweh. The sheep are provided for by the Shepherd in the beginning, throughout the events experienced in the life of a sheep, and then at the end. In the course of the action all of the relationships between Yahweh and the believer develop, but the sheep are still sheep enjoying the blessings of the Good Shepherd. The Psalm is not intended to demonstrate Christian growth but rather to praise and to rejoice in the provisions of Yahweh, the Good Shepherd, for His own, the sheep. Although the eight Yahweh relationships are all contained in the Psalm, the believer's progress in faith is not the issue, as presented in Exo. 6:6-8.

The Approach of Chapter 5 and Beyond

It is now appropriate to pause a minute to look back over the manuscript to comprehend how we got here and then to briefly look forward to where we are going.

Up to this point in our study of the names of God, it is clear that the particular name under consideration must be a title of deity, that is, the term is a particular and specific appellation indicating the dignity, distinction or preeminence assumed by God because of His rank, office and attributes.

We have specifically considered the generic names, the personal name YHWH, and an abundance of compound expressions and titles that must be considered identifiers and hence, names of God. To assist our understanding we have gone beyond simple observation of the names to examine the Scriptural application, purpose and support arguments for each of these appellations. It should be understood that every name has a special purpose, given at the time of its introduction in order that God may better communicate Himself to man, His master creation. The name used might be interchangeable with another; but the applied name is a maximization of identity for that particular occasion. The use of any other identifier at the given time would not be as effective in portraying or displaying the character of God.

As we look forward in the progress of the study detailed in Chapter 5 and beyond, it is noticed that the names of God take on a somewhat different quality. The attributes and characteristics of God are frequently incorporated into figure-of-speech words and phrases using metaphors, similes and in some cases epithets recorded by the inspired writers. So, many times, it appears that these writers seem to be trying to sum up the personal satisfaction they have in God by expressing their feelings in a figures-of-speech series of words. This implies neither mechanical dictation nor the effacement of the writer's personality, but rather that the Holy spirit infallibly guides the choice of words available in the writer's own vocabulary. Beautiful verbal descriptions of the relationship of God to His people are painted by this technique. For example, David, in his Song of Deliverance (2 Samuel 22:2-3) applies no less than eight metaphorical descriptions of Yahweh God in two verses. Then David sums up the series when he writes, "...my savior; thou savest me from violence." Originally, these descriptive terms and phrases were the expressions and comments of David. But then the people became familiar with them, accepting and using them for the author's intended character description of God, and the expressions became names of God in the people's thinking, speaking, and eventually, writing. Today we speak of these metaphorical terms as names of God, for they generally outline and portray specific characteristics of God, filling our hearts with blessing as we read of His mighty ways and attributes.

The Old Testament Names of God

A Perspective

Chapter 5

Contents

*Appendix Support

5.1 <u>ANCIENT OF DAYS</u>:

	NAME VARIATIONS IN:	INITIAL REFERENCES
BECK	Ancient of Days	Dan. 7:9,13
JER	one of great age	
KJV	Ancient of Days	
TLB	Ancient of Days-the Almighty God	
NAS	Ancient of Days	
NEB	ancient in years	
NIV	Ancient of Days	
NKJV	Ancient of Days	
RSV	ancient of days	

To Whom Does This Name Apply?

The term Ancient of Days is a title of Yahweh-Jesus (It appears in 7 Scripture versions), alternately rendered "one of great age" or "ancient in years" (in 2 versions).

The Argument:

Daniel the prophet writes in Chapter 3 of the content of his two dreams with careful detail. In the first dream the Ancient of Days is described as to His outward appearance, "...whose garment was white as snow, and the hair of his head like the pure wool: his throne was like the fiery flame, and his wheels as burning fire..." (Dan. 7:9). Daniel saw the Ancient of Days. Daniel also saw the purpose of His coming—there was "...Judgment, and the books were opened."

Scripture makes it clear in both the NT (Col. 1:15) and the Old (Exo. 33:20) that man may not see God. So it wasn't Elohim that Daniel saw. And who can see and describe the Holy Spirit? Therefore the Spirit was not in the dream. Yet Daniel saw the Ancient of Days. Who was this person? He was the one who judges at the bema where all men shall stand before Him to be judged. That is not God the Father, for He judges no one; it is Yahweh-Jesus in a manifestation of the preincarnate Christ.

The second dream also speaks of the Lord Christ (Dan. 7:13), but the picture is now one of the incarnate, glorified, risen Savior coming in the clouds of heaven. Criswell[43] sums up the assembly this way:

> And there sat the Ancient of Days, and there was brought near Him the Son of man coming in clouds of glory. The two are face to face, 'pros ton theon.' They are two in the one God. One, the Ancient of Days, God preincarnate, the great Yahweh of the old Covenant, and the other the preincarnate manifestation of God, pros ton theon, face to face, equal, the same.

The Ancient of Days is Yahweh. The Son of Man is Jesus Christ. However, the Ancient of days can also be identified as the preincarnate Christ, Yahweh-Jesus, the judge of all the nations. Much difference of opinion exists in the literature about the identity of the Ancient of Days. In any case, for the purposes of this study, Ancient of Days is certainly a name of God.

The Purpose Of This Name:

In this time of world turmoil, agony, convulsion and distress, the name Ancient of Days continues to remind us that the LORD is still on His throne.

---

[43] Criswell, W. A., *Daniel* Grand Rapids: Zondervan Publishing House, 1976, Vol. 4, p. 39-40.

5.2 ANGEL OF the LORD:

	NAME VARIATIONS IN:	INITIAL REFERENCES
BECK	the LORD's Angel	Gen. 16:7, 9, 10, 11[44]
JER	angel of Yahweh	
KJV	angel of the LORD	
TLB	Angel of the Lord	
NAS	angel of the LORD	
NEB	angel of the LORD	
NIV	angel of the LORD	
NKJV	angel of the LORD	
RSV	angel of the LORD	

To Whom Does This Name Apply?

In his Old Testament appearances, the Angel of Yahweh or Angel of the LORD, is a theophany of the preincarnate Yahweh-Jesus.

The Argument:

The initial appearance or visit of the angel of the LORD to the earth is recorded in Genesis 16:7-11, and it was a moment of unusual significance. This angel was not a created being but the LORD in a theophanic manifestation of Himself to Hagar. From these passages it is evident that the "angel" is Yahweh Himself, present in time and visible at this place. He identifies Himself with Yahweh; He speaks and acts with the authority of God; He is spoken of as God or as Yahweh.[45] Therefore, it is plain that the term "the angel of the LORD" is the name of God. The name is used in all versions of the Scripture of consideration in this study.

---

[44] The name *angel of the LORD* is well documented in the OT. See detail in a concordance.

[45] *The Wycliffe Bible Commentary*, Chicago: Moody Press, Copyright 1962, 13th Printing 1976, p. 22.

The Purpose Of This Name:

Several blessed attributes of Yahweh are displayed that are not only applicable to the needs of Hagar, but are equally applied to man today. Hagar was a runaway slave. The LORD confronted her with kindness and grace. The LORD showed Hagar mercy when she deserved death. The LORD provided encouragement in the hour of despair, and Hagar was given direction for her life by the Omniscient God. The application and need of these blessings in our day is quite plain.

5.3 ANGEL OF GOD:

	NAME VARIATIONS IN:	INITIAL REFERENCES
BECK	God's ANGEL	Gen. 21:17
JER	angel of God	
KJV	angel of God	
TLB	Angel of God	
NAS	angel of God	
NEB	angel of God	
NIV	angel of God	
NKJV	angel of God	
RSV	angel of God	

To Whom Does This Name Apply?

The name angel of God (or angel of Elohim) refers to the identity of a messenger or representative from God.

The Argument:

The name God used in this title refers to Elohim, but there are interesting related considerations. First, the messenger cannot be God the Father Himself, since in certain appearances of the angel, the messenger-angel was seen by the recipient (Jdg. 6:11-21; 13:6-21). In these two cases both Gideon and Manoah saw the messenger, and both believed that they would die because they had seen God; but death didn't happen to either one of them.

In the Jdg. 6:11-21 account, the identifiers "the angel of God" and "the angel of the LORD" are applied interchangeably. For example, "the angel of God" is used in Jdg. 6:20. The same messenger is identified as the "angel of the LORD" in the next verse. The angel of the LORD is Yahweh Himself. The interchange allows the angel of God to also be the preincarnate Yahweh.

The Purpose Of This Name:

It appears that the Angel of God is the incarnate LORD. From the name the Angel of God it can be observed that there is a definite difference in usage between Yahweh and Elohim. They coexist but perform different functions. For the people of the OT, it was demonstrated that God the Creator is not visible, nor can He be. He loves, He creates, He controls but the dealings of God with the covenant people are through Yahweh.

5.4. ANOINTED:

	NAME VARIATIONS IN:	INITIAL REFERENCES
BECK	Anointed	1Sa. 2:10
JER	Anointed	
KJV	anointed	(also see Appendix 5.4)
TLB	anointed	
NAS	anointed	
NEB	anointed	
NIV	anointed	
NKJV	anointed	
RSV	anointed	

To Whom Does This Name Apply?

The word Anointed, commonly supported by an adjective modifier or epithet, is a name of the Messiah, Christ Jesus our Lord.

The Argument:

In the OT, the word anointed applied 84 times to numerous things and people. For example, such items as vessels, wagers, ceremonies and even the tabernacle are spoken of as being rubbed with oil, and therefore, are classed as being anointed. Likewise, many people are anointed on special occasions. These include Israel, Ephraim, David, Saul, Solomon and many others. But along with these ordinary uses of the term there also appears its highest application, where the word or name is employed to designate the One promised of God as the Great Deliverer, and who is, in a preeminent and altogether unique sense, The Anointed, or the Messiah of God.[46]

---

[46] A full listing of the 84 applications of the term anointed is contained in the Appendix.

(Note: The referenced Appendix details 11 verses that seem to apply the name "Anointed" to deity. Careful consideration of the 11 passages indicate that in 10 of them the word anointed is identified as a name of God).

The Purpose Of This Name:

The purpose detail is a part of Appendix 5.4.

5.5 BRANCH:

		NAME VARIATIONS IN:	INITIAL REFERENCES
BECK	son		Psa. 80:15
JER	son		
KJV	branch		(also see Appendix 5.5)
TLB	son		
NAS	son		
NEB	*		
NIV	son		
NKJV	branch		
RSV	*		

* paraphrased out

To Whom Does This Name Apply?

The Branch is a title applied to the Messiah, Christ Jesus our Lord.

The Argument:

In the prayer of Psalm 80, it is requested that the LORD look down from heaven and provide protection for the vine (Israel) against the vicious work of devastation by the Gentiles under the leadership of the Beast (v. 14 & 15). Then the branch (Son) whom God made strong for Himself is mentioned for the first time in this Psalm. The translation of the Hebrew word "ben" (which literally means son) as branch in some versions of our English Bibles appears reasonable, since the Hebrew word "ben" is used figuratively in Genesis 49:22 to mean branch or bough. It may have been a common colloquial expression. (See variations above.)

Some take it that the word cannot mean Christ, the Son of God, but that it must mean the nation Israel. They claim that in prophetic passages there is blending together of the concepts of Son and of Israel, which is destined to be God's firstborn among the nations.[47] Israel is yet to be made strong as the nation of the kingdom. However, in view of the closing statements of this Psalm it seems to be certain that none other than Christ our Lord, the Son of God, is meant. They look to Him, knowing that the once-rejected One is their coming King. And when the calamity is repeated during the culminating days of this age, when the fires rage as never before, then will come His day, the day of their salvation and the day of His glory.[48]

The Purpose Of This Name:

The Purpose detail is a part of Appendix 5.5.

---

[47] See "...Israel is my son, even my firstborn..." (Exo. 4:22) also Hos. 11:1.
[48] Arno C. Gaebelein, *The Book of Psalms,* Wheaton, Ill. Van Kampen Press, 1939, p. 312.

5.6. BREATH OF THE ALMIGHTY:

	NAME VARIATIONS In:	INITIAL REFERENCE
BECK	the Breath of the Almighty	Job 33:4
JER	the breathing of Shaddai	
KJV	the breath of the Almighty	
TLB	the breath of the Almighty	
NAS	the breath of the Almighty	
NEB	the breath of the Almighty	
NIV	the breath of the Almighty	
NKJV	the breath of the Almighty	
RSV	the breath of the Almighty	

To Whom Does This Name Apply?

The name, "breath of the Almighty", applies to Shaddai, the Almighty, the All Powerful One, the Mighty (God).

The Argument:

Our English versions of the Scriptures contain a significant number of identifiers for God wherein the particular name is made up of not merely a single word but a series of words or terms. These are interesting to study, for it is apparent that less than reasonable agreement about them exists among the translators of the various modern versions of the Bible. A case in point is the current name of concern, "the breath of the Almighty". Two considerations have been observed and are discussed as follows:

Consideration 1. "The breath of the Almighty" is a phrase wherein "the breath of" is simply a modifier of the proper noun the Almighty. The term of import is the name the Almighty or, in Hebrew, Shaddai. This name has already been considered in an earlier chapter. As can be seen from the above tabulation, 7 of the versions treat the name in this fashion. The JER Version also accepts the transliterated Hebrew name Shaddai used in place of the Almighty.

Consideration 2. The Beck version of the Scripture treats the name somewhat differently by employing capital letters so as to read, "the Breath of the Almighty". Now we have two nouns, the Breath and the Almighty connected by a conjunction and the whole phrase, "the Breath of the Almighty", becomes the name of concern.

Why was this phrase used at all? Job's three "friends" Eliphaz, Bildad and Zophar had involved Job in lengthy discussions as to why Job suffered. Now Elihu, a young and angry man steps forward to speak. Elihu, as was the custom, had waited till now in deference to the other three older men. But they had failed to resolve the question, at least in Elihu's thinking, so Elihu says to Job, "Hear my speech, and listen to everything I say. Look, I've opened my mouth, and in it my tongue speaks. I talk straight from my heart and speak sincerely the knowledge coming from my lips. God's Spirit made me, the Breath of the Almighty gives me life,"[49] (or the Spirit of God imparts the life and the wisdom of the LORD to me). But Elihu does no better than the others. Then God speaks to settle the matter for Job (Job 38:1).

The Purpose Of This Name:

Remember that this portion of Scripture is poetry. Elihu speaks his thoughts in couplets. In verse 33:4, Elihu says two things. First, "the Holy Spirit of God has made

---

[49] William F. Beck, *The Holy Bible In the Language of Today*, Philadelphia & N.Y., Leader Press, 1976, p. 610.

me." And secondly, "the breath of the Almighty gives me life." The reader is reminded that God is the Creator of man and his mind, a view needed by mankind in Job's day as well as in this day.

5.7 CREATOR:

	NAME VARIATIONS In:		INITIAL REFERENCE
	Ecc. 12:1	Isa. 40:28	Isa. 43:15
BECK	Creator	made	Creator
JER	Creator	created	creator
KJV	Creator	Creator	creator
TLB	Creator	Creator	Creator
NAS	Creator	creator	Creator
NEB	Creator	creator	creator
NIV	Creator	Creator	Creator
NKJV	Creator	Creator	Creator
RSV	Creator	Creator	Creator

To Whom Does This Name Apply?

The name Creator, as shown in the above Variation Table, occurs in only 3 passages of the OT. In the initial verse (Ecclesiastes 12:1), God (Elohim) is implicitly identified as the One who has created us. However, in the Isaiah verses, the Creator is explicitly identified as the everlasting God (Elohim), the Holy One, the Creator of Israel and the ends of the earth, the King and the LORD.

The Argument:

"In the beginning God created the heaven and the earth." (Gen. 1:1.) God (Elohim) brought into existence out of nothingness the heaven and the earth and all that is therein. He created or He made them by the power of His Word. "God spoke and it was done..." (Psa. 33:9). This word create, clearly stating what God (Elohim) has done, is the root of the word appearing in Ecclesiastes and Isaiah naming the Creator.

He is the Maker, the One who brought the universe into being, the fabricator of all things.

One other special observation: The various Scripture versions treat the capitalization of the word creator differently. For example, in the Ecc. 12:1 passage, eight of the nine versions treat the term creator as a proper noun with capitalization. There is only a single exception where the lower case is used. In the Isaiah passages there are greater variations in style among the versions, apparently due to editorial preferences. However, it should be noted that even though these variances are present, the basic Biblical truths are not changed. The Everlasting God, the LORD, the Creator of Israel and even the very ends of the earth; He is the Creator, and that is one of His names.

The Purpose Of The Name:

Man needs to be reminded continually of just who God is: He is the Maker and the Creator, who has created heaven and earth and all that is in them including man and all that man knows or is to know, sees, controls or possesses.

5.8 CREATOR OF ISRAEL:

	NAME VARIATIONS In:	INITIAL REFERENCE
BECK	your Creator, Israel	Isa. 43:15
JER	the creator of Israel	
KJV	the creator of Israel	Only entry in OT
TLB	Israel's Creator	
NAS	The Creator Israel	
NEB	your creator, Israel	
NIV	Israel's Creator	
NKJV	The Creator of Israel	
RSV	the Creator of Israel	

To Whom Does This Name Apply?

"Creator of Israel" is a genitive phrase, and when applied in total, it is used as a substitute for the name of God (Elohim). Examination of the Variations list indicates that some of the more recent translations of the Scriptures remove the genitive phrase and simply identify the "Creator of Israel" as your Creator, meaning your Elohim or your God.

The Argument:

Comparing Isaiah 43:15 with 40:28 presents interesting identifier observations: Verse 40:28 relates to God as the "everlasting God (El Olam), "the LORD" (Yahweh), and "the Creator of the ends of the earth..." Verse 43:15 relates to God as "the LORD" (Yahweh), "Holy One" (LORD thy God, cf. - Isa. 43:3), "creator of Israel" and your "King" (LORD of hosts - Jer. 48:15). These verses contain a series of names of God. Some are substitutes for His name that exalt Him by referring to his wonderful acts (i.e.,

Creator of the ends of the earth or Creator of Israel). Other identifiers are titles (i.e., Holy One and King). Still others are names (i.e., everlasting God and LORD).

The Purpose Of This Name:

The name "Creator of Israel" is a reminder of just who God is and what He has done. He is the Creator of Israel that made His people a nation out of nothing.

5.9 CROWN:

	NAME VARIATIONS In:	INITIAL REFERENCE
BECK	beautiful garland	Isa. 28:5
JER	crown of glory	
KJV	crown of glory	
TLB	crowning glory	
NAS	beautiful crown	
NEB	lovely garland	
NIV	glorious crown	
NKJV	crown of glory	
RSV	crown of glory	

To Whom Does This Name Apply?

The word Crown or, more exactly, the Crown of Glory is figuratively applied to the LORD of hosts, Yahweh Sabaoth.

The Argument:

The computer concordance indicates that the word "crown" appears in the OT 51 times. Careful review of these words, their uses and origins indicate that the 51 are derived from 5 different Hebrew words that are translated into several English words such as top, pate, scalp, separation, conservation, head and crown belonging to royalty. Twenty-three words of the 51 are translated from the Hebrew word 'atarah (SRN 5850) and are of particular interest because the word crown in this translation means a garland, wreath or circlet worn literally for figuratively to indicate royalty, sovereignty, power, authority or honor.

Review of these applications display 9 literal uses of the word crown and can be disregarded as possible deity identifications. There are 10 applications of the word crown that are of continued interest because of their possible figurative application. There are also 4 verses where crown might be interpreted as either literal or figurative. But in these cases these 4 are not of interest in this study as they do not relate to deity identity.

By this slow and careful process of elimination we have accomplished the two factors: (1) removing from further interest the verse applications where the word crown is not a possible identification of deity and, (2) we have selected the unique metaphor found in Isa. 28:5 where it is stated that the LORD who will be a "crown" of splendor and a diadem or crown of beauty unto the remnant of His people or nation. The LORD is spoken of as a Crown of Glory and Beauty as the Prophet Isaiah, in figurative language, tries to express the way he feels about his God.

It is interesting to observe the variations in the various Scripture versions in this crown phraseology. Seven versions agree in the translation of the Hebrew into the English word crown with modifier glory, beautiful or glorious. Two of the versions translate the Hebrew into the English with the word lovely as a modifier, so there is some lack of agreement at this point.

Some feel the phrase "Crown of glory" is not a name at all. If anything, it is used to express the thought that the greatest blessing and honor that Israel will enjoy during the Kingdom is the privilege of being formally associated with the Lord of hosts as His chosen people, His nation of priests.

Others raise an interesting question. If "crown of glory" is a name of God, why isn't "diadem of beauty" also a name?

Certainly this thinking is challenging and further investigation is left to the reader. However, this author feels that the Hebrew, in smoothest translation, reads crown and when combined with its modifier produces the name of God, "Crown of glory" or perhaps "Glorious Crown." In that day we shall see the LORD as the "Glorious Crown" of His people.

The Purpose Of This Name:

The Ephraimites of long ago as well as the people of today need a reminder that God Almighty the LORD of hosts is still very much in control of His creation and one day coming soon His people will see Him in power and great glory even as their Crown.

The Old Testament Names of God

A Perspective

Chapter 6

Contents

*Appendix Support

6.1 DELIVERER:

	NAME VARIATIONS In:	INITIAL REFERENCES
BECK	Deliverer	2Sa. 22:2
JER	deliverer	
KJV	deliverer	"Deliverer" appears 5 times in the OT in connection with a name of deity. See Appendix 6.1
TLB	Savior	
NAS	deliverer	
NEB	champion	
NIV	deliverer	
RSV	deliverer	

To Whom Does This Name Apply?

David addressed his God as Yahweh, as Elohim, and as Adonai in the verses of consideration and then in each case proceeds to embellish these names of God with the metaphor, my deliverer.

The Argument:

Strong's Concordance indicates there are only 8 references to the word deliverer in the OT. The term is not really an official name or title of deity but is epithetically used in an effort by the Scripture writers to strengthen their expressions and feelings of God. Then, because this word was applied so frequently by the authorities of that day, it became like a name and so appears to us today.

Now consider the 8 passages. Five are metaphors, either directly substituting for the names of LORD (Yahweh) or for God (Elohim). David adds metaphorical term upon term in extensive word series, as he does in so many of his writings, trying to sum up the satisfaction he has in God. We will discuss only 2 of the interrelating passages in this proof-of-name argument. The other 3 applications are reserved for Appendix 6.1 for the reader wishing more detail.

In addition, remember that there are yet 3 other occasions[50] where the term deliverer appears. These are not names of deity at all; rather they speak of specific people or specific needs in that far off day. However, since they are not pertinent to this study, they will receive no further consideration.

Of course it is only necessary for a name of Deity to appear once in the OT to be accepted as a name of God. But in the case before us, as in other situations, multiple passages applying the word as a name simply strengthen the particular argument. The supplemental arguments appear in the appropriate Appendix.

Now let us compare the passages 2Sa. 22:2-3 and Psa. 18:2. They are essentially the same, the Psa. 18:2 passage being an insert by David from his earlier 2Sa. writings. He first composes 2Sa. for his own harp. Then he reinserts the verses as a song of praise for his life-long deliverance.[51]

---

[50] Othniel a judge in Jdg. 3:9, Ehud a judge in Jdg. 3:15 and a discussion of the desire for a deliverer by the people of the city of Laish from the Danites, Jdg. 18:28.
[51] *Matthew Henry's Commentary,* Zondervan Publishing House, Ed. 13, 1974, p. 357.

Compare:		**With:**	
2Sa. 22:2 & 3		Psa. 18:2	
"The LORD is my"		"The LORD is my"	
rock	fortress	rock	fortress
deliverer	shield	deliverer	God (El)
high tower	horn of salvation	high tower	horn of salvation
refuge	savior	strength	buckler

In 2Sa. 22:2 David sings praises unto the LORD, speaking of Him as his Rock, his Fortress and Deliverer. He goes on in the next verse, referring to Yahweh as his Shield, Horn of Salvation, High Tower, Refuge and Savior. Then in the Psa. 18 passage he almost repeats himself, except that he refers to the LORD, in addition to the other epithets, as his God, his El or the One with great strength, the Almighty. David praised his God with these epithetical terms describing the Deliverer and His great power, protection and salvation. David equates the name deliverer to the others in the series, including the name God (El).

Therefore, we must conclude the word deliverer is a name of God.

We are concerned only with the epithetical term deliverer here, but keep in mind that the other epithets experienced here are also names of God and will be considered in their alphabetical turn.

The Purpose Of This Name:

The word deliverer speaks of deliverance from a foe as do the words fortress, shield, refuge and high tower speak of protection. David spoke of his God using all these epithetical enhancers. The enhancers were certainly applicable to David and his deliverance from his military foe. But the words are also significant whenever Satan is involved as our foe. This was true for David as well as for the children of God in all ages. He is God our Deliverer.

6.2 FATHER:

	NAME VARIATION In:				INITIAL REFERENCES			
REF.	BECK	JER	KJV	TLV	NAS	NIV	NKJV	RSV
Deu. 32:6	Father		father					
2Sa. 7:14	Father		father					
1Ch. 17:13	Father		father		See Appendix 6.2 for additional			
1Ch. 22:10	Father		father		support information			
1Ch. 28:6	Father		father					
Psa. 89:26	Father		father					
Psa. 103:13	father		father					
Isa. 9:6	Father		father					
Isa. 63:16	Father		father					
Isa. 64:8	Father		father					
Jer. 3:19	Father		father					
Jer. 31:19	Father		father					
Mal. 1:6	Father		father					
Mal. 2:10	Father		father					

To Whom Does This Name Apply?

In all verses except one, it is God the LORD (Yahweh) who is being addressed. Only in Isaiah 9:6 does this vary. There it is the Messiah, the Christ, that is spoken of or addressed.

Argument:

The concordance indicates that the term father appears 541 times in the OT. By individually examining each usage, it has been determined that the great predominance is applied to a progenitor or a forefather, or an ancestor in the direct family line. There are also a few instances where the term father has to do with nations.[52]

In search of the confirmation of names of God it has been determined that the word *Father* is used at least fourteen times to signify Deity. These Scripture references are listed in the Name Variation Chart. As in previous cases where a group of passages all contain the word in question, only sufficient information is displayed in this text to satisfy the argument that a name of God is presented in the given verse(s). The balance of any passages involved with the name are discussed in the Appendix. In the case of the word Father, Appendix 6.2 presents additional argument.

For the argument in this Text, first consider the Deu. 32:6 passage. In the Song of Moses there is initially an invocation where a summons is given to the earth and the heavens. They are to be a witness of the covenant about to be delivered. But before the writer can speak of that, he needs to proclaim the identify of the LORD, and he does so in terms of the perfectness of God, the Rock, Then Moses goes on to contrast God's righteousness and the perversity of the nation Israel. They are sons of God, yet due to their corruptness and sin, they are set aside as "not-sons" (v5). Moses says they are foolish and unwise people who seem to have forgotten the God who created and called them out of Egypt. And the question is, is this any way to treat your *Father* who established you and made you strong? Is this how you repay the LORD

[52] See Jeremiah 31:9. "I am father to Israel..."

(Yahweh)...Isn't He your *Father*? And that is another one of the names by which the LORD is known.

The Purpose Of This Name:

God associates with man in the special characteristics of Yahweh because man needed to be called back close to God, summoned to relate to this One who had given him life and every position. But man has always had a difficult time responding to God because of disobedience and sin. So God said, I want to be to you like a Father, that's how close I want the relationship. If you will obey Me and honor Me, then you will be My children and call Me *Father*. That will be My name, *Father*.

6.3 EVERLASTING FATHER:

	NAME VARIATIONS In:	REFERENCE
BECK	Everlasting Father	Isa. 9:6
JER	Eternal Father	
KJV	everlasting Father	
TLB	Everlasting Father	
NAS	Eternal Father	
NIV	Everlasting Father	
NKJV	Everlasting Father	
RSV	Everlasting Father	

To Whom Does This Name Apply?

The Messiah, the LORD Jesus the Christ

The Argument:

The title, Everlasting Father appears only once in the Old Testament. Isaiah uses it in his writings to help outline the place that the coming Messiah will have among His people. It is this name, Everlasting Father, selected from among the several Messianic names in Isaiah 9:6, that will be considered here. The other titles will each be studied in their turn.

Isaiah speaks of the coming deliverance for Israel and then proceeds to describe the characteristics of the Immanuel who will bring this to pass. The Wycliffe Commentary[53] summarizes these attributes this way:

"He will come into the world as a baby born to the Hebrew people, a gracious gift of God to them." "He will rule God's kingdom with God's authority. He will be a Wonder of

---

[53] *Wycliffe Bible Commentary*, Moody Press, Chicago, Ed. 13, 1976, p. 619.

a Counselor. That is a person of two distinct natures—God and man. He will truly be a wonder from Yahweh, and as the One who alone has the words of eternal life. He will be a counselor like none other. As Mighty God[54], He will be the irresistible battle champion (as this word for mighty implies), who will obtain the final victory in the arena of history. As everlasting Father (literally, Father of Eternity), He will be not only Lord of eternity but the author of eternal life to the redeemed. As Prince of Peace, He will bestow what shalom, 'peace', implies in its fullest meaning: health to the sin-sick soul; a sound and healthy relation between sinners and God, as well as between sinners and fellow sinners; and a sound condition of universal righteousness and prosperity prevailing over the earth."

Let us look more closely at the title, Everlasting Father. The word everlasting is rather frequently used in the Old Testament. There are everlasting hills, statutes, arms, doors, covenants, priesthoods and many other items. Most of these applications have been translated into English as everlasting from the Hebrew word 'olam. Here we must be careful, because the word 'olam, although applied to God[55] six times in the Old Testament, is not the same Hebrew word used in the Isa. 9:6 passage. There the Hebrew word is 'ad[56] and is translated into the English with connotations of terminus, duration, perpetuity, forever and eternity. For example, in Isaiah 57:15 we are told that "His existence is eternal." In Psalm 111:3 and 112:9, "His righteousness endures

---

[54] A term clearly applied to the LORD in Deu. 10:17; Isa. 10:21 and Jer. 32:18.
[55] See Olam applied in the name Everlasting God in Chapter 1.
[56] See SRN 5703.

forever." In Micah 7:18, "His anger does not last forever." Finally, in Isa. 9:6 we have everlasting Father or Eternal Father. The word everlasting used alone is not a name of God, but when it is added to the name Father as an epithet or enhancer, the two words constitute a name of God.

The Purpose Of The Name:

In the time to come, all the heathen enemies and persecutors of God's people will be utterly crushed. "For every warrior's boot used in battle and every garment rolled in blood will be destined for burning, and will be fuel for the fire." (Isa. 9:5 NIV.) Then Isaiah, as directed by the Holy Spirit, sets forth the characteristics of the One who will bring this deliverance. Man continually needs to be reminded of who this is: His four-fold name includes Wonderful Counsellor, The Mighty God, The Everlasting Father, The Prince of Peace. Amen.

6.4 <u>FEAR OF ISAAC</u>:

	NAME VARIATIONS In:	REFERENCE
BECK	Awesome One of Isaac	Gen. 31:42
JER	Kinsman of Isaac	
KJV	fear of Isaac	
TLB	God of Isaac	
NAS	fear of Isaac	
NIV	Fear of Isaac	
NKJV	Fear of Isaac	
RSV	Fear of Isaac	

To Whom Does This Name Belong?

The interesting name or title, *Fear of Isaac*, is a Figure of Speech called a Metonymy of the Adjunct or Relation. In this arrangement the word Fear is substituted for the term God or Elohim, who is feared. The phrase can be rewritten, *the God whom Isaac feared* whereby the title is applied to God (Elohim). (Notice: this name is in the genitive, and all of the words of the phrase must be present to complete the name.)

The Argument:

There is less than good agreement in the translation of this name. However, the fact that the phrase is a title of deity is everywhere directly or indirectly established in the literature. This is demonstrated in our limited comparison of the eight Scripture versions displayed in the Name Variation Chart. We observe that the phrase Fear of Isaac appears 5 times, Awesome One once, Kinsman once and God of Isaac once. All of these phrases are names of God with some variation. Concerning this variation let us examine a paraphrase of the context in one encyclopedia.[57]

Fear of Isaac, the name or designation of the deity by whom Jacob swore an oath as part of his covenant with Laban (Gen. 31:42; in v. 53 it is slightly altered to the "Fear of his father Isaac"). The name has been interpreted in three basic ways. Some scholars thought it meant the fear that proceeded from the deity Isaac. Another approach interpreted the Hebrew word translated fear to mean "kinsman". This proposal was emotionally more palatable than "fear" and was widely accepted for awhile. In more recent times, however, this approach has been more or less rejected. The third possibility, and the one that has been perhaps most widely accepted, argues that it is the name of a deity who terrified Isaac and whom Isaac therefore worshipped. It is further pointed out in this analysis that the *Fear of Isaac* parallels in form *God of Abraham* and *Mighty One of Jacob,* the names of God associated with patriarchs, and there is no reason to change it.

Finally then, the main sense of Gen. 31:42 is that the *God of my father, the God of Abraham*, and *Fear of Isaac* are all identical; these are simply different names or titles of the same or one and only God.

The Purpose Of This Name:

The spiritual role of fear in the OT must not be isolated from the other major elements in OT religion, especially when the "fear of the Lord" is seen as the

---

[57] *The ISBE*, Eerdmans Publishing Co, Vol. 2, C. 1982, Reprinted 1988 p. 291.

fundamental OT expression for religion. The concept "fear of the Lord" involves two elements that always have affected the people of God, namely, Divine holiness and human sinfulness. The holiness of God requires and produces Judgment. The people's awareness of this caused dread and fear of Him. But the grace that characterizes God and His forgiveness of sin causes the dread and fear to change to reverential awe.[58] It was true then and it continues today.

[58] Ibid., p. 291.

6.5 <u>FIRST AND LAST</u>:

	NAME VARIATIONS In:		REFERENCES
	ISA. 41:4	ISA. 44:6	ISA. 48:12
VERSION			
BECK	First and Last	First and Last	First and Last
JER	first and last	first and last	first and last
KJV	first with last	first and last	first and last
TLB	First and Last	First and Last	the First-the Last
NAS	first and last	the first-the last	first and last.
NEB	first to the last	first and last	first and last
NIV	with first and last	first and last	first and last
NKJV	first-with last	First and Last	First and Last
RSV	first-with last	first and last	first and last.

To Whom Does This Name Apply?

"I am the First and I am the Last" refers to the LORD (Yahweh).

The Argument:

Looking at the phrase "First and Last" as a possible name of God, we need to remember two requirements. First, a name must be supported by Scripture as an appellation or title of God. Then the title must present a manifestation of His presence in such a manner as to illustrate who He is. Indeed, one or more attributes may be featured in the name in order to show to man characteristic(s) of God; that is a primary purpose of His name(s), to make Himself known to His creation.

Returning to the phrase First and Last, we find that the LORD, speaking through Isaiah, clearly uses it to describe Himself in three different verses, "I the LORD, the First and with the Last" (Isaiah 41:4); "Thus saith the LORD the King of Israel and His

Redeemer the LORD of hosts; I am the First and I am the Last; and beside me there is no God." (Isaiah 44:6); and then in 48:12, "...I am He; I am the First and I also am the Last."

These verses apply the phrase First and Last (all the words must be present) in a manner to meet the requirements for a name of God. Therefore, we have here another name, "First and Last."

The Purpose Of This Name:

Man, being continually prone to place his own ego or self on the throne of life, needs to be reminded again and again that it is God first, last, and all the time who initiates, control and finalizes all affairs of life. We are to remember God first, for He was before the beginning, and last, for He will certainly be there at the end and will bring blessing, joy and peace. To forget that God is indeed First and Last in all things, as His name here clearly indicates, is to lose the blessing, joy and peace God has prepared for His own.

6.6 FORTRESS:

VERSION	NAME VARIATIONS In:	REFERENCES
		2Sa. 22:2
BECK	fortress	There are 6 additional passages that apply the word fortress to deity. Please see these in the 6.6 Appendix.
JER	bastion	
KJV	fortress	
TLB	fortress	
NAS	fortress	
NEB	fortress	
NIV	fortress	
NKJV	fortress	
RSV	fortress	

To Whom Does This Name Apply?

The English word Fortress is used in various metaphoric expressions addressing the LORD (Yahweh).

Strong's Concordance indicates there are fifteen references to the word fortress in the OT However, only seven of these passages apply this word to deity. The other eight applications speak of select fortified places, forts or defensive walls and will receive no further consideration in this study.

The seven passages of interest displayed in the Name Variation Chart (see Appendix 6.6), where applications of the word fortress occur to address God, illustrate again the colorful metaphorical use of the common and well understood words of the writer's era to indicate deity. Certainly this is different today, for the particular use of the word fortress to represent God, apart from the Scriptures, has become most unusual. We don't think or talk in terms of forts and fortresses. They are obsolete. We defend cities and oil fields, airports and military concentrations but not forts or fortresses. So the word fortress has lost much of its significance for today's society.

But in David's time, the people thought in terms of the strength and safety of the fortress, so David wrote of this bulwark to illustrate important attributes of God. Bible scholars agreeably attribute four of the seven passages of concern to David.[59] Two of the other passages (Psa. 71:3 and 91:12) are not necessarily assigned to David by all, but their style and verbiage is certainly Davidic. Then Jeremiah came along some 450 years later and apparently incorporated some of David's metaphors for deity into his writings, for, certainly, the same Davidic descriptive addresses are similar in all seven of the passages.

Having established the verses containing the word fortress as an address for God, let us look more carefully at the word usage to verify that this term is indeed a name of God. Remember, this verification needs to be done only once, but in this case of multiple verses the other six uses are considered in the Appendix 6.6.

It was observed earlier that many of the writings of David are filled with metaphors expressing David's strong satisfaction with God.[60] For example, in the earlier study of the metaphorical name, Deliverer, it was observed that this word or name was only one of several in a series of figures of speech used by David to extol God for His protection and deliverance. We might also remember that one of the other

---

[59] See 2Sa. 22:2; Psa. 18:2; 31:3; 144:2.
[60] See Chapter 6.1 Text.

names in that series, along with Deliverer, was Fortress. David simply said, "the LORD is my Fortress," and so for us was established the name of God, "Fortress".

The Purpose Of This Name

The LORD has many names, each with a purpose and designed all to manifest that He is God. Although the significance of the term Fortress, in our daily conversation, has largely been lost, the fundamental meanings of the word remains clear. A fortress is a defence, a stronghold and represents one great attribute of God for that era and also for our day.

The Old Testament Names of God

A Perspective

Chapter 7

*The Of-(Genitive) Names of God

*Appendix Support

7.1 GENITIVE INTRODUCTION:

In Chapter 1 of this study of the names of God consideration was given at length to the primary names El, Elohim and Yahweh. We then were introduced to an alphabetical list of metaphorical and epithetical identifiers of deity. These, as has been pointed out, may not strictly be names in the classic sense, but since they are handled as names of deity in the Scriptures, this study looks at each one as if it were as solid an identifier as the primary and compound groups. Also, be aware that the list of metaphorical and epithetical identifiers has not been exhausted by any means. However, the alphabetical name presentation plan being followed now requires an interruption in order to consider a name-group called the Of-(Genitive) Names of God.

Close study has determined that this group contains at least 52 names of God.[61] To belong in the of-(Genitive) Names of God aggregation certain easily recognizable conditions must exist. Each name contains a prepositional phrase with the preposition "of". In addition, the 52 names all begin with the word God (sometimes prefaced by other modifiers such as the name LORD or LORD of hosts). Therefore, the names are very similar in construction, yet each defines an attribute, a specific act or a designation of our God. For example, He is "the" God of Israel and is so addressed 201 times in the OT writings. Or again, He is "the" God of Abraham and is called by that specific name many times in the OT.

---

[61] Fifty-two of-(Genitive) names of deity have been located and their validity verified. However, there may well be other Names of God not yet discovered. (See Chapter 7 Appendix for the search detail.)

Let us pause now and further consider this expression "of-(genitive) name of God." The purpose of this prepositional phrase "of-(genitive) name of God" is to provide an English working appellation for the primary form of the possessive case. The phrase contains the of-(genitive) names of God in the form "God of__" as well as other forms. For example, the name King of Glory (Psa. 24:7, 8, 9,10), and the name King of Israel (Isa. 44:6), and even again the name Holy One of Israel (2Ki. 19:22) are all correctly classed as of-(genitive) names of God. But, recognizing this, we will for convenience in this part of our study limit the of-(genitive) names of God to only those names with the form "God of—". The other forms do indeed occur as names of God in their own right, and each will be considered as the alphabetical approach to the names proceeds.

The textbook English Grammar[62] tells us that the central idea of the genitive is that of "sphere", indicating that a person or thing belongs to the sphere of another, having close relations to it or forming an integral part of it. "God of" names include Attributive Genetives, Possessive Genetives and the Partitive Genitive. There are multiple categories of the Attributive Genitive with sphere, but only those of specific interest to this names of God study will be mentioned.

Of first concern is the category Possessive Genitive, expressing possession, sphere, a belonging to, association with an inherent relationship. For example, again consider the name God of Abraham. He is Abraham's God—that is, He is the One

---

[62] George O. Curme, *English Grammar*, Barnes & Nobel Books, Harper Row, p. 126.

God, Yahweh the LORD, that the Patriarch associated with and trusted so that it was counted to Abraham for righteousness (Gen. 15:6). Now, of course, Abraham didn't own God, but the sphere of relationship of Abraham included the sphere of God, and because of the faith of Abraham God identifies Himself as the God of Abraham in numerous passages (Gen. 26:24; 28:13; Exo. 3:6; 4:5).

Now look at the second category, the Appositive Genitive, in which the modifying term explains or clarifies the preceding governing noun, usually in the "of__" form, but still sometimes with the old "__'s" form in poetic expressions (i.e., God of Knowledge: He is the God from whom all knowledge comes, 1Sa. 2:3; Dan. 2:20,21,22).

Of final interest here is the Partitive Genitive, denoting the whole of which only a part is taken—a piece of bread; a friend of mine. (The Genitive of Graduation is a variety of the Partitive Generation—God of gods, Deu. 10:17; Jos. 22:22; Psa. 136:2.)

The Argument:

The format of Chapter 7 is different than the other chapters, because in this chapter we have a multitude of very similar names that must be organized and their credibility as names of God verified. In addition to indicating name application, duplicates and multiples (the name of concern appearing more than once in a given verse) must be identified and eliminated in the count.

In this text we will examine only a very limited portion of the 52 of-(genitive) names of God, as we will sufficiently demonstrate the format, group membership and credence of the chosen examples. The remaining names of the 52 are detailed in Appendix 7.

The assembly of 52 of-(genitive) names has been organized into four groups as shown in Table 7.1

Table 7.1

Groupings of the 52 Of-(Genitive) Names of God

Group Number	Classification	Quantity
1	Personal Names	11
2	Groups of People Names	15
3	Names of Locations and Places	7
4	Names of Characteristics	19

In this text let us select one or two examples from each group for detailed examination. Select "God of Abraham" and "God of David" from Group 1. Select "God of Israel" from Group 2. Select "God of Heaven" and "God of Bethel" from Group 3. Finally, select "God of Glory" and "God of gods" from Group 4.

Group 1:

Group 1, displayed in the Appendix as Table A.7.2a, presents 11 names of God in the possessive of-(genitive) case. Scripture clearly indicates that sphere[63] is expressed in the application of each name, that is, God reigns over the sphere or the life style of each person. They all have a very close relationship to Him. He is their

---

[63] Sphere is defined as: the place, range, or extent of action, existence, knowledge, experience, influence, the walk of life or life style.

God and is referred to as the God of Abraham or Daniel or Isaac. These possessive expressions stand as His name. Indeed the name God, or more often the name LORD God, certainly needs no embellishment. Yet the Scripture writers seem to apply these possessive names in a fashion to express their feelings about their God, highlighting His everlasting relationship to them and their progenitors and affirming that He is the Living God of all ages. Looking more closely at example 1 from this Group, the designation "God of Abraham" appears 16 times in the OT. Abraham's sphere of relationship (or his life style) was centered upon his God in his day-to-day living. Abraham believed in God (Elohim) as the Almighty (Gen. 17:1), as the everlasting (Gen. 21:33), as the most high God, the possessor of heaven and earth (Gen. 14:22), as the actual and lawful LORD of all (Gen. 24:3) and the righteous judge of all the earth (Gen. 18:25). Abraham is referred to as a Friend of God (2Ch. 20:7; Isa. 41:8). Indeed Abraham's lifestyle was centered upon God so completely that God was a part of Abraham's "everything," God was Abraham's all right, and the title for God, as recorded in the AV, is in the form "God of Abraham."

Our second example is the designation "God of David." This title appears only four times in the OT, but because David is classed with Moses in terms of spiritual contributions to mankind, a great many illustrations of the sphere relationship of David to God are unnecessary.

Perhaps the tremendous contributions of David as an author can be placed at the top of his list of achievements. David, in his day-to-day walk with God, entered into a very close relation with Him in the literary sphere. As the Holy Spirit guided, David wrote many of the magnificent psalms. Indeed 75 of the 150 canonized psalms are credited directly to David, with yet others probably credited indirectly. His mouth continually overflowed with a heart-felt praise for God. Ethan the Ezrahite, observing the sphere of relationship, writes of the unique covenant God made with David (Psa. 89:3) that David's dynasty will endure forever. David generally did that which was right in the sight of the LORD, save for his great sin in the matter of Uriah the Hittite. David repented of this and was forgiven by God, but the penalty for this disobedience, the Judgment that the sword would never leave David's house, continued throughout David's life. David was a great statesman and warrior, but he had sufficient blood on his hands to be restricted from building the Temple of God. David, spoken of as a "man after God's own heart" (1Sa. 13:14), had a particularly firm and unshaken trust in God as he intermingled his sphere of life style with that of Elohim, the God of David.

Group 2:

Let us now proceed to the second group of names. These are displayed in Table A.7.2b of the Appendix. Here we have an assemblage of 15 names of God with variations from the first group in the previous Table. The Group 2 listing is referred to as the "Peoples Group" since each name relates God to either a group of people (i.e., God of the Hebrews or God of Israel) or to progenitors (i.e., God of their father or God of his father).

In contrast to the entries in Table A.7.2a, the uniqueness of some of the Table A.7.2b names needs some consideration, but not in terms of their credibility, for all are properly applied as names of God in the Scriptures. However, application of metonymy in some modern Bible versions tends to produce certain limited changes in the meaning from that of the AV. We will look at this. Then the prominence of application of any given name, such as "God of Israel," should receive special attention. Since we are interested in "Groups of People," let's look at a range of group sizes from a group consisting of one or a few, as in names associated with fathers, to a very large group, such as the nation of Israel. Lastly, the exceptional name "God of my lord" needs special scrutiny. Let us examine these names but, for convenience, not necessarily in the order given in the Table.

Remember that from Group 2 we will discuss in this text only the one selected name. Appropriate comments on the other names will be found in the Chapter 7 Appendix.

The name of God example for Group 2 that has been selected is "the God of Israel." This is the most frequently applied possessive of-(genitive) name in the OT, being used 201 times. God initially established a covenant involving Abraham's posterity and the land. This covenant was passed on to Isaac and then to Jacob (or Israel after his name change). It is Abraham who is referred to as the father of many nations (Gen. 17:5) and, through Isaac, is the father of the Israelite nation. Jacob's part in all this was two fold. First the nation Israel is his posterity by natural descent, and secondly in Israel, the transformed Jacob, the spiritual aspects of the nation Israel are typified. It is interesting to observe that in the name the God of Jacob, sometimes Jacob refers to the man Jacob. Three times Jacob refers to the nation (Psa. 8:11; Isa. 2:3; Mic. 4:2). Throughout the early portions of the Pentateuch the name "the God of Abraham, the God of Isaac and the God of Jacob," appears. Abraham and Isaac are the retrospectively identified patriarchs in these cases. When the name "the God of Jacob" is used, Jacob and the nation Israel share in that name jointly. However, when we look at the name "the God of Israel," the reference is to the spiritual sphere of influence or life style of the nation and not to that of the man. True, God is the God of Jacob and hence Israel, but the Scripture references relate to the great God who has been in and out of the sphere or relationship of the nation Israel throughout the history of that nation. One Encyclopedia suggests these comments.[64] From the days of Abraham the LORD has shown Himself to be the God of faithfulness, election, mercy and love. He is the God of creation, and He rules over the nations according to His sovereign will and power. He is the God who works in history, the God who has chosen the people of Abraham, Isaac and Jacob as the first object of His revealing and reconciling actions. As the God of these people, He is the covenant God, the God of relationships. He is entitled "the God of Israel." The nation Israel has responded poorly and inconsistently, only sometimes relating closely to God and wanting Him deeply involved in their relationship sphere. At other times these people have disobeyed Him,

---

[64] *The International Standard Bible Encyclopedia, Vol. 2*, Eerdmans Pub. Co., p. 498.

going their own way, leaving the great God out of their national life completely. Nevertheless He still bears the name "the God of Israel" and will ultimately be truly such to these, His beloved people.

Before closing the consideration regarding the name "the God of Israel," there is a related possessive of-(genitive) substitute name that should be mentioned--the name, "God of Jeshurun." This title appears in Deu. 33:26 and is apparently applied there as a hypocorism or term of endearment for the name Israel. Therefore, the comments relating to the God of Israel are also appropriate for this name.

Group 3:

The next group has only seven members as displayed in Table A.7.2c in Appendix 7. These names are categorized as the "Locations and Places" group, because in the OT Scriptures God is associated in these names with certain locations and places. Of course, this actually relates God to the inhabitants of these places, since these locations and places with their collective spheres contain inhabitants with their own individual spheres of influence. It seems totally plausible regarding each of the names of God in this group to be quite ambivalent as to whether the place or the collective people of the place are being considered.

Two examples have been selected in Group 3 for consideration in this Text, "the God of Bethel" and "the God of Heaven." The opposite extremes of inhabitant quantity are present in these appellations. In the first name the involved spheres are limited to those of God and Jacob. The second location involves the potential for large quantities of inhabitants since Heaven contains the vast family of God. Look first at the title the God of Bethel. Jacob, as he travels to Padan-aram in search of a wife, camps at a certain place one night. There Jacob has a vision of God in a dream of such consequence that Jacob names that place Bethel (Gen. 28:19), meaning the House of God, for Jacob experienced the sphere of the LORD and His covenant reaffirmation there.

Some 20 years go by. Jacob, still in Padan-aram, is now wealthy and the father of 11 sons. Then God speaks to Jacob saying, "I am the God of Bethel where thou anointed the pillar." (Gen. 31:3.) God called Jacob to return to this special place, Bethel, and in so doing refers to Himself as the "God of Bethel." Bethel was the place, but the events of that place were about God in the life of Jacob. At Bethel Jacob embraced and possessed God for a short time, for God was in Jacob's sphere at Bethel. Well, the trip back to Canaan was far from uneventful, what with threatening meetings with his father-in-law, Laban, and with Esau, his brother. Jacob knew he deserved just punishment for his evil treatment of both Laban and Esau, but the LORD saw him safely home to Bethel. Jacob builds an altar and calls the place El-beth-el. It is not just Bethel the place now. Rather, it is the God of the place. Jacob remembers God after all the years spent in the world lying and cheating. He remembered that it was at Bethel that he first encountered God, where God was first in his sphere of life. And Jacob remembers the God who brought him back to that place. Jacob had come back to the influence, the way, the sphere of the "God of Bethel."

Now look at the second Group 3 example. The name variations God of Heaven and God of earth appear in the OT in three separate combinations.[65] Abraham uses the two names "God of Heaven" and "the God of Heaven and the God of the Earth" as he prepares for the securing of a bride for his son Isaac (Gen. 24:3). The Patriarch requires his most trusted servant to swear an oath by the LORD, the God of Heaven and the God of the Earth, not to take a wife of the Canaanites for Isaac. In the discourse Abraham says that it was the LORD God of Heaven (Gen. 24:7) who brought him to Canaan and who covenanted to give the Patriarch and his seed the land. Isaac can't go elsewhere and expect to take part in these promises. It is obvious that Abraham feels very strongly about this, for he identifies the LORD as the God of Heaven and then again as the God of both Heaven and Earth in these five verses. It is this God that the servant swears by. Where does this name come from? The OT writers repeatedly refer to heaven as the abode of God.[66] He lives there, writes Isaiah. The Psalmist says that God looks down on the earth from His throne in Heaven. The ancient Hebrew did not exactly know where heaven was or what it was, but he knew that God dwelled there. He is enthroned there; it is His sanctuary, it is His home, it is His place. Heaven is a possession of God.[67] God is referred to as the God of Heaven no less than 20 times in the OT When Abraham desired to implement an oath at the

---

[65] God of Heaven (Gen. 24:7); the God of Heaven and the God of the Earth (Gen. 24:3); God of Heaven and Earth (Ezr. 5:11).
[66] Psa. 14:2; 33:14; 102:19; Isa. 63:15.
[67] Gen. 14:19, 22; Exo. 31:17; Deu. 4:39; Ch. 6:14.

highest level he could think of, he called on the name of the "God of Heaven" (Gen. 24:3) and then reinforced this name with the related idea, "and the God of the Earth...."

Ezra uses the third of our heaven and earth name combinations, God of Heaven and Earth (Ezr. 5:11). The Prophet records that the adversaries of temple restoration wrote letters of complaint to King Darius. In this document they quote the Jewish leaders and their helpers referring to themselves as the servants of the God of Heaven and Earth. This statement, which explains just who God is, appears only once in the OT It is a declaration of the sovereignty of God.

Group 4:

Table A.7.2d in Appendix 7 lists a group called the Characteristics of-(genitive) names of God. They are predominantly employed in the OT to express certain of the specific characteristics and attributes of God. With a single exception (Deu. 10:17) the entries all fall in the appositive category of genitives, wherein the Scripture writer explains or identifies who the Person of God is (Sometimes El and other times Elohim) by the descriptive genitive phrase. For example, He is the God of Judgment (Isa. 30:18) and the God of Truth (Deu. 32:4). Certainly these are appropriate names, because God is referred to as a judge in numerous passages (Deu. 32:4; Psa. 9:8) and all His ways are truth (Psa. 25:10). Or again, consider the simple expression God of my Rock (2Sa. 22:3). The writers frequently use the simple form of this metaphor to represent God as the strength of His people (Deu. 32:4; Psa. 18:2; 62:7; Isa. 17:10. These examples and many others point out that these of-(genitive) names present distinguishing characteristics of God that are also defined in other places in the Scriptures in other than the genitive. Another thing: remember that the groupings we have established are only for convenience. Names might be interchanged from Group to Group at the desire of the reader.

Now look at our chosen examples for this Group. First consider the name "the God of Glory." This is an unusual title that memorializes the wonderful theophanies that ancient Israel witnessed, those awe-inspiring appearances of God that revealed the holiness of God, His incomparable power, and His transcendent majesty that humbles all that is in earth and heaven. This name, "the God of glory," reminds us of those great theophanies, but it stands out from other references to them by ascribing to Him glory as a permanent accompaniment. The word glory, when used of God, is particularly appropriate for describing the moral uniqueness and the grandeur of God as Lord of the universe. Any endeavor to specifically qualify or quantify this use of the word glory produces an endless series of adjectives. He is the God of all this. How can He ever be adequately described?

Finally, consider this Group's example "God of gods." As was stated, there is an exception to the Group 4 listing of genitive names—namely, God of gods. This special variety of the partitive genitive denotes the whole, gods, of which only a part, that is God, is taken to express a genitive of graduation.[68]

---

[68] Geo. O. Curme, English Grammar, Harper and Row Publishers, New York, p. 128.

Remember this Text only considers a few of the appellations of God found in the of-(genitive) format. Let us again recommend that the reader read Appendix 7 for details of the complete lists, their composition and methodology.

The Old Testament Names of God

A Perspective

Chapter 8

Contents

*Appendix Support

8.1 <u>GOVERNOR AMONG THE NATIONS</u>:

NAME VARIATIONS In: Psa. 22:28

BECK	"because the LORD is King and rules the nations."
JER	"For Yahweh reigns, the ruler of nations."
KJV	"For the kingdom is the LORD's: And he is the governor among the nations."
LIV. BIBLE	"For the Lord is King and rules the nations."
NAS	"For the kingdom is the LORD's, And He rules over the nations."
NEB	"For kingly power belongs to the LORD, and dominion over the nations is his."
NIV	"for dominion belongs to the LORD and he rules over the nations."
NKJV	"For the kingdom is the Lord's, And He rules over the nations."
RSV	"For dominion belongs to the LORD, and he rules over the nations."

To Whom Does This Name Apply?

In this study of the Names of God the meaning of words and phrases are particularly important, so special attention has been given to variations in name content between Scripture versions.[69] Therefore, in this study flow it is important to examine any specific verse and its content where significant differences between versions seem to be present. Let us look carefully at the Psa. 22:28 passage for two reasons. First, because it contains the alleged Name of God, "Governor of the nations" and secondly, because this declared name appears only in the A V, the guide version, but not in the other studied versions.

---

[69] It is a given that all modern Scripture versions have been prepared by scholars of the highest capability with intent to produce Bible translations with maximum accuracy and minimum individual viewpoint expression, while stimulating thoughts and concepts generally understandable by the average lay person. This is difficult, since a version that corrects one perspective, problem or error may well leave another argument open and unsolved. The quantity of Scripture versions becomes most numerous, each differing slightly from the other. Even the versions (limited to 9) that have been examined in this study develop great appreciation for the efforts of the scholars and producers of the texts. A reasonably good view of the versional differences are also displayed for all to see...and wonder at!

Comparison of the 9 Scripture versions indicate that three of them—the Beck, the LB and the Jerusalem have reasonable agreement in the wording of the second phrase, "rules the nations." Five other versions have the personal pronoun "He" inserted to assist in determining who is ruling. The NEB contains a personal pronoun but with other variations in the wording. The Living Bible and the KJV both apply the name Lord (Adonai) in place of the name Yahweh (LORD).

Let us look again at the inserted pronoun "he." Who is this "he?" Upon this answer hangs much of the meaning of the verse.

This is difficult material, because the Persons of the LORD and the Lord (Jesus Christ) are intermingled in David's writings. Both the LORD and Jesus Christ are frequently referred to by means of pronouns, so careful consideration must be given in order to ascertain who is being indicated. We must ask, is it the LORD (Yahweh, the personal name of the God of the Hebrews) or is it Christ Jesus (the Messiah, the Lord of all and yet to come)? Matthew Henry[70] teaches that they can be identified in each passage by their distinct spheres of sovereignty. He says, "The kingdom of nature is the LORD's, and His providence rules among the nations. The kingdom of grace is the Lord Christ's and He, as Mediator, is appointed Governor among the nations, head over all things to His Church."

The Scofield notes[71] provide an interesting comment regarding this verse:

---

[70] Matthew Henry, *Commentary*, Zondervan Pub. House, Grand Rapids, 1961, p. 600.
[71] C. I. Scofield, *The Holy Bible*, Oxford Press, New York: 1909, 1917, 1945, p. 609.

> The kingdom is the LORD's. In verse 30, Adonai (Christ Jesus) is in view as ruling on behalf of the LORD. The great end object of the rule of Adonai (the LORD) is the restoration of the kingdom to The LORD.

Arno Gaeblein[72] says the following:

> The Kingdoms of this earth will be His, and in that Kingdom He will rule in righteousness among the nations. To receive the Kingdom, He left this earth and is now at the right hand of God. He waits patiently for the appointed time, when God will make His enemies His footstool. When he returns He will receive that Kingdom. All the ends of the earth, all the families of the nations will then turn to Him and do homage.

Finally, compare Jeremiah 30:21 with Psalm 22:28. Chapter 30 of Jeremiah contains a description of the conditions at the end time in the land given to Abraham. Then Jeremiah writes of the "Governor" who comes from the people and is Ruler and Mediator, fully acceptable to God. The proper work and office of Christ, as Mediator, is to draw near and approach unto God to intercede for us and in our name and stead, as high priest of our profession. God the Father caused Jesus Christ thus to draw near and approach to Him as Mediator. He anointed Christ for this purpose, and God declared Himself well pleased in Jesus.[73]

---

[72] Arno C. Gaebelein, *The Book of Psalms*, Van Kampen Press, Wheaton, 1939, p. 109.
[73] Matthew Henry, *Commentary*, Zondervan Pub. House, Grand Rapids, 1961, p. 992.

Because of these referenced arguments it is obvious that the name "Governor among the nations" applies to the Messiah, the Lord Jesus Christ, not to the LORD (Yahweh). This fact, examined in additional detail, is further discussed in Appendix 8.

The Purpose Of This Name:

There are several interesting things observable in the 28th verse. First we must remember that this writing is prophetic. It was not fulfilled in the days of David. For the most part it has not happened even yet today. But a day is coming when this verse will be fulfilled. Elohim, Yahweh, the LORD, Adonai, as God, will take charge of the kingdom or the whole world, which has always been His. That day will be very special, for Jesus Christ will take control as Governor and rule in the hearts of men in all nations throughout the world.

8.2 GREAT:

NAME VARIATIONS In: 1 Ch. 16:25

BECK	because the LORD is great and ought to be praised
JER	Yahweh is great, loud must be his praise,
KJV	For great is the LORD and greatly to be praised:
LIV. BIBLE	For the Lord is great, and should be highly praised;
NAS	For great is the LORD, and greatly to be praised;
NEB	Great is the LORD and worthy of all praise.
NIV	For great is the Lord and most worthy of praise;
NKJV	For the LORD is great and greatly to be praised;
RSV	For great is the LORD and greatly to be praised,

To Whom Does This Name Belong?

The word "great" is used in a relationship to the LORD.

The Argument:

The Hebrew word gadal (SRN 1419), meaning to be or become great, can be applied to God in either a quantitative or a qualitative fashion. In the quantitative sense, the word is used as an adjective modifier for expressions having to do with physical size—or potency. Great appears in such examples as "great lights" (Gen. 1:16), "great darkness" (Gen. 15:12), "great nation" (Gen. 17:20) and "great plenty" (Gen. 41:29). The word "great," used in the quantitative sense, is not applied as a name of God in the Old Testament.

But in qualitative applications such as "great is the LORD" (1Ch. 16:25; Psa. 145:3; 147:5) or "thou are great O LORD God" (2Sa. 7:22) there is a close possibility that the qualitative word "great" describes an attribute of God and, therefore, qualifies as a name of deity. If we take this approach then the synonyms for the word "great" might include excellent, eminent, superior and remarkable. We will look at one example, "Great is the LORD" (Psa. 145:3). Quantitatively this would indicate that the LORD is larger or more intense. All are true statements, for the word "great" is simply an adjective modifier of "the LORD" and is not a name. But if we consider the word in the qualitative sense then we have an appropriate phrase, especially when written "the LORD is great," as some versions prefer. Indeed, the word might be replaced by a synonym whereby the phrase could read Excellent or Superior is the LORD.

One final observation: In all of the OT, the word "great," used in the sense of qualification, is not found as a stand alone name for God.

There are reasonable objections regarding the use of this word as a name of God, and for that reason "Great" will not be accepted as a name of God in this study—but it is certainly worth thinking about.

8.3 HOPE OF ISRAEL:

Strong's Concordance Index indicates there are only 2 references in the OT to the name of God "Hope of Israel." Both passages appear in Jeremiah; however, the application of the phrase is different in the two verses, requiring careful and separate consideration of each entry.

The passages are listed below as they appear in the 9 Bible versions involved in this study.

Reference	Jer. 14:8	Jer. 17:13
BECK	You are Israel's hope	O LORD, the hope of Israel
JER	Yahweh, hope of Israel	Hope of Israel, Yahweh
KJV	O the hope of Israel	O LORD, the hope of Israel
TLB	O Hope of Israel	O LORD, the hope of Israel
NAS	Thou Hope of Israel	O LORD, the hope of Israel
NEB	O hope of Israel	O LORD, on whom Israel's hope is fixed
NIV	O Hope of Israel	O LORD, the hope of Israel
NKJV	O Hope of Israel	O LORD, the hope of Israel
RSV	O thou hope of Israel	O LORD, the hope of Israel

To Whom Does This Name Apply?

In both passages the name applies to the LORD.

The Argument:

In the Jeremiah 14:8 passage, 4 of the versions in our study apply the of- (genitive) possessive phrase, "Hope of Israel," as a name of the Lord. In these cases (TLB, NAS, NIV, and NKJV) the phrase is treated as a name of God with appropriate capitalization. This is similar to the use of the word Savior in the same verse. Savior refers to the Person who saves Israel, a clear reference to the LORD. Savior is the participle formed from the verb to save. The Beck version comes close to the same approach, but the word hope is not augmented with capitalization, thus eliminating this "s" genitive phrase, "Israel's hope" as a name of deity. The phrase "hope of Israel," (no caps on hope) in several versions (JER, KJV, NEB, RSV) makes for problematic reading, since the text in these versions seems to apply the phrase to deity but fails to set the word off with capitalization.

In summary, then, the phrase "Hope of Israel" will be treated as a name of God in this study even though the AV, used as our standard, does not do so. This is simply based on the weight of the evidence from the other versions.[74]

In the Jeremiah 17:13 passage only one of the studied versions (TLB) seems to treat the of-(genitive) phrase "Hope of Israel" as a name of deity. The other versions treat the word as an adjective or a descriptive phrase modifying the noun LORD, i.e., O LORD the hope of Israel. Certainly this is correctly interpreted. The LORD is "the" hope of Israel through all the ages. In Jeremiah's day, time and time again the LORD delivered Israel until the nation looked at divine rescue as their certain, sure expectation. Salvation from trouble was expected as something the Lord would bring as the hope of Israel. And this continues to be true today; the only hope for Israel is the LORD. Therefore, whether these words are applied as a name, "Hope of Israel," or as

---

[74] 44% of the 9 versions in our consideration elect to capitalize the word hope in the application of the word in the name of God "Hope of Israel".

an adjective phrase, none the less it is one of His attributes and, consequently, one of His names. He is "the Hope of Israel."

Purpose Of This Name:

The LORD is the certain, sure expectation or hope for Israel and for all that trust in Him. As such a hope, one of His names is the Hope of Israel. Indeed, all believers have their hope in the LORD, the Hope of Israel.

8.4 HORN OF MY SALVATION:

The name "Horn of my Salvation" appears only twice in the OT; in 2Sa. 22:3 and in Psa. 18:2. The interrelationship of the 2 passages has been observed previously.[75] Further comment is unnecessary except to remind the reader that similarity of the original texts is expected since David was the author of both passages. It can be seen in the Scripture version comparisons, shown below, that only about 50 percent agreement exists between the versions. However, much closer agreement occurs in the meanings of the passages. They all speak of the One in whom the strength of salvation rests.

Version	2Sa. 22:3	Psa. 18:2
BECK	mighty One who saved me	my Horn of salvation
JER	my horn of salvation	my horn of salvation
KJV	the horn of my salvation	the horn of my salvation
TLB	and my salvation	the strong horn of a mighty fighting bull
NASB	the horn of my salvation	the horn of my salvation
NEB	my mountain fastness	my mountain refuge
NIV	horn of my salvation	the horn of my salvation
NKJV	horn of my salvation	horn of my salvation
RSV	horn of my salvation	horn of my salvation

To Whom Does This Name Apply?

David, the servant of the LORD, applies this name to his LORD. Likely David was thinking of the many magnificent deliverances he had experienced in his own day as his God led and protected him. However, this psalm expresses much more, for it is

[75] See Chapter 6 page 97.

also prophetic, speaking of the Messiah/Christ in His sufferings and deliverance from above, as well as of His exaltation and His coming kingdom.

The Argument:

The circumstances involved in the writing of this psalm need not be repeated here. However, it is appropriate to consider the meaning of the words in the phrase making up the name. First consider the word "horn". Several meanings are associated with the original Hebrew word qeren (SRN 7161), literally an animal's horn, then a musical instrument, a flask or container for liquid, a projection at the corners of an offering altar, the summit or top of a hill or, most important here, the symbol of power associated first with animals and then with men. One dictionary[76] indicates that when God exalts the horn of an individual He confers great power and prosperity on that person. Unger writes, "There are two principal applications of this metaphor, strength and honor." (Psa. 18:2).[77] So we can expect that this word implies strength, power and honor.

Then look at the word salvation. It means safety, deliverance, to rescue, and to save. For example, the Old Testament prophecies speak of the One to come, the Messiah, who will bring peace, joy and salvation.

---

[76] Henry Snyder Gehman, *The Westminster Dictionary of The Bible*, Westminster Press, Philadelphia, 1944, p. 255.
[77] Merrill F. Unger, *The New Unger's Bible Dictionary*, Moody Press, Chicago, Renewed, 1985, p. 588.

So this descriptive name means the One with great strength and power, in whom is my deliverance and safety. This often refers to physical safety, to be sure, but it also relates to deliverance from the power of sin.

As for the individual passages, both 2Sa. 22:3 and Psa. 18:2 are from songs of David. In the first case, David waxes forth with a series of metaphors extolling the strength and greatness of the LORD his God. Likely he accompanied himself on a stringed instrument in solo fashion. When we get to the canonical psalm we find again the music of David but modified this time for use in the place of worship.

The Purpose Of This Name:

Man needs to be reminded again and again of the marvelous deliverances God has wrought and will yet provide in the lives of His children.

The Old Testament Names of God

A Perspective

Chapter 9

Contents

*Appendix Support

9.1 HOLY:

The beginning of the study of the word "holy" imposes certain interesting limitations and impressions not encountered previously. The English word holy may be translated from anyone of six Hebrew words. Therefore, this assemblage of Hebrew words needs to be established first. Then an identification will be made of the specific Hebrew word from which the term of interest is derived. Finally, applications and locations of the word holy, if applied as a name of God, are presented. This collection of prospective divine names is assembled in an effort to identify the locations of the stand alone name "holy" when applied to deity. Whereas some of the compound word applications to be studied are easily recognized as names of God (e.g., Holy One), other singly occurring uses of holy are much more difficult to accept as names of deity. They seem more like adjective modifiers instead. Perhaps one reason that the stand alone word holy is difficult to accept as a name for deity is that it is too easy to consider a given occurrence of holy to be a noun, even though it is more likely to be an adjective. For example, in the KJV consider "For thus saith the high and lofty One that inhabiteth eternity, whose name is Holy..." (Isa. 57:15). It appears that the author is writing about One whose name is "Holy." Indeed, one reference book[78] actually makes this statement, "Holiness is such an essential attribute of God that 'holy' becomes a descriptive name." However, other Scripture versions do not agree, simply indicating

---

[78] G. W. Bromiley, Ed., *The International Standard Bible Encyclopedia*, Vol. 2 Eerdmans Pub., Grand Rapids, 1988, Reprint p. 508.

that the name of the high and lofty One is of holy quality but that a name of deity is not suggested.

In numerous places the OT[79] presents the LORD declaring, "I am holy." This could mean that He is called Holy especially because His identifying name is "Holy." Or it could indicate that the LORD is simply speaking of His innate attribute or character of holiness. Of course this is absolutely proper, for two of the primary characteristics of God are His righteousness and holiness,[80] these being displayed and spoken of frequently throughout the Scripture.

Let's look further into the meaning of the term holy or holiness. One source states that holiness[81] is a general term used to indicate sanctity or separation from all that is sinful, impure, or morally imperfect. The term is used with reference to persons, places and things. Holiness is one of the essential attributes of the divine nature. God's holiness is absolute and unvarying, and it is the standard of all holiness.

Zondervan's Dictionary[82] speaks of holiness and holy as words derived from the Hebrew root word qadash (SRN 6942). The basic meaning is separateness or the state of being withdrawn. It is first applied to God, and it is early associated with the ideas of

---

[79] Lev. 11:44, 45; 19:2; 20:26; 21:8 and others.
[80] In a search for words exactly synonymous with holy, none were found. Righteousness, meaning just, is close but different than holy, meaning separated or set apart. God is righteous, He is just. God is also set apart, that is, apart from all others. He is apart from the sin and degradation of mortals. Therefore, holy and righteous mean different things and are not synonymous.
[81] M. F. Unger, *The New Unger's Bible Dictionary*, Moody Press, Chicago, Rev. 1988, p. 581.
[82] M. C. Tenney, *The Zondervan Pictorial Bible Dictionary*, Zondervan Pub. Rev. 1978, p. 357.

purity and righteousness. In the OT holiness in its positive sense refers to the pure, loving divine nature, which is wholly separate from evil yet unwilling to retreat before it, aggressively seeking to universalize life itself and spiritually transforming human beings who have entered into personal relations with God. It is interesting to note that the words "holiness" and "holy" do not appear in Genesis, even though the discovery of God's holiness is implied in the dread or awe which the presence of God inspires. Remember the name "the Fear of Isaac" (Gen. 31:42, and vs. 53). But from Exodus 3:4 and onward, wherever God reveals His name and nature holiness is stressed.

The Argument:

The word "holy" generally appears in compound with other terms, for example Holy One or Holy Spirit. But in two places (Pro. 9:10 and 30:3) in the King James Version the term "holy" (SRN 6918) appears as a stand alone name. This has been changed to "Holy One" in the NKJV, but it continues as a stand alone name in the current KJV. Bible. For this and the other reasons in the above argument, the term "holy" is accepted as a stand alone name of God.

Effort to identify stand alone applications is important, since the word holy is not only a name of God per se but is involved in many other compound names. See Appendix 9 for further consideration, argument, detail and explanation.

9.2 HOLY ONE:

Previous considerations of the basic word "holy" in this text and in the supporting Appendix provide not only information about stand alone names but also yield facts about the compound names incorporating it. We learned that there are 6 Hebrew words that can be translated into the English word "holy." Of these Hebrew words only 3—chasiyd (SRN 2623), qadosh (SRN 6918) and qaddiysh (SRN 6922)—are translated into the English compound expression "the holy One," wherein both of the English words Holy and One are required to form a name of God. However, the words chasiyd and qadosh can have the sense "The Holy One" in Hebrew without technically requiring the actual presence of helping words such as "the...one." Researching the English compound the Holy One, translated from the Hebrew chasiyd, shows that there are but three Scriptural applications. In Deu. 33:8 (your holy man) and again in Psa. 89:19 (your holy one) the Hebrew word is applied to the high Priest. But in Psa. 16:10, the word is translated your Holy One with reference to the Christ and His suffering and death. Therefore, Holy One is considered a name of deity. Then let us look briefly at qaddiysh (SRN 6922). This Hebrew word is used twice in Daniel Chapter 4 to describe a watcher or angel. Neither of these applications involve a name of deity. But look now at qadosh. Eight times the Hebrew is translated to mean the Holy One and is easily accepted as a name of God.

Summation: The stand alone word Holy has been accepted as a name of God, as has the compound expression the Holy One. Eight of the English applications are derived from the Hebrew word qadosh (6918). One is derived from the Hebrew word chasiyd (SRN 2623). It is easily understood why some Scripture versions translate the Hebrew to mean the Holy One while other versions arrive at the stand alone word Holy. The details of the verse locations and the use of these words are presented in Appendix 9.

9.3 HOLY ONE OF ISRAEL:

The "of"-(genitive) expression, "the Holy One of Israel," is the third name of God to be considered in this "holy" series. The previous examination of the names "Holy" and "the Holy One" have produced significant information for this segment of the study. For example, the Hebrew word chasiyd (SRN 2623), is not used in the phrase and deity name, the Holy One of Israel. Only the Hebrew words qadosh and qadowsh (SRN 6918) are used in this name. They appear 40 times in the OT. Isaiah applies this expression 30 times and is certainly its major user. Jeremiah employs the phrase only twice in his writings. Psalms contains this possible name of God three times, and it is recorded in 2Ki. 19:22 that Isaiah used this favorite identifier in his dealings with Hezekiah. It is also interesting to note that the English phrase the Holy One of Israel is translated from two Hebrew words in combination, qadosh (the Holy One) and yisrael (Israel). Both words are required to form this genitive compound name of God. This is important when we remember that it is the possessive genitive that shows sphere or life style interrelationship between the members of the compound, in this case Israel and the LORD. Consult Appendix 9, Table A.9.3. for further details.

Just as it was expedient to examine the words Holy and the Holy One and then to demonstrate their applications as names of God, so the use of the genitive compound, the Holy One of Israel will now be examined as a possible name of God.

The most direct approach to verifying that the phrase, "the Holy One of Israel" is indeed a name of God is simply to seek confirmation of that fact in the OT. As has been previously stated, both Isaiah and Jeremiah clearly apply this compound name to identify the Person of the God-head being addressed on numerous occasions. For example, Isaiah 10:20 reads, "And it shall come to pass in that day, that the remnant of Israel, and such as are escaped of the house of Jacob, shall no more again stay upon him that smote them; but shall stay upon the LORD, the Holy One of Israel, in truth." Isaiah clearly identifies the LORD or Yahweh as the Holy One of Israel.[83] Then in Isaiah 30:15 God is referred to as the Lord God, or Adonai Yahweh, the Holy One of Israel. In Isaiah 43:3, the writer provides multiple identifications saying that Yahweh is your God (Elohim), the Holy One of Israel, your Savior. Then in Jeremiah 50:29 the LORD and the Holy One of Israel are applied as synonyms, as is very frequently done by Isaiah, Jeremiah and writers of the Psalms.[84] After this brief review certainly no doubt remains that the phrase the Holy One of Israel, is a title of God.

[83] For other strong identification of the LORD, see passages such as Isa. 41:14; 43:14; 45:11; 48:17 and many other verses.
[84] Psa. 71:22; 78:41.

9.4 HOLY ONE OF JACOB:

Earlier in this chapter, examination of the Hebrew word qadosh (SRN 6918) has shown that this Hebrew expression translates into the English words Holy One, which clearly is a name of God. It has also been seen that Holy One *per se* is sometimes applied as a name of God but more frequently is coupled with the word Israel to form the name the Holy One of Israel.[85]

However, on just one occasion, occurring in Isa. 29:23, the writer employs the same Hebrew word, qadosh, coupled with the name Jacob to arrive at a new name of God, "the Holy One of Jacob." This appears unusual, since Jacob and Israel are the same person (Gen. 32:28), so why is the new name applied?

The Argument:

The concerned passage (Isa. 29:22-23) basically reads as follows: Thus said the LORD, who redeemed Abraham, concerning the people of Jacob (natural posterity of Jacob elsewhere called Israel). Jacob's family (his descendents or natural Israel) will not be ashamed or be pale faced, for when Jacob's natural family, Israel, sees what I the LORD have done among them, Jacob's people will treat My name (Elohim) as holy and treat the Holy One of Jacob as holy and stand in awe of the God of Israel (spiritual Israel).

---

[85] See the previous study in this chapter on the Holy One of Israel.

The house of Jacob represents the non-spiritual part of Israel that was cast out of the land of promise because of their evil doings. Meanwhile, throughout the land a remnant held on to the promise of restoration and blessing (Gen. 28:15). The exiled group is to be called back to the LORD in Christ, and at that time this part of Jacob's house will marvel at His name, that is, the name of Christ. They will now treat this Holy One of Jacob, even Christ—so long neglected—with honor and respect. Then they will stand in awe at the God of Israel, the God of that spiritual remnant of Israel that knew Christ all along.

The Purpose of this Name:

Obviously there is a need for two names, the Holy One of Israel and the Holy One of Jacob, because the patriarch Jacob relates to his progeny under two conditions, the natural man and the spiritual. These two will be united spiritually into one family in Christ at that day.

9.5 <u>HOLY SPIRIT</u>:

The fifth and final identifier to be considered in this holy name series is the Holy Spirit. Both parts in this two-fold appellation are required in order to fully express the name in either English or Hebrew. The English name "the Holy spirit" is translated from two Hebrew words, qodesh (SRN 6944) and ruwach (SRN 7307), which make up the compound. Qodesh has been considered earlier and means, among other related things, holiness, apartness, or sanctity. The word ruwach means breath or life, spirit or, on occasion, the Spirit of God or the Spirit of the LORD.

Any significant examination of the name the Holy Spirit will touch on details of the Doctrine of the Holy Spirit. His name is prominent in the OT, being applied in multiple locations in the form Spirit, the Spirit, the Spirit of God, the Spirit of the LORD, or the Holy Spirit. The full range of these names is beyond the scope of this manuscript. Therefore, an effort will be made to limit this examination to the name Holy Spirit in the three places where it occurs.

The Argument:

The compound name the Holy Spirit is applied in only three passages in the OT First, in Psa. 51:11 David, in deep contrition for his sin with Bathsheba, addresses God (Elohim). David is concerned about being cast away from the presence of God and the loss of His Spirit, who here is called Holy, establishing the name the Holy Spirit.

Then in Isa. 63:10, 11 the writer discusses the goodness, kindness and mercy of God and the great work of the LORD on behalf of Israel. God was their Savior and friend in all their troubles. He loved them and pitied them. God redeemed them. He took them up and carried them all the days of long ago. "But they rebelled and grieved His Holy Spirit. So He turned to be their enemy and fought against them. Then His people remembered the days of old and Moses: Where is He who brought them up out of the sea with the shepherd of His flock? Where is He who put within them His Holy Spirit?"[86]

The people of Israel had been greatly blessed by God in the days of old, but now they rebelled, and Scripture says that they grieved not the Person of Yahweh (or the LORD) but rather the Person of His Holy Spirit.

These instances clearly show that two Persons are involved—the person of the LORD (Elohim) and the Person of the Holy Spirit. Each has a name and each is addressed by his name.

The word Holy, either as a stand alone name or in the three compound names studied in this chapter, denotes that aspect of God's greatness involving His being set apart from and far above all His creations. The revelation of this aspect of God's status has always been needed by man, for it drives home to our hearts just who God is.

---

[86] William F. Beck, *The Holy Bible in the Language of Today*, Copyright 1976, A. J. Holman, Leader Press, Philadelphia, p. 862.

The Old Testament Names of God

A Perspective

Chapter 10

Contents

*Appendix Support

10.1 I AM THAT I AM:

	NAME VARIATIONS IN:	REFERENCE
BECK	I AM WHO I AM	Exo. 3:14
JER	I Am who I Am	
KJV	I AM THAT I AM	
TLV	The Sovereign God	
NAS	I AM WHO I AM	
NEB	I AM; that is who I am	
NIV	I Am Who I Am	
NKJV	I AM WHO I AM	

To Whom Does This Name Apply?

"God revealed Himself to Moses not as the Creator-God of power, Elohim, but rather as the personal God of Salvation," whom we recognize from other descriptive passages as the LORD, or Yahweh. All that the name "I am" contains shall be manifested through the ages to come, culminating in Jesus Christ, whose "I AM" illuminates the pages of the New Testament.[87]

The Argument:

Moses had been called of God to lead the children of Israel out of Egypt. Moses, feeling somewhat insecure and apprehensive at such an assignment, asks Elohim for special information so he will be able to respond to the people when they ask what God's name is. "And God said unto Moses, 'I AM THAT I AM': and He said, 'Thus shalt thou say unto the children of Israel, I AM hath sent me unto you'." (Exo. 3:14). God

---

[87] Philip C. Johnson, "Exodus," *The Wycliffe Bible Commentary*, The Moody Press, 13th Printing, 1976, Chicago, p. 55.

said, "I AM THAT I AM, but you, Moses, shall tell the people that my name is simply, 'I AM'." "And God said moreover unto Moses, 'Thus shalt thou say unto the children of Israel, "The LORD God of your fathers, the God of Abraham, the God of Isaac, and the God of Jacob, hath sent me unto you": this is my name forever, and this is my memorial unto all generations'." (Exo. 3:15).

How absolutely amazing! The great God of the universe speaks to the man Moses and declares, "I have a name, I Am That I Am," (in Hebrew, 'ehyeh 'ªsher 'ehyeh). Hebrew scholars[88] point out that the verb 'ehyeh is imperfect qal and is linked to the tetragrammation. Of the two possible senses for it, "I am who/what I am" and "I will be who/what I will be," the latter is preferable, because the verb hayah has a more dynamic sense of being—not abstract pure existence, but becoming, happening, being present. The historical and theological context of the early chapters of Exodus shows that God was revealed to Moses, and subsequently to the whole people—not the inner nature of His being, but His active, redemptive intentions on their behalf. He "will be" to them "what" His deeds will show Him "to be."

Now in a discussion such as this, don't lose track of the supreme truth that is presented, for that is most important. God is not an abstraction, He is the living God, and He calls Himself by the name "I AM That I AM." Remember that Moses had been informed of God's name but that God also told Moses to say unto the children of Israel,

---

[88] G. W. Bromley, General Ed. *The International Standard Bible Encyclopedia,* Eerdmans Publishing Co., Grand Rapids, CR. 1982/88, Vol. II, p. 507.

"I AM hath sent me to you." But what does this mean? One suggestion is that[89] the name Yahweh expresses active manifestation of existence, that is, not what God is in Himself, rather what God will approve Himself to be to others. He will be to Moses and his people what He will be—something which is undefined but which, as His full nature is more completely unfolded by the lessons of history and the teachings of the prophets, will prove to be more than words can express." The meaning of the name is certainly not the same to everyone, because all people do not perceive Him equally. This does not mean at all that Yahweh is a variable but rather that people vary in their personal sensitivity, observations and interpretations of His acts and deeds. Even His self-description, as listed in the 9 Scripture versions earlier in this chapter, is variously translated. Six versions see His name as I Am Who I Am.[90] Three versions prefer different name renderings, yet all nine viewpoints are from the same original language.

This name is echoed throughout the Scriptures as the writers continually use the verb "I am," the very same identifier that God used with Himself to Moses, with additional words identifying God. For example,[91] God identifies Himself clearly by the phrase "I am the LORD" some 161 times in the OT. He refers to Himself by the expression "I am God" some nine times and states that "I am He" 11 times, and yet some have failed to recognize Him. Other identifiers are used like the comforting

---

[89] *The Wycliffe Bible Commentary*, The Moody Press, 13th Printing, 1976, Chicago, p. 55.

[90] with capitalization variables that are not repeated here.

[91] The peculiar thing about Hebrew is that in this kind of phrase there is no verb such as <u>is</u> or <u>am</u>. It's structured very much like Tonto's English—"that man very bad," or "I hungry." The phrase rendered "I am

phrase "I am with thee" which appears 10 times. And there are many individual uses of the statement "I am" in such phrases as "I am gracious" (Exo. 22:27), "I am merciful" (Jer. 3:12), "I am jealous" (Zec. 1:14) and "I am a great king" (Mal. 1:14). Then the statement is applied in a negative way in some 16 verses where the LORD emphasizes His "no vote" concerning a specific condition.[92]

The Purpose Of This Name

The name "I AM THAT I AM" calls attention to the indescribable nature of God, who provides our marvelous salvation. Many identifiers are contained in this names of God manuscript, but they all inclusively fail to begin to describe the total essence of His character; how can one single name identify Him? Yet the Holy Spirit presents here in one place a name that represents what God has done in the past, is doing now and that which He will yet do in the future.

---

the LORD," is actually (in Hebrew) "I the LORD," and you may spot such phrases in those translations which supply the missing words using italic type.

[92] Jer. 21:3; 23:30; Eze. 5:8; 13:8; 21:3; Nah. 2:13; 3:5, etc.

10.2 JUDGE
JUDGE OF ALL THE EARTH
JUDGE OF THE EARTH
THE LORD IS OUR JUDGE

In the beginning, the OT computer concordance was carefully searched for information concerning the use of the term "judge" as applied to deity. This proved most interesting, for while the names God and the LORD are referred to nearly 50 times in action statements specifying that they are involved in judging people, only on the listed four occasions does the Scripture refer to deity specifically by the name judge. It is these four applications that are of special interest here, since the intent is to accept or reject the given usage as a name of God.

The meaningful practice of Scripture version comparison has been applied to the candidate verses and the phrases of interest listed in Table 10.1. This means that initially an examination has been made for the presence of stand alone names. In the process of searching for them, other applications were located in which the name YHWH was combined with the term judge. The name Judge and the compound names are all presented together because of the similarity of the compounds.

Table 10.1

Scripture Version Variations

Ver.	Gen. 18:25	Jdg. 11:27	Psa. 94:2	Isa. 33:22
Beck	the Judge of the whole world	the LORD, the judge	Judge of the world	the LORD is our Judge
JER	the judge of the whole earth	Yahweh the judge	judge of the world	Yahweh is our judge
KJV	Judge of all the earth	the LORD the Judge	Thou judge of the earth	the LORD is our judge
TLB	Judge of all the earth	the judge	judge the earth	the Lord is our Judge
NAS	Judge of all the earth	the LORD, the Judge	O Judge of the earth	the Lord is our judge
NEB	the judge of all the earth	LORD who is judge	judge of the earth	the LORD our judge
NIV	Judge of all the earth	the LORD, the judge	Judge of the earth	the LORD is our judge
NKJV	the Judge of all the earth	the LORD, the Judge	O Judge of the earth	the LORD is our Judge
RSV	Judge of all the earth	the LORD, the Judge	judge of the earth	the LORD is our judge

The Argument:

From Table 10.1, it can immediately be observed that only in a single case (Judges 11:27) is there initial agreement in all examined versions that the LORD is the Judge. Grammatically, He has judged, He is judging and He will yet judge. The LORD is the Judge. It is not merely an attribute; Judge is a name.

Examination of the more controversial verse Psa. 94:2 results in the observation that there are some differences of opinion among the Scripture versions concerning the meaning of the phrase, "judge of the earth." For example, the NKJV interpretation of verses 1 and 2, in keeping with the general tenor of the early portion of this psalm, addresses deity with a series of titles. First appears the formal name, Yahweh Elohim. This is followed immediately with the ascription "to whom vengeance belongs." Then God is addressed a second time as Elohim, again with an ascription "to whom vengeance belongs." The psalm writer pleads in this series of titles, "show thyself" to this miserable group of wicked enemies. Then the psalmist goes on and says, "Lift up thyself, O Judge of the earth," or the One Judging the earth; or, converting to the "s" genitive, "earth's Judge." Here it seems obvious that direct address of Yahweh using His rightful title "Judge" is occurring in the form "O Judge...." But more than that, Yahweh is the Judge, supreme Judge, Judge of all, the only Judge. Therefore "Judge of all the earth" as applied in this verse in the NKJV version is considered a name of God.

In the older KJV version, the same phrase, "judge of the earth," is set forth in another form of direct address, "Thou judge...." Those translators do not seem to consider either the single word judge or even the whole phrase to be a name of God. So care needs to be taken regarding the version being studied. Or, better yet, intercompare several versions. In the older KJV version, the phrase, "judge of the earth" is not considered a name of God. Yet in the newer NKJV the same phrase, "Judge of the earth," is accepted as a compound name of God.

Now examine the phrase, "the Judge of all the earth," as found in Gen. 18:25. Scripture version comparison indicates good agreement between the several versions considered. Yahweh is the Judge of all the earth. Clearly, the Genesis writer seems to feel that (in the "s" possessive genitive) "all the earth's Judge" or "the Judge of all the earth" is an appropriate name of God.

Finally, look at the phrase "The LORD is our Judge" found in Isa. 33:22. Scripture intercomparison shows that all the versions agree on a similar English metaphoric translation meaning that the LORD is represented as our Judge. He is the Person qualified to give an assessment or decide on the relative worth of anything. Indeed the LORD is our arbiter, with emphasis on the authoritativeness of decision of One whose Judgment in a particular matter is considered indisputable. For these reasons the phrase, "the Lord is our Judge" is accepted as a compound name of God.

The Purpose Of This Name:

God is the arbiter in all things: He knows our histories from yesterday, the demands upon us today and the events to come tomorrow. Truly, be reminded, He is the wise personal Judge of each of us.

10.3 <u>KING</u>:

In the OT the word "king" is commonly applied to a male ruler, sovereign or monarch. He may be either limited or absolute in his authority over a nation, state, principality or, sometimes, only a city, the ruled domain usually being called a kingdom regardless of size. According to the computer concordance the use of the term king occurs some 1677 times in the OT. However, this study has only a passing interest in most of these officials. It is the relatively few occurrences applied to deity—only 26 times by concordance count (see Appendix 10, Table A.10.1) that become possible entries as names of God.

To Whom Does The Name Apply?

The usage of "King" that draws our interest is closely associated with the name LORD (Yahweh), LORD of hosts or God (Elohim) in all but 3 of the 26 select verses. In those three passages the name "King" closely relates to the Messiah.

The Argument:

The word king is very commonly used in the OT with genitive qualifiers to define or name a person. For example, "Melchizedek king of Salem..." (Gen. 14:18). The term is also frequently found in a general relationship to royalty, for example, "...before there reigned any king over the children of Israel" (Gen. 36:31), or "there was no king in Israel" (Jdg. 21:25). Such uses as these, as well as the relatively few applications where deity is referenced, need consideration.

The word King, relating to deity, is of such a nature in the text as to require no proof or credential. The Scripture simply states that God is King.[93] The term is a valid name of God. It is not of concern in the cases where the word King is applied to deity whether the word can be justified as a name of God, for this is a given.

The Purpose Of The Name:

In the world economies of today, where the governing power is largely democratic, the true meaning and application of the word King has largely been lost. But the word King still identifies a person with authority and power in the very top echelon of the system. God is King. It is His world and He is in full control now and forever.

[93] Examples of King-related deity statements are: "the LORD is King" (Psa. 10:16); "my King and my God" (Psa. 5:2); "the LORD is a great God and a great King" (Psa. 95:3).

10.4 KING OF GLORY:

The word King, when used in relationship to deity, requires no proof or defense, as demonstrated in connection with Table A.10.1. The statement is absolute, the King is unquestionably God or the LORD. He is the King. But when it is applied to Deity the word King can be combined with other appropriate compound members to form other names of God. We will look at these compounds with the intent to determine their authenticity.

Before the phrase, "King of Glory," as a possible name of God can be objectively considered, the word glory requires special study and investigation. What does glory mean? It appears 214 times in the OT. In addition there are numerous secondary verbs like glorify and glorified, plus adjectives like glorious and adverbs like gloriously. Scripture speaks of the glory of certain people such as Jacob (Gen. 31:1) or Joseph while he was in Egypt (Gen. 45:13). Moses uses the word glory addressing King Pharaoh in an idiomatic expression, "glory over me" (Exo. 8:9). Moses effectively says, "Honor yourself, King, by selecting the time for me to pray about this frog problem."

Then, in addition to people, inanimate objects such as garments and houses (Exo. 28:2, 40 and 1Ch. 22:5) seem to have glory. Even heaven itself is spoken of as displaying glory. Then, of course, the Scriptures refer to the glory of deity some 123 times in phrases like "ye shall see the glory of the LORD" or "ye shall give glory unto the God of Israel" (Exo. 16:7 and Isa. 6:5). So glory is something that was seen or perceived in the OT. Now, the term glory is translated into English not from a single

Hebrew word but from 14 different Hebrew words. But more complex than this, the 14 are also sometimes translated into the word glory and other times into words like honor or majesty or beauty—or one of 24 other words more or less related to the concordance's definition of the word glory.

Even today, in our daily personal walk with our God, we repeatedly apply the word glory in expressions like "let me see Your glory" or "let my actions bring glory to Your name." So we must know what glory means! Actually, we should stop and ask questions. What do we mean? What are we saying? What does this word glory signify? It's difficult to come to grips with the subject. For instance, consider the definition of glory from the academic or scholastic point of view. One encyclopedia offers this comment:[94]

> Glory is a comprehensive term applicable to both men and God, reflecting such qualities as esteem, reputation, essential worth, prestige, fame and honor. As used of God, it is deemed particularly appropriate for describing His moral uniqueness and grandeur as Lord of the universe.

On the other hand, a Bible Dictionary[95] defines glory as...

> the exhibition of the excellence of the subject to which it is ascribed. Concerning God, it is the display of His divine attributes and perfections.

---

[94] Edward F. Harrison, "Glory," in *The International Standard Bible Encyclopedia*, Eerdmans Publishing Co., Grand Rapids, CR 1982/1988, Vol. II, p. 478.
[95] Merrill C. Tenney, General Ed., *The Zondervan Pictorial Bible Dictionary*, Zondervan Publishing House, Grand Rapids, CR 1967, p. 315.

> Concerning man, it is the manifestation of His commendable qualities such as wisdom, righteousness, self control and ability. A connotation of splendor is included, such as `the glory of the moon and the stars.'

The New Unger's Bible Dictionary[96] speaks of glory as...

> the exercise and display of what constitutes the distinctive excellence of the subject to which it is spoken; thus, in respect to God, His glory is the manifestation of His divine attributes and perfections, or such a visible splendor as indicates the possession and presence of these (Exo. 33:18-22; 16:7, 10). God's glory is the correlative of His holiness, that is, in which holiness comes to expression. Glory is the expression of holiness, as beauty is the expression of health. In respect to man, God's glory is found in the things that reveal His honorable state and character, such as wisdom, righteousness, superiority to passion, or that outward magnificence that is expressive of what, in the lower sphere, bespeaks the high position of its possessor.

Certainly there is agreement with these definitions; however, before the word glory can be fully understood, at least the predominant variations in Scriptural use must be comprehended. These include what can be seen, what fills, what can be given, declares, moves about, departs or abides; what sanctifies, what can be owned, and at least a dozen other similar characteristics.

Realizing the extensive detail peculiar to the subject "The Names of God," it was early on elected to limit this study to the OT. That has proven to be a wise choice and quite satisfactory on all but a few names. For instance, this limit has imposed difficulties both with the word glory and in the previous considerations of names involving the term holy. In both cases, the option to apply textual information from the New Testament would have significantly eased the search for appropriate descriptive examples. This is particularly true when instances from the life and actions of our Lord must be omitted. However, the restriction has been rigorously applied, remembering that the term glory can be more easily grasped when viewed in relation to our Lord and His beauty and attributes.

Others have written appropriate comments applicable to this study, and they will be included here. Dr. Charles Rolls has this to say:[97]

> Glory is as difficult to define as light, because it constitutes the exclusive excellence of the divine character in its essence and entirety, and consists of all the attributes essential to Deity blended harmoniously in perfect unity. Each characteristic is of equal proportion whether it is divine goodness, graciousness, gentleness, greatness, righteousness, repleteness, restfulness, pureness, perfectness, peacefulness, preciousness, loving-kindness, fullness, tenderness, mercifulness,

---

[96] Merrill F. Unger, *The New Unger's Bible Dictionary*, CR 1957/88, Moody Press, Chicago, p. 479.
[97] Charles J. Rolls, *The Indescribable Christ,* CR by Loizeaux Brothers, Neptune, NJ, 1984/88, p. 179.

> changelessness, truthfulness, meekness, holiness, blessedness, joyfulness or the score of other qualities that comprise the very nature of the Godhead. Christ in person is the exponent and full expression of every feature of Deity.

There is no doubt that a great deal more could be said about the word "glory" and what it means to the child of God, but this study must press on.

To Whom Does This Name Belong?

The "King of glory" or the "glorious King" is clearly identified as Yahweh, the LORD of hosts (Psa. 24:7, 8, 9, 10).

The Argument:

In Psalm 24, David writes of the earth's ownership and they that dwell therein. All belong to Yahweh by right of creation. But in support of this declaration, the Psalmist goes on to the consider the rule of this vast array. Who shall rule this creation? It is a matter of worthiness. Scofield, in his notes, comments[98], "...and no one is worthy but the Lamb." David writes of the One he knows through long experience, the One who is fully qualified, and he carefully names this Person. He is Yahweh, the LORD God of hosts; He is worthy, He is "the King of Glory" or "the Glorious King." That is His name.

---

[98] Scofield, *The Scofield Reference Bible*, notes, Oxford University Press, New York, CR 1909/45, 610.

The Purpose of the Name:

"The King of Glory." This particular name of God has required a fuller study than other names for at least two reasons. First, there is an effort being made to define in limited English terms thoughts and meanings that are simply beyond description. How is one to put into words in one place all the attributes and characteristics of God? It cannot be accomplished, and yet that is the object, and that is the effort. Indeed, even to take any single attribute of God and attempt to fully examine and document it is beyond reason. Yet He is the King of Glory; that is, God's glory is infinite in nature and extent.

Secondly, the concept of glory is near and dear to the heart of God. It is closely associated with worship, which He deserves from all men (cf. Isa. 42:8). After all, this word so grand and full of meanings, applied in so many ways in the Scripture, refers to His praiseworthiness, which is most wonderful and awe-inspiring in extent. It is in the display of some of the given aspects of His glory that His children can begin to understand that His attributes are limitless in perfection.

10.5 KING OF HEAVEN:

The Old Testament contains a significant quantity of of-(genitive) expressions, frequently appearing in names of God. Several of this type of construction have already been studied. The expression King of heaven, now to be considered, is an example of an of-(genitive) used in a name of God.

Chapter seven presented at some length names of the "of-genitive" type. Even so, the following reflective comment seems appropriate here. Remember that the central idea of the genitive is that of "sphere," indicating that a person or thing belongs to a particular sphere of another, that is, having a close relationship to it or forming an integral part of it. The name "King of heaven," appearing only in Daniel 4:37, illustrates such a sphere, for certainly heaven is in close relationship to God.

To Whom Does This Name Apply?

The Person given honor and praise in Daniel 4:34 and referred to there as the "Most High" or "El Elyon" is the same Person honored and praised again and identified as the "King of heaven" in verse 37.

The Argument:

The name "King of heaven" appears in the OT only a single time, namely, in the autobiographical sketch of King Nebuchadnezzar involving his humbling experience in coming to know the true God (Dan. 4:37). Indeed, this great heathen king puts in writing his conversion experiences and calls attention to the writings by addressing them to "...all people and languages that dwell in all the earth." No conversion testimony is without excitement, and at that time a royal soul was turned to God and eternity. But the story this king writes is most unusual, for he suffered a Judgment of God upon his sins called lycanthropy, that is, disease involving the afflicted person's delusion that he is an animal.

To start at the beginning, the mighty King Nebuchadnezzer had a dream which both terrified and alarmed. It is interesting to note here that the fright was caused by a dream—one undoubtedly sent by God, but only a dream. God, who has all power, could communicate with this king in any one of many ways, but God chose a dream. That is often the way God deals with His creatures. He applies the usual, the common, the familiar so that the person will understand and not get mixed up with special, unusual happenings that have no bearing on the situation. God used a scary dream, and the king paid immediate attention.

The king said that he was living without a worry, prospering in his palace, when he had the vision that neither he nor any of his wise men, sorcerers or astrologers understood, though he called them all. At last Daniel came in. The king told him the contents of the dream, that a great tree grew in the middle of the earth, large enough to be seen from the farthest part of the world. Now this tree was very beautiful, with leaves and fruit enough to feed everybody. The animals found shade under it, and the birds nested in the branches. It fed every living thing. The king said that he dreamed that a holy one came down from heaven and directed that the tree be cut down. Strip off the leaves and scatter the fruit. Drive the animals away from beneath it and the birds from the branches, but leave the stump with its roots in the ground. Leave the stump bound with a band of iron and bronze in the tender grass of the field. Then, speaking as if the bound stump were a person, the holy one continued: ...let him lose his human mind and be given the mind of an animal. And let him remain like this for seven years.

Daniel was speechless for awhile. What should be do? What should he say? He didn't want to offend this heathen king and stir up his ruthless nature. Daniel immediately knew the interpretation, but he was slow to speak, because this king was a cruel and violent man. It was this king who heated the oven seven times hotter in order to roast three young Hebrew men who refused to bow down before his golden image. It was this king who had the eyes of Judah's king Zedekiah put out after he had the man's sons slain before his very face. Certainly Daniel had reason to be a bit hesitant in his response to Nebuchadnezzar. On the other hand, maybe Daniel had even grown to like this king. At any rate, after some delay, Daniel says, "It is thou O king..." and Daniel follows up with a recommendation, "...break off thy sins by righteousness, and thine inequities by showing mercy to the poor..." (Dan. 4:22-27). Well, the king didn't change, so God didn't change, and the Judgment occurred at the end of 12 months exactly as it had been spelled out. For seven years Nebuchadnezzar acted like a wild beast, living in the fields, eating grass, drinking water from the rains. His head was down and away from God. But the best part is yet to be told. At the end of the appointed time this king was returned to normal, even as he had been, except for one thing. He had a changed heart. He looked up to God; he had a personal experience with God, and it made a great difference; for in the king's own words he says, "My reason returned unto me, my glory, my honor, and my brightness all returned, and I was established in my kingdom and excellent majesty was added to me." But the king had abandoned his pride, and I think that he had also lost his old cruel, bitter, vindictive spirit. He had learned that not Nebuchadnezzar but God had done it all. So he says, "Now I, Nebuchadnezzar, praise and extol and honor the King of heaven, all whose works are truth, and His ways Judgment: and those that walk in pride He is able to abase." (Dan. 4:37.) It was a very difficult lesson, but now the king of Babylon knew God by the name the King of heaven.

The Purpose Of The Name:

There are a multitude of God's characteristics displayed in this amazing portion of Scripture. Judgment of the king for his sin is paramount. But then there is a demonstration of the great outpouring of God's long-suffering and mercy in the life of Nebuchadnezzar. The glory and power of God are very obvious to both Daniel and the king. But then, we can't miss the patience of God as He waits for the king to have a change of heart. Finally, the king is just amazed at the seven years of preservation through derangement and then the full restoration of God in his personal affairs. All these aspects of God's sovereignty are experienced by the king, and he gives a great testimony of praise, honor and exaltation to this great God, the very God of heaven.

10.6 KING OF ISRAEL:

	NAME VARIATIONS In:	INITIAL REFERENCES
BECK	King of Israel	Isa. 44:6
JER	Israel's king	
KJV	King of Israel	
TLB	King of Israel	
NAS	King of Israel	
NEB	Israel's King	
NIV	Israel's King	
NKJV	King of Israel	
RSV	King of Israel	

To Whom Does This Name Apply?

The name basically belongs to Yahweh, the LORD, the King of Israel, the Redeemer, the Lord of hosts. But prophetically the title the King of Israel correctly applies to Jesus Christ the King.

The Argument:

The genitive expression "king of Israel" occurs 129 times in the OT whereby various kings are introduced, spoken of or spoken to. But the phrase "the King of Israel", used in addressing or identifying God, is found only once. In Isaiah 44:6 the LORD God is clearly titled with a series of epithets as the King, Israel's Redeemer and the Lord of hosts. The One is proclaimed as the First and the Last, and beside Him there is no God.

The Purpose Of The Name:

The title "King" has lost much of its royal meaning in today's culture. Titles such as President, Ruler and Majesty are more popular and common. But in the OT world, the term king was the nearly universal title of office for the top ruler with complete authority over his kingdom. Yahweh asserted His right to be the King of Israel. The divine identity of the promised Messianic King was poorly understood in those times. He is the unaccepted King of Israel today, but the day is coming when He will be acknowledged as King of Israel and of the whole world.

10.7 KING OF JACOB:

	NAME VARIATIONS In:	INITIAL REFERENCES
BECK	King of Jacob	Isa. 41:21
JER	Jacob's King	
KJV	the King of Jacob	
TLB	King of Israel	
NAS	King of Jacob	
NEB	Jacob's King	
NIV	Jacob's King	
NKJV	King of Jacob	
RSV	King of Jacob	

To Whom Does This Name Apply?

Yahweh, the God of Israel, the King of Jacob—or as some versions read, Jacob's King—is speaking and reminding His people of His might and of the nothingness of the heathen idols.

The Argument:

The of-(genitive) "King of Jacob" occurs but a single time in the OT, and that's here in Isaiah 41:21. A contest is under way at this point. God has challenged the heathen idols to show their power, and how He challenges the heathen idols to speak out as to their abilities and knowledge; but of course there is no response from these pieces of wood and bits of metal. God has identified Himself as the Holy One of Israel, the First and the Last. Then for the sake of His audience he reminds them of their heritage through Jacob, for even then the LORD was in control as the King of Jacob.

The Purpose Of This Name:

The LORD, in connection with the demonstration of true divinity being presented to this court of Judgment, calls for a display of greatness and power. But there is no real contest, because the LORD, the only God, leads and protects His people Israel, for they are His servants. The heathen gods are no match, for they are as nothing. Even before Jacob was renamed Israel, God was watching over him. But it has always been that way. The Lord cares for His own even before His ownership is manifested.

10.8 KING OF NATIONS:

	NAME VARIATIONS In:	INITIAL REFERENCES
BECK	King of the nations	Jer. 10:7
JER	King of nations	
KJV	King of nations	
TLB	King of nations	
NAS	King of the nations	
NEB	king of the nations	
NIV	King of the nations	
NKJV	King of the nations	
RSV	King of the nations	

To Whom Does This Name Apply?

"Forasmuch as there is none like unto thee, O LORD; thou art great, and thy name is great in might. Who would not fear thee, O King of nations?" (Jer. 10:7). Obviously, it is the LORD being spoken to by this phrase.

The Argument:

This portion of Jeremiah attacks the uselessness of idols in a manner similar to that observed in the previous Isaiah study involving the "King of Jacob." Again we read of the vast contrasts between the incomparable majesty of the LORD and the coarse materialism of idols.

"Thou are great and thy name is great in might O King of nations." This title is unique in the Scripture, but near it are found related expressions like, for example, "For the kingdom is the LORD's and He is the governor among the nations." (Psa. 22:28), or "God reigneth over the heathen: God sitteth upon the throne of His holiness (Psa. 47:8), or "And the LORD shall be King over all the earth: in that day shall there be one

LORD, and His name one." (Zec. 14:9). The LORD is the King of the nations, the true God; He is the living God and the everlasting King. What a tremendous contrast between the true God and an idol or false god. What a tremendous name, "King of the Nations."

The Purpose Of This Name

Kings, rulers and governors of nations we know about and accept in our day, even as the Israelite did in his. But the thing they and we so easily forget is that over these officials rules the King of Nations. He is over all. All that happens occurs because he allows it to happen, and all that doesn't happen doesn't occur because he intervened. Let us remember the true God, the King of the Nations, the everlasting King.

10.0 KING OVER ALL THE EARTH:

	NAME VARIATIONS In:	INITIAL REFERENCES
BECK	King over all the earth	Psa. 47:2
JER	King of the whole world	
KJV	King over all the earth	
TLB	King of all the earth	
NAS	King over all the earth	
NEB	sovereign over all the earth	
NIV	King over all the earth	
NKJV	King over all the earth	
RSV	King over all the earth	

To Whom Does This Name Apply?

"The LORD most high is awesome; He is a great King over all the earth." The LORD...is awesome...is a great King and He reigns over all the earth. There can be no doubt, it is the LORD and His majesty as King that is being discussed.

The Argument:

The phrase "King over all the earth" occurs in only two OT verses, Psa. 47:2 and Zec. 14:9. Both of these verses refer to the LORD in His millennial kingdom, expressing the relationship of the King, the LORD, to all the earth. He is not only the God of the Hebrews, but also the Universal Sovereign Ruler, and one of His names is "King over all the earth."

Now let us make some interesting comparisons. Because "King over all the earth" rightfully belongs as a name, then "King of all the earth" from Psa. 47:7 is also accepted as a name. Both verses boldly indicate that "the King rules all the earth."

It is interesting to observe the variations in translation shown in the above Name Variation Chart. Six versions maintain the word "above" in the translation, preventing the phrase from being an "of" genitive. One version modifies the phrase to the "whole world," and still another version replaces the word "king" with the word "sovereign." These are simply interesting variations in translations, but we keep in mind that all are from the same original Hebrew documents.

The Purpose Of The Name:

God is King of everything—king of Glory, of Heaven, of Israel, of Jacob, of the Nations. God is King over all the earth, over the whole world. Whether His Kingship is considered in its separate aspects or in total. He is King of the whole earth, transcending the Glory of His Heavens, and His believers are His subjects. Let us bear this continually in mind.

The Old Testament Names of God

A Perspective

Chapter 11

Contents

11.1 LAWGIVER

The participial form m^{e}choqeq of the Hebrew word chaqaq) (SRN 2710) is translated into the English word "lawgiver" in six different verses in the AV of the OT. However, only in the Isaiah account is the word to be considered as a direct title of God. In Gen. 49:10 no name or title is directly applied to God, but the word lawgiver is indirectly used in reference to God, or in this case the Messiah.[99] Translation of m^{e}choqeq into the English word lawgiver occurs in four other verses, but since none of these are considered names of God, only minor attention will be given to them.

NAME VARIATIONS

REF.	KJV	NIV	BECK	TLB	MOFFATT
Gen. 49:10	lawgiver	ruler's staff	ruler	scepter	part. Out
Num. 21:18	lawgiver	scepters	scepters	leaders	captains
Deu. 33:21	lawgiver	leader	ruler's	leader	nation's chief
Psa. 60:7	lawgiver	scepter	My scepter	kings	baston
Psa. 108:8	lawgiver	scepter	My scepter	scepter	baston
Isa. 33:22	lawgiver	lawgiver	Ruler	Lawgiver	captain

[99] Gen. 49:10 is one of the great Messianic verses. "Jacob foresees and foretells: 1. That the scepter should come from Judah; 2. Shiloh, that peaceable and prosperous One or Savior, should be of the tribe of Judah; 3. That after the coming of the scepter, it shall remain the tribe of Judah." (Matthew Henry's Commentary, p. 68-69.

In considering the word lawgiver the six verses of primary concern from several Scripture versions will be compared. It is interesting to observe the wide variations in translation in the various versions. The word lawgiver, having been chosen as the reference word, naturally will appear in all the selected KJV verses. However, keep in mind that the word lawgiver is but one of about ten English words that can be translated from the Hebrew verb chaqaq. Some of these are to decree, to inscribe and to engrave, all of which are related to the promulgation and recording of laws and ordinances. Awareness of this prepares the reader for observing the variations in the translations that appear in the other Scripture versions. For example, the NIV elects to use the word lawgiver only in Isaiah 33:22. Neither the Beck nor the Moffatt translations use the word lawgiver at all, and Moffatt even elects to paraphrase the "lawgiver" out completely in the Gen. 49:10 application. Attention to this translation variation is somewhat aside from the mission at hand of finding and verifying names of God. However, the word lawgiver presents a good example of the variation in translations that impedes name study, yet at the same time increasing interest in the study.

To Whom Does This Name Apply?

It is quite clear that the Person referred to in Isaiah 33:22 is the LORD, for we are told that "the LORD is our judge, the LORD is our lawgiver, the LORD is our king..." He is our Lawgiver: that is a name.

The Argument:

Matthew Henry's Commentary summarizes Chapters 32 and 33 of Isaiah in this manner.[100] These Scripture writings relate to the distress and trouble of Judah and Jerusalem brought on by Sennacherib's invasion and to Israel's deliverance by the unusual destruction of the Assyrian army. Additional pertinent details concerning Chapter 33, verses 17 through 24 are gathered from the Wycliffe Bible Commentary as follows.[101]

> This passage, judging from the statement that Jerusalem will be inviolable, is a foreglimpse of the Millennial kingdom. Therefore, the king of Israel must be Christ in His regal splendor, reigning over a world-wide domain (v. 18-19). The Almighty prophesies the complete removal of latter-day 'Assyrians' from the scene, after their abortive siege of Jerusalem. The undisturbed quiet of the Holy City indicates a time after the conclusion of the 'times of the Gentiles.' Yahweh's presence, with a Zion obedient and faithful, will insure her impregnable defense (v21). She will be like a city surrounded by protective moats—impenetrable to enemy ships—and fructifying streams. No mere man is sovereign over Israel, but the LORD God Himself, and this insures her ultimate deliverance. But, the invading ship of Assyria (figuratively speaking) will run helplessly

---

[100] Matthew Henry's Commentary, Zondervan Publishing House, Ed. 13, 1974, p. 874.
[101] Wycliffe Bible Commentary, Moody Press, Chicago, Ed. 13, 1976, p. 632.

aground, with its tackling loosened; and all its contents will become spoil to the Hebrew defenders.

There will be no more spiritual sickness in the cleansed and forgiven land of latter-day Israel, because the LORD is her Judge, her lawgiver, her King and her Savior.

Particular Aspect Of God's Character Highlighted:

The LORD is our Supreme Lawgiver, Judge, Commander, Governor, Enforcer and Interpreter, yet He does it all in love and with perfect concern for His own.

The Special Need Of Man Met By The Revelation Of This Aspect Of His Character:

Man begins to assume that he is the provider of the law, that he is the judge, governor and enforcer. But man is not the true lawgiver, for all that man has comes from the LORD, who is the ultimate Lawgiver and Judge. It is needful that man be reminded of his dependence upon God.

11.2 LEADER:

The word "leader" (naqiyd, SRN 5057) specifically appears in three verses in the OT; however, only in the Isaiah 55:4 passage can it be considered a possible name of God. Here, even if the verse is simply referring to David, it would certainly be applicable. David was a witness to the nations, a leader and a commander to the people, exalting the Lord among these he conquered.[102] Of course, in that case the word leader would not be considered a name of God. Many commentators—Wolf, Bultema, Matthew Henry and Gleason Archer[103]—take the viewpoint that the leader of Isaiah 55:4 is the same person as Messiah the Prince (or Leader) spoken of in Daniel 9:25. Then, from the information at hand, it is concluded that the Isaiah 55:4 passage does indeed pertain directly to the word Leader and is used as a name of God in this verse.

NAME VARIATIONS

REF.	KJV	NIV	BECK	TLB	Moffatt
Isa. 55:4	leader	leader	prince	para.out	leader
Dan. 9:25	Messiah the prince	Anointed One	anointed Prince	Anointed One	high priest

[102] Herbert M. Wolf, *Interpreting Isaiah*, Academie Books. Zondervan Pub., Grand Rapids, CR 1985, p. 221.

[103] (a) Ibid., p. 222.
(b) Wycliffe Bible Commentary, Gleason Archer, *Isaiah*, Moody Press, Chicago, Ed 13, 1976, p. 648.

Comparison of name variations in various Scripture versions provides interesting word observations. The Hebrew word nagid means a person high in importance, a commander or captain, a chief, a leader, a ruler or a prince. From the varying translations of the Hebrew into English it can be seen that differences of opinion exist as to its meanings. The KJV, NIV and Moffatt agree that the proper translation is the English word leader. On the other hand Beck has chosen another of the Hebrew meanings, namely, prince. In either case the word Leader or Prince can well refer to the Lord Jesus Christ.

Pursuing the Hebrew word nagid a bit further shows that the word prince, applied in the KJV version of Daniel 9:25, is the same word that both the NIV and the Living Bible translate into the ruler. At the same time, the Beck version uses anointed prince and Moffatt uses supreme high priest. Probably none of these translations are any more right or wrong than any other, because all come from the same Hebrew root word. Of course, in the Daniel verse, this name study accepts only the word leader; the other English words are left for proper consideration elsewhere in this study.

To Whom Does This Name Apply?

As previously discussed, the name Leader in the Isaiah 55 verse might refer either to David or to Christ; however, this study accepts the word as a title of God, applying to Jesus Christ in the ages to come.

The Argument:

Some considerable differences exist among commentaries as to who the "Him" refers to in the Isaiah verse. However, the arguments identifying this person as the Lord Jesus are sufficient, so that, as mentioned above, this manuscript agrees that this person is Christ at His second coming.

Two quotations from the literature will be included here in the application of the name "Leader." First consider excerpts from Bultema's Commentary.[104]

> (1) The word 'behold' always demands special attention and is very often used before Messianic predictions to call special attention to the Messiah. (cf. 7:14; 42:1; Jer. 23:5; 33:14; Zec. 6:12.
>
> (2) The language used here is far too strong to refer to David, Cyrus or any other famous person.
>
> (3) The Lord Jesus as the Messiah is emphatically called <u>nagid</u>, leader in Daniel 9:25. In 1Ch. 9:20 and 11:2 that word is translated ruler. That is what the Lord Jesus will be to all nations after His return. By right he is this already; He will be this actually at His coming again.
>
> (4) The word witness in Isa. 55:4 anticipates His prophetic work at His Second Coming. The word leader points to His additional office as King. In Jeremiah 30:9; Eze. 34:23-24; 37:24-25 and Hosea 3.5 the

---

[104] Harry Bultema, *Commentary On Isaiah*, Kregal Publications, Grand Rapids, CR 1981, p. 551.

> Lord Jesus is presented as the great King David. After His return the Lord Jesus will rule as the King of kings and Lord of lords. The word commander designates Him as the royal Lawgiver who will command and instruct all nations.

Or yet again, consider the following excerpt from Matthew Henry.[105]

> Jesus Christ is promised {to us} for the making good of all the other promises which we are here invited to accept (Isa. 55:4). He is that David whose sure mercies all the blessings and benefits of the covenant are. There was nothing in us to merit such a favour, but Christ is the gift of God. We know not how to find the way to the waters where we are to be supplied, but Christ is given to be *a leader*. We know not what to do, but He is given for a *commander,* to show us what to do and enable us to do it. Christ is a commander by His precept and a Leader by His example; our business is to obey Him and follow Him.

Particular Aspect Of God's Character Highlighted

Three aspects of the character of the Lord Jesus are mentioned in Isaiah 55:4. He is to be a witness to the people, a Leader of the people and a Commander enabling the people.

---

[105] Matthew Henry Commentary. Zondervan Publishing House, Ed. 13, 1974, p. 911.

The Special Need Of Man Met By The Revelation Of This Aspect Of His Character

So many of the world's leaders and rulers of today think that they can provide the direction and guidance that this old world needs, but they can't, and the world staggers on blindly. The only possible satisfying Ruler, Commander and Leader that will ever fulfill the needs of the world is revealed in the Lord Jesus at His second coming. His leadership is the greatest need of the world today.

The Old Testament Names of God

A Perspective

Chapter 12

Contents

*Appendix Support

12.1 INTRODUCTION TO THE LORD, Lord, lord SERIES OF NAMES:

In the beginning of this study of these names it should be immediately understood that any argument of whether or not it is deity in discussion is unnecessary, since LORD is translated from the Hebrew word Yahweh, and to say Yahweh is to say God. "The Lord," translated from the Hebrew word 'adōnāy, is used only as an honorific name of God. So, obviously, the words LORD and Lord are names of God. However, the consideration of the word lord requires some special investigation because the basic Hebrew word 'adōwn or its cognates are, on occasion, addressed to God.

The expanded review of these names immediately brings to mind two questions: (1) hasn't this material been considered previously, and (2) why take a series of names at one time, instead of the usual single name approach. These are good questions, so let us provide immediate answers. First, this manuscript examined earlier and in some detail the LORD, Lord, lord series of names. It was then obvious that the names Lord or LORD, as singular entries, and Lord or LORD in compound with other support names (as well as the word lord addressed to man and sometimes God) are very common throughout the Old Testament. The results of these investigations were recorded in earlier portions of this manuscript, particularly in Chapters 1,2 and 3. However, as the alphabetical arrangement of the names of God now arrives sequentially at the name Lord, there is a need to supplement and add to the earlier work. This will be done in a style similar to that used with regard to the other names. However, the previous entries will be allowed to remain in their places, because it was appropriate that some very early consideration of these very important names be presented. Chapter 12 refers back to the previous information whenever necessary in order to present a more complete study of the names. The prior information location is displayed in Table 12.1.

The second question was concerned with the reason for examining a series of names rather than a single name. This approach does not actually interfere with the intention to consider the various names lord, Lord and LORD and their appropriate compounds in singular fashion. The series nomenclature is applied only as a convenient referencing procedure.

12.2 LORD:

Now, to begin the study of the name LORD, consider Table 12.1. Here are listed for cross reference purposes the initial appearances in the Old Testament of the single and compounded names of the LORD that have previously been studied. The three KJV appearances of the word "Jehovah" in the AV, even though not yet considered in this study and, therefore, marked N/A, are listed for completeness. Some variations in the applications of the name LORD are also displayed and then discussed.

It is also appropriate to call special attention to Jer. 23:6. In the KJV the compound name of Yahweh is rendered "THE LORD OUR RIGHTEOUSNESS" (all capital letters). This same title in the NIV is given as The Lord Our Righteousness, while in the Jerusalem Bible this name is written Yahweh-our-integrity.. This verse is one of 15 cases[106] where all letters are capitalized in a word or phrase in the OT Presumably this uniqueness in printing style indicates the importance which translators along the way have attached to these words.

[106] Large capital letters are used in the AV in Exo. 3:14 (twice); Exo. 6:3; Exo. 28:36; Exo. 39:30; Deu. 28:58; Psa. 68:4; 83:18; Isa. 26:4; Jer. 23:6; Dan. 5:25-28; Zec. 3:8; Zec. 6:12 and Zec. 14:20.

Table 12.1

THE NAME THE LORD

Name	Ref.	Location	KJV	NIV	Beck	Jer.	Mof.
LORD	GEN. 4:1	Chap. 1, p.1	the LORD	LORD	LORD	Yahweh	Eternal
LORD God	Gen. 2:4	Chap. 1, p.1	the LORD	LORD	LORD	Yahweh	Eternal
LORD of Hosts	1Sa. 1:3	Chap. 1, p.19	the LORD	LORD	LORD	Yahweh	Lord
LORD our Maker	Psa. 95:6	Chap. 2, p.3	the LORD	LORD	LORD	Yahweh	Eternal
LORD Most High	Psa. 7:17	Chap. 1, p.18	the LORD	LORD	LORD	Most Hi.	Eternal
LORD Who Heals	Exo. 15:26	Chap. 3, p.8	the LORD	LORD	LORD	Yahweh	Eternal
LORD our Righteousness	Jer. 23:6	Chap. 3, p.15	the LORD	LORD	LORD	Yahweh	Eternal
LORD who Sanctifies	Lev. 20:8	Chap. 3, p.12	the LORD	LORD	LORD	Yahweh	Eternal
LORD is Shammah	Eze. 48:35	Chap. 3, p.19	the LORD	LORD	LORD	Yahweh	Eternal
LORD our Shepherd	Eze. 34:15	Chap. 3, p.17	Lord God	Sover. LORD	Lord God	Lord Yah.	Lord Eternal
Jehovahjireh	Gen. 22:14	Chap. 3, p.6	Jehovah	LORD	LORD	Yahweh	Yahweh
Jehovahnissi	Exo. 17:15	Chap. 3, p.10	Jehovah	LORD	LORD	Yahweh	Eternal
Jehovahshalom	Jdg. 6:24	Chap. 3, p.13	Jehovah	LORD	Lord	Yahweh	Eternal
Jehovah	Exo. 6:3	N/A	Jehovah	LORD	LORD	Yahweh	Eternal
Jehovah	Psa. 83:18	N/A	Jehovah	LORD	LORD	Yahweh	Eternal
Jehovah	Isa. 12:2	N/A	Jehovah	LORD	LORD	Yahweh	Eternal
Jehovah	Isa. 26:4	N/A	Jehovah	LORD	LORD	Yahweh	Eternal

The above Table clearly indicates that translation of the English word the LORD (from the Hebrew word Yahweh), must be somewhat discretionary. For example, although the use of the name the LORD is predominant in many popular English Scripture versions, there are some variations. For instance, the NIV uses the word consistently. However, while the Old Testament of the AV normally conforms to this practice, in seven verses the translators have elected to use the un-translated word Jehovah rather than the LORD. Three of these seven are component parts of compound names. The other four are those yet to be considered.[107] It must also be noted that the Jerusalem Bible generally applies Yahweh in place of the word the LORD, but there are exceptions. Moffatt translates the original term into the word Eternal most of the time, but he is not fully consistent, either.

Beck's version has one strange application in Judges 6:24, where the Lord is used in place of the LORD. This may simply be a printing error in that particular version.

Why do the Scripture versions differ in translating the name the LORD? In order to answer this question we will look for clues in the text material and also in the prefaces and introductions to each of the versions we are using. That information is included in this text in order to assist in understanding this name.

---

[107] The other four applications of the word Jehovah, not yet discussed, appear in Exo. 6:3; Psa. 83:18; Isa. 12:2 and 26:4.

What Some of the Selected Versions say about the name "LORD"

NIV

The Preface reads,

> "In regard to the divine name YHWH, commonly referred to as the Tetragammaton, the translators adopted the device used in most English versions of rendering that name as "LORD" in capital letters to distinguish it from *Adonai*, another Hebrew word rendered 'Lord', for which small letters are used."[108]

Beck

In regard to the divine name YHWH nothing is specifically mentioned in the Beck version[109] about the use of the word "LORD" (all capital letters) as a translation of the *Tetragrammaton*. However, this practice consistently prevails throughout the version with the word "Lord" or "the Lord" being a translation from the Hebrew word 'adonay.

Jerusalem

In regard to the divine name YHWH, commonly referred to as the Tetragrammaton, this version elects to transliterate the Hebrew name Yahweh in place of "the LORD," attesting to this form as accurate but possibly a problem maker, especially in the Psalms, even to the point of being unacceptable. Where

---

[108] *The Holy Bible*, New International Version, Zondervan Bible Pub. Grand Rapids, CR 1973, 1978, 1984, Preface, p. x.
[109] *The Holy Bible, In The Language of Today*, William F. Beck, A. J. Holman Co/Leader Press, CR 1976.

this occurs the reader may elect to substitute the traditional "the Lord." This improperly implies that Yahweh is translatable to the name "the Lord" rather to the name "LORD" or "the LORD." (See the paragraph on Hebrew Scripture Considerations that follows.)

KJV

The Preface to the basic KJV version does not discuss the name "LORD." However, this word is used to indicate the God of Israel multitudinous times in the Old Testament. The name Jehovah, per se, appears but seven times, with three of these applications in compound with other support names. From this it can be surmised that the name the LORD, meaning the God of Israel, is paramount. Jehovah, as a name, barely ranks in frequency of occurrence, perhaps being used for accentuation purposes, while the true personal name of God, "YHWH" or "Yahweh" is not used at all.

MOFFATT

In the introduction to the Moffatt version[110] there is a rather detailed discussion of the translators' problems in moving from Hebrew to reasonable, meaningful and correct English. This difficulty is repeatedly caused by the fact that no English equivalent exactly corresponds to the original word's meaning. Moffatt goes on to point out a crucial example of this difficulty, found in a Hebrew term which lies in the prehistoric

---

[110] *A New Translation of The Bible*, James Moffatt, Harper & Brothers Publishing, CR 1935, p. xx and xxi.

name given at the exodus by the Hebrews to their God. Moffatt says, strictly speaking, this should be rendered "Yahweh," which is familiar to modern readers in the erroneous form of "Jehovah." Were this version intended for students of the original, there would be no hesitation whatever in printing "Yahweh." But almost at the last moment Moffatt says he decided with some reluctance to follow the practice of the French scholars and translate this name by the words "the Eternal" except in an enigmatic title like "the Lord of hosts." Moffatt goes on to say that there is a distinct loss in this--that is, to drop the racial, archaic term is to miss something of what it meant for the Hebrew nation. On the other hand there is a certain gain, especially in a book of lyrics like the Psalter. Moffatt comments that in this version his present choice will be understood even by those who may be slow to pardon it.

Hebrew Scripture Considerations: Jehovah

The variations observed in Table 12.1, together with the additional support from the comments following that Table, encourage further investigation into the name LORD. As a matter of fact, the decision made by the English translators to use the word LORD is based on ancient Jewish practice. For example, the first translation of the Old Testament into a foreign language was the Greek Septuagint, which translated YHWH into the Greek word for Lord, Kurios. All Jewish literature followed the same custom—literature in Hebrew, Aramaic and Greek–and Christians accepted that tradition and made it their own. However, Jehovah, the form of the name that's most familiar, is incorrect. Here's why.

The original Hebrew was written without vowel letters, so every time reference was made to the proper name of the God of Israel, it was simply written YHWH (the Tetragrammaton). During the intertestamental period and on into New Testament times because the scribes and devout Jews feared using the name YHWH in a profane way, they would not pronounce the word at all. When they came to the written word YHWH, they substituted the word 'adonay. Later, when the Masoretes came along with their vowel pointing system, whenever they came to the Tetragrammaton, they actually put the vowel points for the word 'adonay in the text. The four letters, with the points for the substitute word 'adōnāy, came to represent the name of the God of Israel. Literally it means "my Lord" par excellence, which was considered to be a suitable alternative for the Tetragrammaton. But this isn't all. Not only is there this linguistic oddity in the Hebrew, but the English translators misunderstanding the modified Hebrew and choosing to set aside in certain passages the normal practice of substituting the word Lord, clumsily transliterated the word directly into English as Jehovah. According to the rules of Hebrew linguistics, however, the name should be pronounced Yahweh. So now there exists the choice of Yahweh or LORD in English, while in Hebrew, Scripture readers continue to read an improperly pointed Tetragrammaton with the vowels for 'adōnāy (my Lord). No wonder there is confusion.

Included here are Unger's[111] concise comments on the hybrid name Jehovah.

---

[111] Merrill F. Unger, *The New Unger's Bible Dictionary,* Moody Press, CR 1985, p. 781.

The true pronunciation of the name YHWH, by which God was known to the Hebrews, has been entirely lost; the Jews themselves scrupulously avoiding every mention of it. In its stead they substituted one or the other of the words with whose proper vowel points it may happen to be written, usually the Adonai (Heb. 'adōnāy). They continued to write YHWH but read Adonai. Where God is called "My Lord Jehovah" (Heb. Adōnāy YHWH), Elohim was substituted to avoid the double Adonay. When the vowel points were added to the Hebrew text, the rule, in the case of words written but not read, was to attach to these words the vowels belonging to the words read in place of them. Thus they attached to YHWH the points of 'adonay; hence the form Y^{e}h'v'h.

To Whom Does The Name LORD Belong?

From this discussion it is clear that the English name "the LORD" applies to Yahweh or YHWH, the only truly personal name of God in Israel's faith. The initial introduction of this name, in stand alone fashion, appears in Gen. 4:1.

What Is Involved In The Application Of The Name?

The name or Yahweh appears more than 6500 times in the Old Testament, so it is important to understand something of these applications. As can be seen in Table 12.1, sometimes the name stands alone as LORD, and at other times the name is a part of a compound expression, all components of which must be present for the name to be complete. Now, when the basic word LORD is carefully examined, several interesting details appear. First, in Strong's Hebrew and Chaldee Dictionary, the SRN of the word LORD is given as 3068 and of course remains so whether the name is alone or compounded. Strong goes on to say that the transliteration of the Hebrew is Y^{e}hovah, meaning the self-Existent or Eternal Jehovah, the Jewish national name of God-Jehovah the Lord.[112]

The Brown-Driver-Briggs Hebrew and English Lexicon comments on page 217b that YHWH, when properly pointed, produces the Hebrew word Yahweh and means the proper name of the God of Israel. This lexicon also indicates "the pronunciation Jehovah was unknown until 1520, when it was introduced by Galatinus,[113] only to be immediately contested by Le Mercier, J. Drusius and Capellus as against grammatical and historical propriety." Unfortunately, the pronunciation Jehovah became popular and remains with us to this day.

---

[112] Refer to the name Jehovah in Chapter 1, p, 4.
[113] Petrus Galatinus, confessor of Leo X, AD 1518.

12.3 lord:

As this manuscript progresses, it is convenient to next examine the name lord. As we do so, it will soon become apparent that the nicety of the application of the English word "lord" only to deity has been lost, for this name is used to address both God and man.

Two Hebrew words are translated "lord" in the OT. One is 'adown (according to Strong) or (according to modern usage) 'ădōn. The other is 'ădōnāy. It is intended here to consider these terms individually. However, because of subtle differences in the traditional English rendering of these words some discussion of the interrelationship between the two is necessary.

The word 'ădōn can be translated into English, as owner, master, husband or lord. It is most commonly applied to man as a term of respect, often being used with reference to an acknowledged superior. When man is addressed the English word is usually written "lord," with no capital letters, and it has been assigned the SRN 113. The word lord initially appears in Gen. 18:12, where Sarah uses it in reference to her husband. But this word in the plural is also used by Lot in addressing angelic visitors (Gen. 19:2). The Pharaoh of Egypt was called by this title (Gen. 40:1). Hannah addressed Eli the priest with this same title (1Sa. 1:15). Indeed, the word lord appears some 321 times in 278 verses in the OT; 289 occurrences address man, 31 apply to God. Obviously, when applied to man it is not a name of God.

It should be noted that the form 'ādōni (my lord, 1Sa. 29:8) of the word 'adown has a plural, 'adōnay (my lords, Gen. 19:2). The word 'ādōnay can be a problem if care is not exercised to distinguish it from the special emphatic divine title 'adōnāy, (SRN 136; Eng. Adonai), meaning my Lord, Lord or O Lord. This last word is carefully distinguished from the word used in Gen. 19:2, but one must look closely to see the difference. Only when reference is made to the Lord is there a long "a" in the last syllable. More on this will follow, but first look again at this Hebrew word 'adōwn as it applies to God in numerous places in the OT. For example, it is found in Deu. 10:17 in the comparative expression "Lord of lords." Lord is applied there to God compared with other gods or even with great men, but both expressions, Lord and lord, bear the same SRN. 'Adōwn is used to address God especially in the Books of 2 Samuel, Psalms and Isaiah. When it occurs the translated word in English is usually written with a capital "L", with the other letters in lower case, as in "Lord."

12.4 **Lord**:

Then Consider the Word Lord Applied to Deity:

'Adōwn also appears in the special plural form, with a first common singular pronominal suffix ('ădōnāy, SRN 136). In this form it always refers to deity, and it is translated into English as "the Lord," or "my Lord," or simply "Lord." This special intensified form is found some 416 times in the OT, and although closely related to 'adōwn, it is to be counted as a separate name of God. English translations generally, again, use an upper case "L" with the other letters lower case.

Summarize the Names lord/Lord

1. The word 'adōwn, the form 'ădōni and its plural 'ădōnay, are applied to man. English translations are usually written lord or lords. Obviously these words are not names of God.

2. The word 'adōwn is applied to God on some occasions, while its special emphatic form 'ădōnāy is applied only to deity. The Masoretic vowel pointing's difference between 'ădōnay and 'ădōnāy must be observed. 'ădōnay means lords or my lords in the plural. The second word translates to "the lord" or "my Lord." The first word is not a name of God. The second word is a name of God.

3. Even though only three Hebrew words are involved ('ădōn, 'ădōnay, and 'ădōnāy), the English translation into lord, my lord, my lords and the Lord all sound disconcertingly similar. Obviously, English usage is not the best way to locate a given name of God here.

There are three other Hebrew words that are sometimes translated into the English word "lord." These are g^{e}biyr (SRN 1376), shalosh (SRN 7969) and Yahh (SRN 3050). The first two words are used only to address man. The Hebrew word Yahh is a name of God, appearing most often in the praise term, "Hallelu Yah." This will be examined in detail in proper alphabetical sequence.

4. Individual English Scripture versions are not very helpful in ascertaining whether a particular application of lord is a name of God due to variations in translation. However, comparison of several versions is a good way to select names. Indeed it was Miles Coverdale in about 1538 who said, "one translation declareth, openeth and illustrateth another."

5. Last of all, the hybridization of God's name YHWH by the Hebrew substitution of the vowels for 'ădōnāy can be confusing when searching for and selecting God's name.

THE COMPOUNDS

It has been observed that the names LORD (Heb. YHWH), Lord (Heb. 'ădōnāy) and lord (Heb. 'ădōn with special considerations) can be stand alone or single element names with or without appropriately attached pronouns and the definite article. In the true sense a combination of a pronoun and a name of deity constitutes a multiple-element expression or name. Therefore, we count these phrases as names of God even though the words LORD, Lord and sometimes lord are names of God independent of any other pronouns and/or the definite article. For example, Lord vs. my Lord or Lord vs. the Lord. Lord is a name of God with or without the attached pronoun or definite article.

Now we want to investigate compound expressions applying to LORD, Lord and lord where all members of the compound phrase must be present to produce a name of God.

Table A.12.4 from the Appendix, summarizing the names, is copied below to provide rapid identification of these names. The arrangement and details of the revealed LORD/Lord/lord compound names of God are fully discussed in Appendix 12.

Table A.12.4

Summation of the LORD/Lord/lord names of God from Chapter 12

01 LORD God	17 LORD God of Israel
02 Lord God	18 LORD, the God of heaven and the God of earth
03 LORD of hosts	19 LORD my God
04 Lord of hosts	20 LORD our God
05 LORD God of hosts	21 LORD thy God
06 Lord GOD of hosts	22 LORD your God
07 LORD Who Heals	23 LORD their God
08 LORD Our Righteousness	24 LORD his God
09 LORD Who Sanctifies	25 Lord of the whole earth
10 LORD is Present	26 Lord of all the earth
11 LORD Our Shepherd	27 Lord of lords
12 LORD will Provide	28 Lord my God
13 LORD Our Banner	29 Lord our God
14 LORD is Peace	30 Lord my God
15 LORD, the God of heaven	31 Lord our God
16 LORD God of heaven	

The Old Testament Names of God

A Perspective

Chapter 13

Contents

*Appendix Support

13.1 MAKER:

The Hebrew verb 'asah (SRN 6213) may be translated into the English expressions "to do (a deed)," to work, or "to make" in the broadest sense and widest application. For example, the list of definitions of interest might include "to earn, to prepare, and to accomplish" (to do or complete). This list continues with words like "use" (to employ) or "yield" (to produce). But in this list of some 70 words relating "to do (a deed)" or "to make" is the English term "to fashion." In narrowing our focus to the two ideas "to fashion" and "to prepare" we soon arrive at the basic English translation of the Hebrew word which is of special interest here.

Let us reinforce what has been stated: a maker is one who makes or fashions an object; if it was performed in the past it may be referred to as a deed that is already done. It is easy for human beings to understand the meaning of maker. Man is a maker in that he makes, he fashions or he produces.

But God is also a Maker, that is, One who fashions or One who modifies an object or person already here. Today man is already here; that is, he exists and he reproduces his genetic line. But God still fashions, makes and molds man.

Let us examine the meanings of the word Maker a little further. There is another Hebrew word, bara', similar in meaning to the Hebrew word 'asah. The Hebrew word bara' sometimes means to make or fashion, but its basic meaning is to create a new thing from something that was not there, from "nothing." For example, "...God created the heavens and the earth" (Gen. 1:1); that is, He fashioned them from nothing.

Another example is, "...in the image of God created He him; male and female created He them" (Gen 1:27). God didn't merely make man, He created him in His own image. Here the action is something that only God can do.

Both man and God make or fashion things from material at hand, but only God the Creator makes, fashions, initiates or creates a new item from nothingness.

This manuscript has already considered the title of God as Creator (Chapter 5). Now we want to examine the name Maker as applied to God.

The Argument:

The term Maker appears 19 times in the OT. Twice man is specifically referred to (Isa. 17:7; Job 4:17). These two verses will not be given further consideration. But what of the remaining 17 applications We are seeking to vindicate the word maker as a distinct name of God.

References to the maker compounded with possessive pronouns appear eight times in the books of Job, Proverbs, Isaiah and Hosea. Twice in the book of Job the expression "my maker" is used (32:22; 36:3). In each case the Creator is being referred to as the maker or molder. Job 35:10 uses the more expansive expression, "God my maker." Psalm 95:6 applies the phrase "the LORD our maker," whereas Isaiah 45:11 uses the name of God, "the LORD...his maker" (using the Hebrew synonym yōtzrō). Isaiah 51:13 uses the more archaic form, "the LORD thy maker," and Isaiah 54:5 combines several expressions to produce the elegant series, "thy maker is thy husband; the LORD of hosts is his name; and thy Redeemer the holy One of Israel; the God of the whole earth shall he be called." Once the term "the LORD the maker" (Jer. 33:2) and once the name "the maker" (Isa. 22:11) are used. In all, the word maker, directly applying to Deity, appears eight times. This vindicates the word Maker as a name of God, not once, but these eight occasions.[114] There are another eight indirect applications of the word Maker wherein God, as Maker, is addressed indirectly.

Now this is a lot of information to try to follow, so these particulars have been assembled in a list of the verses containing the word maker and is provided in the Chapter 13 Appendix. The members of this list have been examined and the particular applications of the term maker in several versions of Scripture detailed.

---

[114] It must be remembered that the variations in word translation between Scripture versions will result in a variance in what are and what are not considered Names of God. For example, the KJV Jer. 10:16a reads, "The portion of Jacob is not like them for he is the former of all things; and Jer. 10:16a in the NIV reads, "He who is the Portion of Jacob is not like these, for he is the Maker of all things,..." The phrase, "the former of all things," probably would not be located as containing a name of God; whereas, the phrase, "the Maker of all things" contains the word Maker, which is a name of God.

13.2 MASTER:

A rapid mental review of Scripture may well place the word master high on a list of terms applied often to Deity. For the New Testament this is especially correct, for Jesus is the Master; this one of His names. And any thesis about Him will naturally, again and again, apply this name to Him. However, in the OT a serious search must be made to locate such use of the term master, even once, in connection with Deity; the word master is generally limited to the sphere of authority over slaves and servants in the OT. Yet the application is there, for in Malachi 1:6 is recorded the statement of the LORD of hosts applying to Himself the relative position of Master to His servants.

The Argument:

Both Strong's Concordance and the Computer Dictionary indicates that there are 77 referenced verses, applying various Hebrew words, all translated into the English word master and applied to man. But of the 77 instances only once, in the Malachi passage of interest, is Deity being discussed or addressed.

In Malachi 1:6 the KJV text seems to argue that Israel's priests have failed to fear and honor the LORD, begrudging Him even the respect normally expected from children and from servants.

If I be Israel's father, why don't you honor me? And if I be your Master, where is my reverence? These Jews were speaking of God as their Father (Isa. 63:16; 64:8), at least in name if not in faith, but were not obeying this One they called Father. Father is a name of God and, by association, so is Master a name of God.

Purpose Of This Name:

The LORD is speaking hypothetically to His people, through His prophet Malachi, referring to Himself as Father and Master. The word Master is associated with legitimate authority and sovereign ownership.

13.3 MESSIAH:

The Hebrew word mashiyach (SRN 4899) appears 38 times in the OT. It basically means anointed and by extension an anointed one or a consecrated person. However, the KJV and certain other versions of the OT[115] translate this Hebrew term as the Messiah in two verses of the OT (Daniel 9:25,26). Mashiyach in many places is used as a title of honor describing certain of the kings of Israel as being consecrated to God by anointing and, therefore, holy. For example, 1Sa. 24:6 speaks about Saul as the LORD's anointed. The word is also used as an honorific title for both priests and prophets. It is also applied to select persons as they perform their tasks. Moses anointed Aaron as high priest (Exo. 28:41; 29:7). Aaron anointed his successor as well as the lower priesthood. They were spoken of as anointed but were never referred to as messiahs. Since the KJV is being used as the primary guide in this study it is important that careful attention be given to the word Messiah. Shall it be considered a title of God as applied in the OT?

NAME VARIATIONS:

	Dan. 9:25	Dan. 9:26
KJV	the Messiah the Prince	Messiah
NIV	the Anointed One, the ruler	the Anointed One
JER	an Anointed Prince (or Prince Messiah)	an anointed one
Beck	the anointed Prince	the Anointed
Moffatt	a supreme high priest	the consecrated priest
TLB	the Anointed One	the Anointed One

[115] The Hebrew word mashiyach is translated Messiah in Dan. 9:25, 26 in some Bible versions, including at least the following: KJV, Modern Language Bible, Septuagint (Charles Thomson) and the Helen Spurrel translation of the OT. The JER Version carries "the Prince Messiah" note in the footnotes.

Comparison of these two verses in various Scripture versions quickly verifies that there is less than agreement as to who the Person is that the KJV addresses as the Messiah and how this Person should be titled.

Looking first at the Daniel 9:25 list, it is interesting to note that only the Moffatt version fails to refer to the subject of the passage as the royal Messiah, keeping in mind the fact that the words Messiah and Anointed or Anointed One are normally equated. Also some consideration must be given to what the versions signify when the word anointed is not capitalized in English.

Consideration of the Daniel 9:26 list results in similar observations as those for the prior verse. It seems that more care with the English capitalization is in order and the term "the consecrated priest" seems questionable as the optimum translation of the Hebrew word mashiyach.

Now it is the intent in all this to determine if the word Messiah is a title of God in the Daniel passages. In some Scripture versions it appears that the basic Hebrew word, transliterated into English as Messiah, gives a strong impression of who is being discussed. Even when the Hebrew is translated Anointed or Anointed One the Person identified is the Lord Jesus. In these situations, instead of using the word Messiah, the word Anointed is applied and the reader is left to make the right connection. Of course in all this critique one cannot help but be influenced and biased by NT information where the Messiah is carefully identified.

Restricting this part of the consideration to the various Scripture versions and comparing one with another, we observe that they apply the Daniel verses to the Messiah about as frequently as to the less specific future Anointed or Anointed One. This seems to be sufficient evidence for a choice in the matter, and the specific word Messiah has been selected in this study as a title of God.

To Whom Does This Name Apply?

The specific title Messiah in the OT applies to the Lord Jesus, the coming Messiah. The title appears in only two places, Daniel 9:25,26. Consideration of the word anointed or anointed one (from the root of the word transliterated as messiah) appears elsewhere in this study (See Chapter 5.).

The Argument:

The Theological Wordbook comments that the extensive use of the term Messiah (Christ) as a title of the coming great Son of David is primarily a NT phenomenon.[116] Arnold C. Schultz comments that "with the possible exception of Daniel 9:25, 26, the title Messiah as a reference to Israel's eschatological king does not occur in the OT."[117] Not all agree that the root word mashiyach (whether the word is translated anointed or transliterated as messiah) in Daniel 25, 26 refers to Christ.

---

[116] R. L. Harris Ed., *Theological Wordbook of the Old Testament*, Moody Press, Chicago, 12 Printing/RM/Year 92,91, Vol. 1, p. 530-531.

[117] Merrill C. Tenney. Ed., *The Zondervan Pictorial Bible Dictionary,* Zondervan Publishing House, Grand Rapids, CR 1963, 64, 65, 25th Printing, p. 528-529.

However, it should be stressed that the OT did employ the term mashiah to designate the coming Savior Jesus.[118]

Another source[119] says that it is debatable as to how clearly the OT presents a coming Messiah. However, the Jewish people in Jesus' day saw several well developed and popular doctrines based upon the OT. As God's Anointed, He would redeem Israel. Not only this but the common people, aside from the direct followers of Jesus, argued fervently about the coming Messiah and His role.

As has been discussed, both the terms messiah and anointed come from the same Hebrew root word mashiyach. Either term seems to be used almost at the discretion of the translator in the various Scripture versions of the Daniel 9 verses. This seems also true of the commentary and reference writings. For these reasons either the word Anointed or the name Messiah, referring to Christ, are accepted as titles of the Son of God.

Purpose Of This Name:

Man was introduced to the Messiah through the doctrine taught in the OT, but man failed to grasp these truths. Mankind wanted a prince who would be a military hero, a political leader, a king and a deliverer. Man wanted to be freed from bondage under the yoke of despotic kings and governments. His concept of the Messiah was centered on that hope, namely that the Messiah would be that kind of deliverer. But

---

[118] Ibid., footnote 116.

[119] Lawrence O. Richerds, *Expository Dictionary Of Bible Words*, Zondervan Publishing House, Grand Rapids, CR 1985, p. 162.

man needed, and still needs, much more than a physical deliverer. Mankind needs the Messiah who will deliver not just the body but, much more important, also the soul. Man missed the point of the Messiah spoken of in Daniel. This Messiah appeared at the first advent. But this same Messiah will come again to completely deliver the believer. This is the need of man.

13.4 MESSIAH THE PRINCE:

The previous consideration of the title Messiah as a name of God is primarily based upon OT usage of the term anointed as a single Hebrew word. Remember that this happens, for example, in Daniel 9:26 in the KJV. But there is also the occurrence in Daniel 9:25 of compound title consisting of the phrase, "the Messiah the Prince." Some special consideration needs to be given this compound expression, since the second half of the title further identifies the Messiah.

The formation of a compound title or name is not unusual. This is found in expressions like Creator of Israel; Holy Spirit or Holy One; King of Glory and many others, including the particular title of our consideration, Messiah the Prince. Of course, for this consideration to apply, all the words of the compound phrase must be considered in the formation of the complex name or title, otherwise, there is no need for anything beyond the simply name or title.

Now, some will argue that the compounding is achieved merely by adding adjectives, modifying the simpler title, and in some cases this may be true. But in the case under consideration, the word Prince is an epithet providing additional definition to the simpler name Messiah. The augmented name reveals more than the simpler name, but both the simple name Messiah and the compound name Messiah the Prince are valid names of The Son of God in their own right.

During the study of the title Messiah it was observed that the word messiah means "anointed one." The kings of Israel were anointed with holy oil and so were "anointed ones." They were referred to frequently as "the Lord's anointed, Mine anointed, Thine anointed, etc." But they were never referred to as messiahs in the specialized prophetic sense even though this word means anointed one. One reference comments,

> It is obvious that there must be some historical connection between the designation "the Lord's anointed," "mine anointed," "thine anointed," "the anointed one," and the title "Messiah." The term "Messiah" apparently is a later expression and is an abbreviation of the fuller title, "the Lord's anointed." It shows that the Messiah of Israel's Messianic hope derived His title from the sacred title of the kings of David's line.[120]

NAME VARIATIONS:

The compound title "Messiah the Prince" is unique, occurring only in Daniel 9:25. Although the word messiah means anointed one, and the expression anointed one occurs rather frequently in the OT, the term messiah the prince does not appear elsewhere.

To Whom Does This Title Apply:

There is general agreement in the literature that this compound title refers to the Lord Jesus Christ. He is Messiah the Prince, the Anointed Prince, the Prince of Peace.

---

[120] Merrill C. Tenney, Ed., *The Zondervan Pictorial Bible Dictionary*, Zondervan Pub. House, Grand Rapids, CR 1963, 64, 65, 25th printing, p. 528.

The Argument:

Daniel writes of his encounter with Gabriel and their conversations regarding the timing and the chief events of the end time for the children of God. Gabriel speaks of being aware that Daniel is having trouble comprehending God's plan, so he has come to help Daniel grasp the issues of the end time. Gabriel lays out before Daniel the timing of the program of God expressed in weeks of years or heptads. The timing and the contents of the years are most interesting, but the occurrence of outstanding significance to this study is that Gabriel relates that the presence of the Messiah the Prince will be a major temporal event.

Through the years countless numbers of students of Scripture have studied these writings of Daniel. Many agreements and disagreements have been developed concerning the title the Messiah the Prince. Some argue about who the Person is with this title. Others disagree with the title itself, stating that the Hebrew word mashiyach should be translated into the term "anointed one" and not "Messiah." However, if the time sequence developed in the Daniel verses is compared with history, it seems apparent that those who argue that the Person with the compound name "the Messiah the Prince," is the Lord Jesus Christ have correctly followed the dominant view. Daniel may not have understood what he wrote, for he spoke of a leader or Prince to come, who would have extreme influence on the events of the time of the end. Daniel also wrote of the death of this One, which was even more difficult for him to understand. Probably Daniel would have been totally perplexed had he known that in the sequence of events, he wrote about was included a vast interval that he never envisioned called the church period. Daniel simply wrote as directed, identifying One called "the Messiah the Prince" and thereby establishing this compound phrase as a title of God.

The Purpose Of This Name:

It is through God's Prince the Messiah, the Anointed One, that all the plans involving mankind and the universe will be completed. Let us not miss the purpose to show that this "Messiah the Prince" is the Son of God, possessing all the attributes and characteristics of God such as those enumerated in this study and others far beyond.

13.5 **MIGHTY:**
13.6 **MIGHTY ONE:**
13.7 **MIGHTY ONE OF ISRAEL:**
13.8 **MIGHTY GOD OF JACOB:**
13.9 **MIGHTY ONE OF JACOB:**

The alphabetical sequence of this study of the names and titles of God has arrived at the term "mighty," and special consideration will be given to this word. Is it a mere modifying adjective or, under certain conditions, does it assume, in combination with other words, a very part of the name of God? To answer this question consider the following: The English word mighty is an adjective in itself and has not been found to be a title or name of God. A computer search of the OT finds that there are 38 different Hebrew words that translate into the English word mighty. Certainly not all of these are of interest here but some are; namely, those that related to names of deity. It is our goal to identify the words that, in combination with the term mighty, produce compound names of God.

The Hebrew words corresponding to the English word mighty and related synonyms are used to modify many Hebrew nouns. For example, there are mighty (SRN 1368) men (Gen. 6:4) and warriors (Gen. 10:8). There is a mighty (SRN 6099) Nation (Gen. 18:18). There is a mighty (SRN 430) prince (Gen. 23:6). The mighty (SRN 6105) children of Israel are spoken of in Exo. 1:7. Then there are mighty hands, winds, waters and many other applications, plus the special occasions relating to deity.

Much is made of the adjective translated into the English mighty, since it is this word that is not only applied prevalently to things, but also the term, when applied to a deity identifier, produces a compound name of God.

The computer initially identified all the appearances of the word mighty. This list was examined to select the possible combinations of the term with words producing a name of God. Twenty-one such possibilities were discovered and arranged into categories for further consideration. Each category was expanded, and any category containing names of God was tabulated. This procedure identified and verified the initial five compound names.

The Argument:

The extreme detail substantiating the selection of the five names of God is presented and discussed in the Chapter 13 Appendix. The reader is referred there for a full explanation and justification of the name selection.

The Purpose Of This Name:

God has power and might to do all things. He has power and might to create and to destroy. He has power and might to install and to remove. But He uses His great power, might and authority only to achieve His goals and plans established in the beginning. The name "Mighty God" reminds of this quality.

The Old Testament Names of God

A Perspective

Chapter 14

Contents

*Appendix Support

The Old Testament Names of God

A Perspective

Chapter 14

Contents

14.1 PORTION OF JACOB:

Scripture contains many genitive expressions of both the “s” type and the “of” type. Some of these were discussed in Chapter 7 as they relate to the possessions of God. But in this current chapter another possessive genitive style becomes of interest—namely, those of the form “_of Jacob.” Eighteen phrases speaking of the certainty of Jacob’s possessions in the form of s-(genitives) are contained in the OT. For example, Jacob’s voice (Gen. 27:22) or Jacob’s mother (Gen. 28:5). But none of them bear relationships to names or titles of God. Then there are 98 “of-(genitive)” phrases. In this group resides the new name of God, “the portion of Jacob.” Indeed this unusual metonym for the name of God occurs twice in the writings of Jeremiah, first in 10:16 and then, in repetition, 51:19. So it is important to examine these verses and to verify the presence of this name of God.

NAME VARIATIONS:

The compound name of God, “the portion of Jacob,” is consistently rendered in this form in several of the more common Scripture versions. However, certain other versions used in this study do not maintain the form so that the phrase loses the name distinction. These variations as found in Jer. 10:16 and 51:19 are shown in Table 14.1.

Table 14.1

The Phrase "the Portion of Jacob" in Selected Scripture Versions

VERSION	JER. 10:16	JER. 51:19
KJV	The portion of Jacob	The portion of Jacob
NKJV	The Portion of Jacob	The Portion of Jacob
NIV	The Portion of Jacob	The Portion of Jacob
RSV	The Portion of Jacob	The Portion of Jacob
JER	The Portion of Jacob	The Portion of Jacob
Beck	Jacob has as his portion	Jacob has as his portion
TLB	God of Jacob	God of Jacob
Moffatt	Jacob's own possession	Verses 15-19 omitted
NEB	God, Jacob's creator	God, Jacob's creator

The first 5 versions listed in the above Table present the phrase and title of interest, "The Portion of Jacob." It is interesting to note that of these 5 versions all except the KJV capitalize the phrase and name, the Portion of Jacob. As seen before this simply indicates that capitalization cannot necessarily be used to indicate proper names in the KJV. The phrase appearing in the Beck version conveys information similar to that of the other versions, but the genitive form required and presented in the first 5 versions is absent, destroying any title possibility. The Living Bible variation listed in the Table is a name of God[121] in a genitive or possessive format but not in the form of

[121] See Chapter 7 for genitive names of God in the form "God of—".

interest. Moffatt and the NEB are not in the required form either, yet they are of interest to show that in some versions the s-(genitive) might be used with text rephrasing. The last four entries also illustrate the manner in which one version of Scripture may be used as a commentary on another.

To Whom Does The Name Apply?

The text clearly states that the name "the Portion of Jacob" is a substitute address for the ancient name Yahweh, The LORD of hosts.

The Argument:

The title "the Portion of Jacob" first appears in Jeremiah 10:16 in connection with the comparison of the relationship between the true God and idolatry. The chapter begins with a discussion of the futility and foolishness of the efforts of those people involved in heathen worship practices. Their acts are useless and, as the Living Bible implies,[122] the man-made idols are nothing more than carved trees that, since they are decorated with gold and silver, must be securely fastened with hammer and nails so they won't fall over. There stands their god like a helpless scarecrow in a garden. It cannot speak, and it must be carried, for it cannot walk. Don't be afraid of such a god, for it can neither harm nor help nor do you any good.

Then at verse 6, the writer abruptly swings into an outpouring of praise as he begins to speak of God, His greatness and His power: "the LORD is the true God, He is

---

[122] The Living Bible, Tyndale House Publishers, CR 1971, p. 689.

the living God, and an everlasting King:" (v10). "He hath made the earth by His power, He hath established the world by His wisdom, and hath stretched out the heavens by His discretion." (v12). "Who would not fear thee, O King of nations?..." (v7).

The writer has said it once and now he says it again, "every man is brutish in his knowledge, every founder is confounded by the graven image: for his molten image is falsehood, and there is no breath in them. They are vanity, and the works of errors, in the time of their office they shall perish" (ver.. 14,15). "The portion of Jacob is not like them. He is the former (or creator) of all things; and Israel is the tribe (or branch) of His inheritance (or possession): The LORD of hosts is His name" (ver16).

Now examine the interesting phrase the portion of Jacob. The word portion (SRN 2506) is certainly not unique, for it appears 90 times in the OT. The word means a share or a part, a possession, inheritance, allotment or lot. In Deu. 32:9 the writer says "...the LORD's portion is his people; Jacob (or the nation of Israel) is the lot of his inheritance." In Num. 18:20 God speaks of Himself as "thy part and thine inheritance." In Psa. 73:26 and 119:57 God is spoken of as "my portion." This expression is also found in Lam: 3:24. There Yahweh is referred to as the "the portion of Jacob," because the nation was created to be His people and worshippers. The two Jeremiah passages of concern speak of "portion" or "part" connecting someone with someone else in a manner indicating the idea of sphere or closeness by means of a genitive phrase similar to "the God of_."[123]

Lastly look at the repetition of Jer. 10:12-16 that occurs in Jer. 51:15-19. The LORD had pronounced judgment upon Babylon, but who is strong enough to bring this about? The writer has previously given an account of the One who is able to do so in the tenth chapter and simply repeats his statements to show that God will convince by His act of judgment those who would not be convinced by His word that He is God.

Particular Aspect Of God's Character Highlighted

Perhaps the Deuteronomy 32:9 passage is among the best statements of the possessive zeal of God towards Israel. Yahweh's possession is His people. Jacob or Israel is His inheritance. Even today national Israel belongs to God. One day out of this nation will come spiritual Israel, which will be the desired possession of the LORD forever.

The Special Need Of Man Met By The Revelation Of This Aspect Of God's Character.

From Jacob or national Israel will come Spiritual Israel. There is a great need for today's man to recognize that God is not finished with the nation of Israel. Much, much more is to yet occur. The nation is to be yet shaped, molded, smoothed and polished until it has become the Spiritual beauty that is the real inheritance of the LORD.

---

[123] "Sphere" as applied in the discussion of genitives in Chapter 7.

14.2 PRINCE:

The English word "prince" is interesting in that it, or its plural, appears prolifically in some 341 verses of the OT. Ninety-one times the singular form prince and 250 times the plural appears, translated not from a single Hebrew word but from a total of eight different Hebrew words. These eight words are variously translated into English words like exalted one, king, captain, ruler, commander and leader. However, in each translation prince or princes appears along with the other synonyms. Yet in the 341 verses, neither the word prince nor its plural alone ever serve as a name of deity. But if the word prince or princes is joined to a compound expression in the form "the prince of_" and the 341 verses are examined again, three titles of God will be identified from the text material. It is these three compound phrases that we will now examine closely to verify that they are names of God.

Considerable information has been developed about the three candidates. All contain the word prince translated from the Hebrew word sar (SRN 8269). Each of the three candidates employs a genitive phrase, closely relating the term "prince" to the other members of that compound. Each candidate appears but once in the OT and, of course, all components of the particular phrase must be present if a name of deity is to be formed.

In addition to separating and identifying the candidate compounds from the 341 possible passages, comparison of several Scripture versions was considered in order to assist in the verification of the possible names. This proved interesting, for it clearly illustrates how a title of God may be hidden by a translation. Indeed, in the 9 versions sampled the single Hebrew word sar is translated into as many as four different English words.

VERSION VARIATIONS:

VERSION	Isa. 9:6	Dan. 8:11	Dan. 8:25
KJV	The Prince of Peace	the prince of the host	the Prince of princes
NIV	Prince of Peace	the Prince of the host	the Prince of princes
RSV	Prince of Peace	the Prince of the host	the Prince of princes
NKJV	Prince of Peace	the Prince of the host	the Prince of princes
JER	Prince-of-Peace	that army's Prince	the Prince of princes
Beck	Prince of Peace	the Ruler of the army	the Ruler of rulers
NAS	Prince of Peace	Commander of the host	Prince of princes
Moffatt	a peaceful prince	the Prince of the starry host	the Prince of the angel-princes
TLB	"the Prince of Peace"	the Commander of the army of heaven	the Prince of Princes

It can also be seen that the compound phrases which form the names of deity vary from version to version. For example, the Isa. 9:6 compound is translated Prince of Peace in eight versions. Only a single version elects to translate the phrase as "a peaceful prince." Another example might be the Dan. 8:11 passage. About half of the versions translate its phrase of interest as the Prince of the host. The other sampled versions translate the phrase otherwise. Such variation certainly makes for confusion and justifies great care in the version selected for basic Bible study.

One other point of interest. The Living Bible is unique in its use of quotation marks to apparently remind the reader that the involved name requires the whole genitive phrase in order to form the name "The Prince of Peace." Would that others might be so helpful.

Consideration of the word prince by itself and then examination of the three phrases using this word in compounds producing names of God clearly illustrate that the four applications of the term prince are closely interrelated. Therefore, in this study the four are arranged in a reasonable order but depend on each other for commonality in order to reduce undue repetition in this text.

14.3 THE PRINCE OF PEACE:

The title "Prince of Peace," (Isaiah 9:6), is one in the series of four names written in word couples. This compound title is applied to One identified as the new King and introduced by His royal accession. Earlier, Isaiah presented the Son of the virgin who would be called Immanuel.[124] But here this same Person is predicted to come again, this time in great splendor, to the throne of His father David, and He will be elevated as the divine Son and Heir. He has been given four names or titles expressing separate functions which belong to the royal office of the King. He will be called "Wonderful Counsellor," "Mighty God or Divine Warrior," "Everlasting Father or Father Forever" and lastly, "Prince of Peace." He came the first time as the suffering Messiah. He will come the second time as the Mighty King worthy of all these titles. He will be known as "The Prince of Peace," for of His government and peace there shall be no end.

---

[124] Isaiah 7:14.

14.4 THE PRINCE OF THE HOST:

The name or title "the Prince of the host" (Daniel 8:11) is but one of a number of OT passages where the phrase "of hosts" is applied to the LORD. Joshua 5:14 and 15 report a dialogue with the Captain of the host of the LORD. Amos 4:13 and 5:27 speak of certain aspects of One named Yahweh the God of hosts. In many other places this phrase appears as a component of a fuller title such as the name Yahweh Sabaoth, the Lord of hosts. The word host is used to describe a large assembly, an organized mass or even a totality of entities as in Gen. 2:1, "the heavens and the earth were finished, and all the host of them." Scripture describes armies and peoples in large groups as hosts. Heavenly items such as stars and angels, and creation itself are spoken of as hosts. God (elohim) and the LORD Yahweh are referred to as the Prince, Ruler, Commander, or Captain of the organized masses called hosts. Daniel, being familiar with the phrase, refers to God as the Prince of the host.

14.5 THE PRINCE OF PRINCES:

The compound title "Prince of princes" is found only in Daniel 8:25 as recorded in 7 of the 9 selected translations. It appears that the author desired to indicate that Yahweh, here referred to as the Prince of princes, is unique among leaders. There is none other like Him, none other with His characteristics, none other in his category. There are other princes, but none are like this Prince. So Daniel used a genitive of graduation to name His God. There is a point of interest observable in the Variation Table. The Beck translation elects to use the title Ruler rather than the word Prince. Of course this has no effect on the title since the words ruler and prince, commander and others all quite properly translate the same basic Hebrew word, sar. However, if one is looking for the compound name the Prince of Princes it will not be found in the Beck translation.

The Moffatt translation uses a hypothetical supplemental identifier with the word princes to arrive at angel-princes. This is certainly different from other versions, and the added epithet is really unnecessary. The Moffatt translation presents only an artificial challenge in qualifying the name Prince of Princes with this added epithet.

Particular Aspect Of God's Character Highlighted

The title "Prince of Peace" highlights the special quality of peace that the prophesied messianic King will bring to His people at His second coming. This King, with this special name given to Him by God as recorded in Scripture, will sit upon the throne of His father David and will be ruler over a peaceful government to which there shall be no end.

The compound titles "the Prince of the host" and "the Prince of princes" are suitable titles for the LORD or Yahweh. Daniel, in describing the actions of the Antichrist in the end times, presents God in terms of authority that the people will easily understand: He is the Commander or Prince of the heavenly army and the Prince who is above every prince. There is no authority or power greater than that of this Prince.

The Special Need Of Man Met By The Revelation Of This Aspect Of God's Character

There is a period coming when the Antichrist will produce conditions so terrible that only the Prince of princes controlling and leading the heavenly host will be able to establish a government of peace. The need of man to seek God grows daily as the prophesied end time destruction approaches.

The Old Testament Names of God

A Perspective

Chapter 15

Contents

*Appendix Support

15.1 REDEEMER:

Continuing the progress in the study of the names and titles of God, we now present the English title Redeemer and the related compound Redeemer of Israel.

The word redeemer is an interesting term, because it is a name of God by definition. Now how does this come about? The OT Hebrew culture provided for a redemption or deliverance plan as specified in Scripture (Exo. 13:2, 12). In commemoration of the Jewish Exodus from Egypt every firstborn male was to be devoted or set apart unto the Lord. Firstborn clean animals were to be sacrificed on the altar; however, the firstborn of humans and of unclean animals could not be sacrificed. Instead a clean lamb was substituted for an unclean animal. The firstborn of humans was redeemed by cash payment. In both cases there was the provision for redemption.[125]

Another aspect of redemption pertained to special provisions for the redemption of land or other property. The background of these laws was the prohibition against selling the land in perpetuity (Lev. 25:23). Hence a right to redemption (Heb. ga'al) was to be granted for inherited land that might pass out of the possession of its owner (V24). If a man by reason of poverty sold part of his possession there were three ways of restoration: (1) A kinsman (Heb. go'el, a participle of ga'al) could redeem or buy back (ga'al) what had been sold. (2) If there was no kinsman to redeem it, the seller himself

---

[125] International Standard Bible Encyclopedia Vol. 4, p. 61.

could redeem the land provided he was financially able to do so (Lev. 25:26). (3) And if neither of these options were possible, the land remained the buyer's possession until the Year of Jubilee, when it was returned to the original owner's possession without cost to him.

Several conclusions derive from this usage: (1) Redemption refers to the restoration of persons or things. (2) A redemption price was necessary for this recovery or restoration. (3) An intermediary, the go'el, acts to secure the redemption.

"In the OT the concept of redemption occurs frequently in reference to the salvation wrought by God for His people. Both the Heb. ga'al and padah appear in this connection."[125a]. But if there is redemption there must be the redeemed, and to have any redeemed there must be a redeemer, a go'el, an intermediary who pays the price. This term is frequently ascribed to the Lord in the OT. He is the redeemer of His people—that is one of His names because of what He does.

But let us continue the investigation of the word redeemer and its source. Strong's Dictionary indicates a multitude of associated English synonyms arising from the Hebrew word ga'al (SRN 1350) and its cognates. These include such words as avenger, deliverer, kinsman, purchase, ransom, redeem and redeemer. These words appear some 99 times in the OT, but there are other Hebrew words that are translated

---

125a Ibid.

into English words that sound much like the translation of ga'al. For example, the synonyms from the Hebrew word padah (SRN 6299) include words like ransom, redeemed, redeem and rescue. Members of this family appear 57 times in the OT. Then there is the family of terms associated with the Hebrew word kopher (SRN 3724) which is translated redemption, price and ransom. Members of this family appear 18 times. Pursuing this course of investigation, it becomes obvious that the participle (go'el, redeemer) of the primary verb ga'al, to redeem, which is limited in use to 18 verses in the OT, always refers to the deity.

Since the word Redeemer has been accepted as a name of God, further consideration of this name could be ended here. But because of the uniqueness of the establishment of this name (simply by definition), further detailed examination is presented in the Chapter 15 Appendix.

Consideration of the compound form the Redeemer of Israel is included in the Appendix, as is coverage of the names Rock and Refuge.

15.2 RIGHTEOUS BRANCH:

The term Righteous Branch is not considered a name or title of God. The word Branch is a title of the Messiah, and the word righteous is an adjective modifier but does not form a compound title. The title Branch has been considered in Chapter 5.

15.3 SERVANT:

The English word servant, or—perhaps even stronger in meaning—slave, is most commonly translated in the OT from the Hebrew word 'ebed (SRN 5650). This Hebrew word is a derivative from 'abad meaning to work or to serve. 'abad appears some 290 times in the OT while 'ebed is used 799 times. Then there are other terms that produce English words with meanings closely related to these. For example, there is sakiyr which is translated hireling, a hired man or servant. Also the Hebrew word na'ar, which means a servant, especially a young person. But it is the word 'ebed that is our chief interest, even to the exclusion of the others, since this word can relate to divine identification in certain applications.

The expressions Servant of the Lord and My servant can refer to various people in the OT—to the Patriarchs (Exo. 32:13), then specifically to David (2Sa. 7:5), to Joshua (Jdg. 2:8), to Moses (Num. 12:7), the Prophets (Zec. 1:6) and many others. But the word servant refers to God[126] only in the five passages in Isaiah where the Messiah seems to be identified as the Servant of God.

The verses where this occurs will be examined carefully with an intention to determine if indeed it is the Messiah that is being addressed as Servant, thereby creating a title of deity, or whether there is reason to believe that another is involved.

---

[126] The five passages of interest have been located by means of a computer search with the word "servant" (SRN 5650) in association with the listings in the Strong Concordance.

The initial step in the study is to compare several other Scripture versions with the basic AV. Look for any variations or changes in the word Servant. We will pay special attention to the capitalization of the word Servant, particularly in the newer versions, where it might be assumed that the more recent translations have been more sensitive to word capitalization, especially proper names and names or titles of deity.[127]

---

[127] Pertinent capitalization rules from three different sources follow:

- "Modern publishers of works in the English language, America perhaps more than British, usually discourage extensive use of capital letters in text. Proper nouns are still capitalized, but many words derived from or associated with them may be lowercased with no loss of clarity."
  The University of Chicago Press, *The Chicago Manual of Style,* 14th Edition, 1993, Section 7.2, page 235.

- "Family Relationships. Capitalize words describing family relationships only when they substitute for a proper noun or are used with the person's name. Do not capitalize the words if they are used with a possessive pronoun."
  L. Sue Baugh, *Essentials of English Grammer*, Passport Books (Trade imprint of National Textbook Co., Lincolnwood, Illinois, 1975, p. 58).

- "Capitalization: Capitalize all proper nouns that are names of individuals. (1) Capitalize epithets added to proper names or applied to people or places. (2) Capitalize nouns like *father* and *mother* when used in address, but do not capitalize such nouns when a possessive pronoun is used with them."
  Margaret Shertzer, *The Elements of Grammer,* Collier Books, Macmillan Publishing Co., 1986, p. 48.

Table 15.1

The Word Servant Variations

	KJV#1	KJV#2	NKJV	NIV	JER	Beck	Moffatt
Isa. 42:1	servant	servant	Servant	servant	servant	Servant	servant
Isa. 49:5	servant	servant	Servant	servant	servant	Servant	to serve
Isa. 50:10	servant	servant	Servant	servant	servant	Servant	servant's
Isa. 52:13	servant	servant	Servant	servant	servant	Servant	servant
Isa. 53:11	servant	servant	Servant	servant	servant	Servant	servant

The columns KJV #1 and 2[128], NIV and Jerusalem all present the text material (words and capitalization) in very similar fashion. The rules shown in the sources given in footnote #127 affect these texts, in that the word servant is not capitalized due to the presence of possessive pronouns. The fact that this occurs is noticed first in the version comparisons, but it will be examined again later as the verses are individually considered.

The NKJV and Beck columns present the word Servant in capitalized form, since these are the titles of a Person, the Messiah.

Moffatt characteristically deviates from the norm of the other versions in two verses, substituting other grammatical forms for the noun in the Hebrew. However,

---

[128] KJV #1 is supported by the 1909, 1917 copyright edition of the KJV.
KJV #2 is supported by the 1984 copyright edition of the KJV.

three times the word servant is used but capitalization is not allowed, presumably because of the presence of possessive pronouns.

Argument:

During the past two or three hundred years scholars have produced an enormous amount of literature on "the servant passage" problem. There is even wide variation in identification of which specific verses are to be included in the problem. There is also less than close agreement as to the textual meaning, interpretation and personage involved. Yet all is not lost, for there are some areas where writers agree on certain important points.

In this manuscript the viewpoints from several authoritative documents will be cited, for the convenience of the reader, and then from this gathering of ideas a determination of whether "the servant passages" contain a title of deity or not will be made.

What Do Others Think?

<u>1. Francis Brown, *The New B-D-B-Gesenius Hebrew and English Lexicon,* Hendrickson Publishers, copyright 1979, p. 714.</u>

This lexicon identifies the Hebrew word '<u>ebed</u> as a masculine noun assigned SRN 5650. The word is applied to a wide variety of servants: slave, servant of households, subject of others (nations, kings, armies, etc.), worshippers of God, servants of Yahweh, Levitical singers, specially recognized prophets including Elijah (2Ki. 9:36; 10:10), Jonah (2Ki. 14:25), and Isaiah (Isa. 20:3). The Scriptures also speak of the faithful of the people of Israel collectively as a servant to Yahweh (Isa. 41:89, 44:2; 49:3 and Psa. 136:22).

"Israel as a people is servant of Yahweh (Isa. 41:8, 9; 44:21), having a mission to the nations (Isa. 42:19) and chosen as a witness of Yahweh (Isa. 43:10). But there is also an ideal servant chosen and endowed with the divine Spirit to be a covenant of Israel and a light of the nations (Isa. 42:1); formed to bring back Jacob, raise up the tribes, and become salvation to the end of the earth (Isa. 49: 5, 6, 7); bearing the sins of all as a lamb and a trespass offering, and yet prospering and justifying many as interposing martyr (Isa. 52:13; 53:11)."

<u>2. Samuel P. Tregelles, *Gesenius' Hebrew and Chaldee Lexicon to the Old Testament,* Baker Book House Co., Copyright 1979, p. 599.</u>

This lexicon begins by translating the Hebrew word '<u>ebed</u> as servant, which was commonly used among the Hebrew people to mean a slave. As in the previous lexicon, here a wide range of applications of the word in the Hebrew is listed out, including a whole nation when subject to another, servants of a king, military officers and even individual soldiers. Also listed are messengers for special purposes and for common conversations between superior persons and their subordinates. Then the word servant or slave is used in describing a worshipper of God, sometimes as a laudatory epithet for pious worshippers like Abraham, Joshua, David, Moses, Isaiah and Zerubbabel. Even the heathen king Nebuchadnezzer is referred to as God's servant, since he was used as an instrument in the chastisement of God's people. According to Gesenius, this name belongs especially to the prophets (Isa. 42:1; 44:26; 49:3; 52:13 and 53:11; but all these passages speak of Christ according to Tregelles).

The nation Israel, which is called the servant of God, is sometimes in other verses called the chosen of God (Isa. 41:8; 42:1; 45:4), sometimes his ambassador and friend (Isa. 42:19), and even, in the plural, His ambassadors (Isa. 44:26).

Gesenius adds, "But, in all the passages concerning the servant of God in the latter half of Isaiah (42:1-7, 49:1-9, 50:4-10, 52:13-53:12), he is represented as the intimate friend and ambassador of God, aided by His Spirit, who is to be the restorer of the tribes of Israel, and the instructor of other nations." (Tregelles disagree, "Most of these passages refer to Christ, and to Him only.")

3. R. Harris, G. Archer Jr. and B. Waltke. *The Theological Wordbook of the Old Testament*, Moody Press, Copyright 1980, Vol. 2, p. 639.

The Wordbook discusses various uses of the Hebrew term servant with mention of a benchmark for those interested in quantity. The form 'ebed appears 799 times in the OT. "The most significant use of the term 'servant' is as a messianic designation, the most prominent, personal, technical term to represent the OT teaching on the Messiah. The central teaching passages on this theme are found in the last 27 chapters of Isaiah."

The Wordbook presents the view of two servants in these passages—the blind failing servant Israel of 42:19 and the healing and restoring Messiah servant of 42:1 and 49:5; 50:10, 52:13 and 53:11.

The Wordbook does agree that the Isaiah passages are heavily involved with the work of the Messiah, but no specific reference is made to these passages.

4. L. O. Richards, *Expository Dictionary of Bible Words, Zondervan,* Copyright, 1985, p. 550-551.

The coverage of the term servant or slave in this dictionary is unusual, because these important words are especially identified in the Isaiah passages where a person called The Servant of the Lord is discussed. This literature makes a point of the possibility that the nation Israel is the Servant of the Lord. But, though chosen and strengthened by the Lord, the servant Israel failed to accomplish God's purposes. So Isaiah introduces another Servant, the Messiah.

Four major passages focus on this coming Servant of the Lord.

1st, Isa. 42:1-9 The Servant will walk humbly and will establish justice on the earth.

2nd, Isa. 49:1-6 The Servant will speak to the nations announcing his credentials. He will call Israel back to the Lord and bring salvation to all mankind.

3rd, Isa. 50:4-10 The Servant will suffer because He is completely obedient to God.

4th, Isa. 52:13 thru 53:12 The Servant is destined for exaltation.

It is pointed out that these passages detail the OT's incredibly graphic portrait of the sacrificial death of Jesus Christ. They also present a picture of Jesus as He modeled servanthood, demonstrating the servant lifestyle.

5. M. C. Tenney, General Editor, *Pictorial Bible Dictionary*, Zondervan, Copyright 1967, p. 774.

"Servant of Jehovah is a term applied to the patriarchs (Exo. 32:13), Moses (Num. 12:7), Joshua (Jdg. 2:8), David (2Sa. 7:5), the prophets (Zec. 1:6) and others. It is used chiefly, however, as a title for the Messiah in Isa. 40-60 (esp. in 42:1-9; 49;1-13; 50:4-11 and 52:13-53:12)."

The Servant's mission is fulfilled only in Christ; election (42:1; 49:7), birth (49:1; 53:2), anointing (42:1; 48:16; 59:21; 61:1), ministry (49:8-13), rejection (49:4, 7; 53:1-3), obedience (50:4-7), new covenant (49:8; 55:3), vicarious death (53:4-12), resurrection (53:10-12), salvation offered (49:8; 61:2), mission to the Gentiles (42:1, 6; 49:6, 12; 60:3, 9), glorification and intercession (49:3; 53:12).

The Isaiah Servant Passages are quoted at least 15 times in the New Testament in relation to the work of Jesus Christ.

6. Roland K. Harrison, *Servant of The Lord, The International Standard Bible Encyclopedia*, Eerdmans Publishing, Copyright 1988, Vol. 4, p. 421-422.

The four Isaiah passages 42:1-9; 49:1-13; 50:1-11 and 52:13-53:12 are referred to in this encyclopedia as the Isaiah "Servant Oracles." In the same article this collection of Scripture is also called the "servant songs." It is pointed out that still another Servant Oracle member may be contained in Isa. 22:1-2 and has simply escaped the attention of scholars' intensive study.

Considerable disagreement among scholars as to the identity of "the Servant" has existed during the last two to three hundred years. "Early Christians usually identified the servant with the righteous, either collectively in terms of the faithful remnant of Israel, or as an individual historical personage." But, following NT tradition, the Christian Church came to see in Isa. 53 a Messianic prophecy that was fulfilled exclusively in the work of Jesus Christ. In modern times, once again some considered the "servant" as the ideal rather than the actual historical Israel.

It is important to notice awareness in this article of the fact that considerable conjecture surrounds the question of who the Servant might be. It cannot be said that Christ is identified consistently as the Servant to the degree of certainty that the term servant can always be assigned as a title of deity.

What Others Have Said, A Summary of Conclusions:

Based on the literature available, it is quite obvious that considerable study has been focused by others on the Isaiah Servant passages. Certainly this blesses this author with confidence for drawing the following conclusions. First, five of the six sources significantly assisted in the positive confirmation that the term Servant is a title of deity. Two of the sources, The Expository Dictionary and the Zondervan Pictorial Dictionary were rated plus in this area. Secondly, as would be expected, all of the sources presented excellent detail concerning the application of the word servant derived from the Hebrew word 'ebed. That assured this author that the correct Hebrew root word was being considered as a possible origin of the word servant, since there are several similar words. In the third place, all of the sources showed that the major Isaiah passages are identified with special names. These included the Servant of Yahweh, the Servant of the Lord, the Servant of God and the Servant passages. These especially named passages agree that Christ, the Messiah, is the topic of concern, thereby assuring that the word Servant in these applications is a title of deity.

To Whom Does This Name Apply?

The title Servant in the Isaiah Oracles applies to the Messiah, our Lord Jesus Christ. This is agreed upon by a significant number of scholars, but not by all. It is interesting to observe the change in textual meaning as the word servant varies from a title of deity to a common noun.

The Purpose of This Name:

There are those who argue that Jesus Christ the Messiah and Savior was not made known and detailed in the OT; that His teachings, actions and relationship to the Father are strictly of the NT. But study of His title "Servant," both from the pre-and post-messianic viewpoints, especially portray His birth, anointing, ministry, rejection, obedience, vicarious death and resurrection. If man is to see Jesus, he must see Him in the OT as well as the new.

15.4 SHEPHERD:
15.5 SHEPHERD OF ISRAEL:

The word Shepherd and its possessive compound, Shepherd of Israel, will be considered together because of their closeness in meaning and application.

The word shepherd appears frequently in the OT in connection with various aspects of God's leadership of His people.[129] The term is also commonly used in relationship to the people of God as certain of their derogatory characteristics are compared to some of the negative attributes of sheep being cared for by a shepherd.[130] However, only in Psalm 80:1 does the word shepherd appear in the unique compound phrase the Shepherd of Israel. Close examination of this compound is necessary in order to determine if it is a title of God.

The word shepherd is the translation of the participle of the Hebrew verb ra'ah (SRN 7462). From this root and its cognates also come the Hebrew words meaning to pasture, pasturing, to tend a flock, to keep or feed (like sheep), and to rule, the compound phrase of interest. Shepherd of Israel appears only once in the OT, but compound titles of similar genitive form appear throughout the OT. For example, in Isa. 43:15 God is referred to as the Creator of Israel. In Psa. 78:41 God is called the Holy One of Israel. Then in Isa. 44:6 God is titled King of Israel, and in 2Sa. 23:3 God

---

[129] God is the Shepherd; there is total dependency of all human beings on Him for existence, survival and common welfare. Gen. 49:24 and Psa. 23:1 speak directly of the Shepherd. Psa. 74:1; 78:52; 95:7; 100:3 and others speak of the sheep led by the Shepherd.

[130] Perhaps some of the most familiar and frequently occurring metaphors comparing people with sheep are those addressing shepherdless sheep. (Num. 22:17; Isa. 53:6; Jer. 50:6; Ezr. 34:5).

is specified as the Rock of Israel. These examples, and the context of Psa. 80, clearly indicate that the initial phrase in this Psalm addresses deity with this compound expression. God is not only the Shepherd of His people, He is explicitly the Shepherd of Israel.

These comments are principally based upon the text in the AV. It is appropriate to consider the same verses in other Scripture versions in order to catch a broader perspective of the words and phrases of interest.

Version Variations:

As has been previously mentioned, the phrase Shepherd of Israel is unique in the OT to Psa. 80:1. The full compound phrase must be present in order to express the title. But the breakdown of the compound into its components yields the more general title Shepherd, the provider for all God's people everywhere, Jew or Gentile. It is the intent now to prepare a table displaying a sampling of Scripture version variations of the word Shepherd and the phrase Shepherd of Israel with special interest in the Hebrew to English translation. Attention will also be paid to capitalization.

Table 15.2

The Word Shepherd and Compound Shepherd of Israel

	Passage Ref.	**Passage Ref.**	**Passage Ref.**
Version	**Gen. 49:24**	**Psa. 23:1**	**Psa. 80:1**
KJV	shepherd	shepherd	Shepherd of Israel
NKJV	Shepherd	shepherd	Shepherd of Israel
NIV	Shepherd	shepherd	Shepherd of Israel
RSV	Shepherd	shepherd	Shepherd of Israel
NAS	Shepherd	shepherd	Shepherd of Israel
JER	name	shepherd	Shepherd of Israel
Beck	Shepherd	Shepherd	Shepherd of Israel
Moffatt	Israel's Strength	shepherds	shepherd of Israel

In the Gen. 49:24 passage, six versions translate the Hebrew word ra'ah—actually the participle ro'eh—to the English word shepherd. It is interesting to note that of the six versions all but one capitalize the word shepherd, as would be expected in this title. The Psalm 23:1 passage translates the Hebrew into the English word shepherd in all but one case. Moffatt somehow forces the Hebrew word to yield the plural form "shepherds" and foregoes capitalization. All versions of Psa. 80:1 translate the Hebrew as Shepherd with only a single capitalization variation. These variations may well result in the student questioning the translation itself. Why do some translators elect to apply one English word while other translators will, from the same Hebrew word, come up with radically different English renderings? And if the translation into various and assorted English synonyms is not enough of a cause for inquiry, the variations in capitalization certainly raise questions. Because of the use of various synonyms and of diverse standards for capitalization, the word of concern may be entirely obscured even though important as a name of deity.

To Whom Do These Names Apply?

The word shepherd is used in many places in the OT. For example, in Gen. 49:24 Jacob gives a final blessing to his sons referring to God (<u>'el</u>) as the Mighty God of Jacob, the Shepherd, the Rock of Israel. Of course, Psa. 23:1 refers to Yahweh as the Shepherd. The people of God are referred to figuratively as God's sheep in numerous passages. For example, Psa. 74:1 refers metaphorically to the sheep of God's pasture, and Psa. 78:52 uses a double simile to describe His people as going forth like sheep. Eze. 34:11-16 speaks of God as the Shepherd seeking, feeding and caring for His sheep. These applications give strong support to the suggestion that the expressions Shepherd and Shepherd of Israel are titles for Yahweh, the LORD.

The Argument:

In Psa. 80:1 the title Shepherd of Israel is used to address God. This appellation is borrowed from the context of the final blessing given by Jacob to his sons where, recorded for the first time (Gen. 49:24), the Mighty God of Jacob is addressed as the Shepherd, the Stone of Israel. The Psalmist envisions the days when the nation of Israel was led by God through the wilderness toward the promised land. He seems to suggest that Jacob was led the same way earlier, like a flock being herded to a better pasture.

Prophetically, the Shepherd of Israel in the coming days will seek His scattered sheep in order to bring them back to their land and take possession of it again. Meanwhile the Shepherd leads and feeds His own people wherever they may be.

The Purpose Of This Name:

Scripture points out that man is prone to wander. "All we like sheep have gone astray, we have turned every one to his own way...." (Isa. 53:6a). We desperately need the Shepherd to save us and to sustain us. If we will become sheep in His fold He will feed us and keep us, leading us in and out to good pastures. Some day the Great Shepherd will come again to gather all His sheep—those already in His fold as well as those of the house of Israel. Man has a tremendous need for this One called the Shepherd. Israel has a tremendous need for the Shepherd of Israel.

15.6 SHIELD:

The word "shield"—can it be a title of deity? Forty-three times this term appears in the OT—particularly in passages relating to armed conflict, military or defense issues. In 16 of these 43 verses shield is used metaphorically, or in some cases descriptively, to detail attributes of God. It is the intent here to separate for discussion the passages pertaining to deity from those relating only to man.

Examination of the 43 passages containing the word shield in the KJV shows that four Hebrew words[131] are involved in the translation to this English word. A fifth Hebrew word shelet, (SRN 7982)[132] also meaning shield, may be removed from this quest for titles of God, since it appears only in the plural within the 43 applications. The most common shield, the magen, was small and the tsinnah was man-sized. However, this detail is not of great interest, since the 16 passages referring to deity apply the word shield to mean a covering or a protection provided by God for His people irrespective of any physical limitations of the particular shield used.

---

[131] These transliterated Hebrew words are kiydown (SRN 3591), magen (SRN 4043), socharah (SRN 5507) and tsinnah (6793).

[132] Recent Hebrew scholars eliminate kiydown (SRN 3591) and socharah (SRN 5507) from this group of synonyms as mis-translations, but they add instead the term agilah (a variation of SRN 5699). The study of the term "shield" is unaffected by these changes, however, because only magen (SRN 4043) and tsinnah (SRN 6793) are applied to God in the OT.

Version Variations:

It is appropriate to list the passages referring to the English word shield, since this word possibly serves as a title of deity. Such a listing also provides an opportunity to examine variations in translation between a sampling of Scripture versions. The following Table 15.3, entitled Variations In The Word Shield presents these 16 passages of interest as they appear in six popular versions of Scripture.

Table 15.3

Variation In The Word Shield

Ref.	KJV	NKJV	NIV	JER	Beck	Moffatt
Gen. 15:1	shield	shield	shield	shield	Shield	shield
Deu. 33:29	shield	shield	shield	shield	shield	shield
2Sa. 22:3	shield	shield	shield	shield	Shield	shield
Psa. 3:3	shield	shield	shield	shield	Shield	shieldest
Psa. 28:7	shield	shield	shield	shield	shield	shield
Psa. 33:20	shield	shield	shield	shield	shields	shield
Psa. 59:11	shield	shield	shield	shield	Shield	shielding
Psa. 84:9	shield	shield	shield	shield	ruler	protector
Psa. 84:11	shield	shield	shield	shield	Shield	shield
Psa. 91:4	shield	shield	shield	shield	shield	shielded
Psa. 115:9	shield	shield	shield	shield	shields	shield
Psa. 115:10	shield	shield	shield	shield	shield	shield
Psa. 115:11	shield	shield	shield	shield	shields	shield
Psa. 119:114	shield	shield	shield	shield	shield	shield
Psa. 144:2	shield	shield	shield	shield	shield	Shield
Pro. 30:5	shield	shield	shield	shield	Shield	shields

It can be seen that the applications are identical in the four columns showing the KJV, NKJV, NIV and JER versions. The word shield, whether used as a title of deity or not, is not capitalized in any of these versions. This restriction on capitalization will be discussed further later. The Beck version contains variations in the capitalization of the word shield that are of special interest to this study. Further examination of this version will be detailed in the appendix. The Moffatt variations have only very minimal affect on this study; further consideration will not be given to them.

To Whom Does This Title Apply?

The AV context presents the LORD as a shield in several verses. For example, Gen. 15:1 speaks of the LORD as declaring, "I am your shield." Metaphorically this simply means, I (the LORD) protect you like a shield. He is Abraham's protector or defense. This metaphor occurs again in examples like Psa. 3:3; 59:11; 84:11 and others. The AV context presents the word shield as a characteristic function of God and is therefore considered a title of deity. This argument is supported by the capitalization of the proper noun shield in certain passages of the Beck version.

In addition to appearing as a title for the LORD the word shield is also used as a title of God (Elohim) in two passages, 2Sa. 22:3 and Psa. 84:9.

The faithfulness and/or veracity of the LORD appears in Psa. 91:4 as that which covers as a shield and buckler. But here the word is not applied as a title. However, sufficient demonstration of the application of the word shield as a title is shown in one or more of the passages, so that we may comfortable accept the word shield as a title of deity.

To facilitate the examination of the occurrence of this word as a divine title in the 16 passages of concern, a comparison of the involved phrases has been prepared and set forth in the Chapter 15 APPENDIX as Table A. 15. 3. Only four versions have been selected for this comparison in order to limit the magnitude of the data. The table can be expanded with other versions for those wishing to do so.

15.7 SHILOH:

The English word Shiloh appears 33 times in the OT; 32 of these appearances provide the name of a city or town that was in the hill country of Ephraim, about 31 km north of Jerusalem (Jdg. 21:19). Shiloh was the prominent center of tribal administration and worship for the 12 Israelite tribes from the time of Joshua until the city's destruction about 1050 BC The modern archeological tell, still under investigation, testifies of Shiloh's violent ruin accompanied by a great fire.

The remaining appearance of the word shiloh is the subject of a controversy of long standing. Most scholars agree on only one point: it is a different word entirely. However, there is widespread disagreement regarding the origin and the meaning of the word. As it stands, it is merely a homonym of the place name used in the other 32 appearances. According to Jewish tradition, this is an epithet of the Messiah that appears in the OT blessing of Jacob to his son Judah (Gen. 49:10).[133] One encyclopedia has this to say about this verse: "The passage is composed of four poetic lines (two couplets) of which the third line has the Hebrew consonants 'd ky yb' shiyloh, translated by the AV to read 'until Shiloh come.' This rendering suggests that Shiloh (Shiyloh, SRN 7886) *might* be a sign of the Messiah or even a metonym for the

[133] According to the ancient synagogue paraphrase, Targum Onkelos, this is a direct reference to the Messiah. Support for this was found in the rabbinic interpretation of Eze. 21:27, which says, "until he comes whose right it is, and I will give it to him." The words "until he comes whose right it is" were regarded as referring directly to Gen. 49:10, and "whose right it is" was considered to be the correct sense of this unique word Shiloh.

Messiah Himself."[134] Such a statement has led this study to investigate and tabulate in some detail how various Scripture versions translate the meaning of the Gen. 49:10 passage involving the word Shiloh.[135] Summation comments from a collection of dictionaries are also included. From this information a reasonable decision as to the application of the word Shiloh as a title of deity will be offered.

---

[134] D. K. Stuart, "Shiloh," _International Standard Bible Encyclopedia_, G. W. Bromiley, Editor, Vol. 4, p. 478.
[135] See Table 15.4 Select Scripture Version Translation of the passage in Gen. 49:10.

NAME VARIATIONS:

Table 15.4

Select Scripture Version Translation of the Gen. 49:10 Passage

Version	Gen. 49:10	Phraseology
KJV (1909/1917)	Shiloh	until Shiloh come
KJV (1984)	Shiloh	until Shiloh come
KJV (1611)	Shiloh	until Shiloh come
NKJV (1982)	Shiloh	Until Shiloh comes
NEB (1976)	**	so long as tribute is brought to him
JER (1966)	**	until he come to whom it belongs
NAS (1975)	Shiloh	Until Shiloh comes or
	Shiloh	Until he comes to Shiloh or
	**	Until he comes to whom it belongs
NIV (1984)	**	Until he comes to whom it belongs
MOF (1935)	**	till he comes into his own
Beck (1976)	SHILOH	Till SHILOH (Man of Rest) comes
TLB (1971)	Shiloh	until Shiloh comes or he to whom it belongs

**Paraphrased out

The comparison of the 11 select Scripture versions demonstrates the variation in translations of the disputed passage. Of the 11 versions, six (including the three KJV date variations) agree that the translation of the debated phrase means, "until Shiloh come(s)," and Shiloh is considered a proper name. But in this group, the NAS and TLB also provide other options. The JER, the NIV and the alternate renderings of the NAS and TLB translate the phrase to mean, "until he come to whom it belongs." The MOF translation, "until he comes into his own," and the NEB's "so long as tribute is brought to him" complete the assortment.

It is interesting to note in the Table that 4 of the versions of 1 of the NAS options have paraphrased the word Shiloh out of their translations completely. Since this study is limited in attention to the word Shiloh, these other translations will receive no further consideration.

The Argument:

Having examined the phraseology of the disputed passage in the various Scripture versions, we turn now to a summation of excerpt interpretations of these phrases as found in select commentaries.

Phrase	Summaries Of What Others Say
Until Shiloh Come(s)	**BDBG Hebrew and English Lexicon: P.1010** (SRN 7886); Proper name of Messiah **Gesenius Hebrew-Chaldee Lexicon to the Old Testament Scripture: P.818** ...Judah shall not lay down the scepter of the ruler, until his enemies be subdued...and he shall rule over many people; an expectation belonging to the Kingdom of the Messiah, who was to spring from the tribe of Judah. **ISBE: Vol. 4, P. 478-479** This translation from the AV and others

suggests that Shiloh might be a sign of the Messiah or even a metonym for the Messiah Himself...However, there are obstacles to this rendering with significant disagreement in the literature. It is also interesting to note that the New Testament ignores Gen. 49:10 and virtually all the ancient versions take the expression sylh as other than a proper name in this verse.

New Unger's Bible Dictionary: P.1182

A title of the Messiah (Gen. 49:10). Though there has been much discussion as to the grammatical interpretation of the word, (Heb. Shiloh) Jewish officialdom and the Christian church agree as to the fact that the patriarch is here proclaiming the coming of the Messiah...When Jacob had before him the founders of the twelve-tribed nation, the question naturally arose, from which of the 12 tribes would the promised Savior proceed?...After reasonable deduction, Jacob states that Judah was to bear the scepter with victorious, lion-like courage, until in the future "Shiloh" was to descend from Judah.

Westminster Dictionary of the Bible: P.557

Aside from the name of a town in central Palestine, Shiloh is a proper name, which designates the Messiah and refers to the peacefulness of his disposition and his reign.

Theological Wordbook of the Old Testament: Vol. 2, P.919

Concerning the phrase, "until Shiloh come(s)," if it is a prophecy of Jesus, the NT nowhere alludes to it. It would be preferable to say it is a prophecy of David as a type of the Messiah, but what does Shiloh add?

Wycliffe Bible Commentary: P.46

The phrase was spoken by Jacob in the midst of his prophetic picture of Judah's place in the plan of God. From ancient times it has been considered a Messianic message. The primary reference must be to Judah, but ultimately the Messiah is the true one who should come.

Zondervan Pictorial Bible Commentary: P.785

The Gen. 49:10 passage is Messianic. The

difficulty of this interpretation is that nowhere else in the OT is Shiloh found as a personal name, and none of the ancient manuscripts apply the word personally to the Messiah.

To Whom Does This Name Apply?

The available evidence in this consideration certainly allows significant latitude as to the interpretation that the term Shiloh is applied as a title of deity in the OT. However, the literature search that has been conducted indicates that even though there is question, there is a predominance of agreement that the word Shiloh should be accepted as a title of the Messiah or a name of God.

The Purpose Of This Name:

This title of deity will be applied to the Messiah at His second coming when the prophecy of Jacob will be fulfilled. From out of the tribe of Judah will come a lawgiver, and the rulership will never depart from Him. Jacob spoke of the coming of the Messiah as sovereign ruler, not seeing the great first coming. Jacob thought that the ruling aspects would occur when the Messiah came. But Jesus came from the tribe of Judah first as a servant. He will come again with all the glory of the God Head.

The Old Testament Names of God

A Perspective

Chapter 16

Contents

*Appendix Support

16.1 SPIRIT OF GOD
16.2 SPIRIT OF THE LORD
16.3 SPIRIT OF THE LORD GOD
16.4 SPIRIT (Including importance Of Word Capitalization)

The computer indicates that in the OT (KJV) there are 228 applications of the Hebrew word ruwach SRN 7307)[136] translated into the English word spirit. Seventy-two of these passages involve indication of deity. The other 156 applications of the word spirit, such as Pharoah's spirit (Gen. 41:8) or the children of Israel's spirit (Exo. 6:9) or David's spirit (Psa. 31:5), do not pertain to deity.[137]

To Whom Do These Names Apply?

Remember, we are interested only in applications where the English word Spirit is a name or title of deity. Several of the compound phrases such as the Spirit of God, the Spirit of the LORD and the Spirit of the Lord GOD are easily recognized as names of God, because these phrases refer directly to God's Spirit or the LORD's Spirit—that is, to the Person of the Holy Spirit. However, the basic word spirit, when applied to deity, may require additional consideration in order to determine whether a particular use of this word does or does not serve as a name of God.

Argument:

It is interesting to note that the compound names in the of-genitive form involve or require that the governing word Spirit, the preposition "of" and the Godhead

---

[136] Note: In 222 verses there are 228 applications (6 multiples).

[137] There is one other Hebrew word, SRN 5397, that sometimes is translated spirit. However, it is of no consequence to this study.

Personage be present as a part of the name. To do otherwise negates the compound as a name. For example, the "spirit of wisdom" (Exo. 28:3) uses the word spirit. The preposition "of" is also present, but the Godhead Personage is not present. Therefore, this phrase is not a name of deity. Similarly, in another example, the "spirit of jealousy" (Num. 5:30) is not a name of deity.

One other variable will be discussed in connection with the names the Spirit of God, the Spirit of the LORD and the Spirit of the Lord GOD. In 14 verses in the KJV the phrase the Spirit of God occurs.[138] In nine of these verses the word spirit is capitalized. But in the other five verses the phrase spirit of God is written without capitalizing the word spirit, suggesting that this compound is not an appellation of deity. But the context of the five applications with no capitalization of the word spirit will not allow any other result than the recognition that the phrase should be considered a title of the Holy Spirit. Therefore, the lack of capitalization must be attributed to editor's or publisher's choice of style.

In the KJV the divine name the Spirit of the LORD occurs in 26 verses.[139] In 21 of these verses the word Spirit is capitalized. Five other times the phrase the spirit of the LORD occurs without capitalization of the word spirit, again suggesting that the phrase is not a compound name of deity. The same reasoning concerning publication style again applies. In this discussion the word spirit should everywhere be capitalized,

---

[138] See Appendix Table A.16.1 for identification.
[139] See Appendix Table A.16.2 for identification.

because in all of these verses the word spirit refers to the Holy Spirit. The phenomenon of inconsistent capitalization together with other details of variations between Scripture versions and their applications of the compound names and the unadorned word spirit are discussed in APPENDIX 16.

16.5 STONE:
16.6 STONE OF ISRAEL:

In the OT the Hebrew word 'eben (SRN 68) is commonly translated into the English word "stone." Because stones are abundant in Israel, the people were well acquainted with this substance and its properties, and the word appears frequently in the OT writings. Strong's Concordance indicates that there are 127 occurrences of the word stone in the OT portion of Scripture. However, only four verses use the word or a synonym, either with an adjective modifier or in a compound genitive expression, to actually or figuratively indicate deity. We will examine these combinations in order to verify their use as names of God. Applications in eight different versions of Scripture are compared,[140] since the Hebrew word 'eben is translated into the English word stone and also into a variety of synonyms. For example, in Gen. 49:24 it is translated the Stone of Israel in the NKJV and into the Rock of Israel in the RSV. Even more variations are observed in the Isa. 28:16 passage. There we find stone and block (of granite) translated from the same Hebrew word 'eben.

---

[140] See Table 16:1.

Table 16.1

The Word Stone Or Synonyms Applied As A Name Of God

REF.	Gen. 49:24	Psa. 118:22	Isa. 8:14	Isa. 28:16
KJV	the stone of Israel	the refused stone	a stone of stumbling	a tried stone
NKJV	the Stone of Israel	rejected stone	stone of stumbling	foundation stone
NIV	the Rock of Israel	the rejected stone	a stone to stumbling	a tested stone
NEB	the Strong One of Israel	the rejected stone	a hardship boulder	a block of granite
JER	Stone of Israel	rejected stone	stumbling stone	stone of witness
NAS	the Stone of Israel	the rejected stone	a stone to strike	a tested stone
RSV	the Rock of Israel	rejected stone	stone of offense	a tested stone
Beck	Rock of Israel	rejected stone	stumbling stone	well-tested Stone

It can be seen from the above version comparison that there is less than agreement in the translation of 'eben to either the word stone or a synonym in these passages where the word figuratively indicates deity.

To Whom Do These Names Apply?

The figurative applications of the Hebrew term stone are most important in this study, since in these four passages the word 'eben or stone is used to indicate deity. Elsewhere Scripture speaks symbolically of the stony or insensitive heart (Eze. 11:19; 36:26). There is also the comparison of human strength or durability with that of stones (Job 6:12). The motionlessness of stone is mentioned in Exo. 15:16. However, the word stone in Gen. 49:24 refers to Yahweh, the stone of Israel or, as some versions read, the Rock of Israel. Then in Isa. 28:16 the phrasing of this passage metaphorically alludes to Christ as a Stone. Isa. 8:14 refers in metaphor to One (Christ) as a Stone of stumbling and Rock of offence to the house of Israel. Psa. 118:22 looks beyond the rejection of the Stone to His exaltation in His coming kingdom. It is plain that the Stone or Rock is used figuratively to refer to Christ.

The Argument:

The term stone is interesting. It appears in all kinds of places and is very common in every type of literature, indicating that the people were very familiar with what is meant by the word. There was the primary use in building and construction. The temple and even the altar were made of stone. In certain locations, the idols were made of stone. Many containers, such as eating and drinking vessels, were often of simple or even ornamental stone. Because of these uses of the material, it is not uncommon to find inscriptions written in stone. On account of its durability, weights were sometimes made of stone as were ownership boundary markers. Weapons were often made of stone. The people threw stones in slings and catapults. Wells were dug and covered over with this material, as were graves. Many of these uses involved common stone, but there were also the precious stones; Scripture mentions some 30 different kinds. They were used in the jewelry of the day. The priests wore breastplates decorated with various kinds of precious stones.

With this suggestive list of applications of stone the reader can immediately form strong mental images of biblical people, places and events, because they involved stone in some manner. For example, Solomon built the temple of prepared stone (1Ki. 6:7). The monument commemorating the Jordan crossover into the promised land was to consist of great stones, plastered over with the words of the law written thereon

(Deu. 27:2,3). The Decalogue was written on two tablets of stone by the finger of the LORD (Exo. 34:1; Deu. 9:10). Then, remember, Jacob used a stone for a pillow at Bethel (Gen. 28:11). Moses sat on a stone with Aaron and Hur supporting his hands while the Israelites defeated Amalek (Exo. 17:12,13). David slew Goliath with a stone (1Sa. 17:49,50), and on and on, story after story, stone upon stone.

The use of the stone in matters of Judgment and related punishment in the Israelite culture must also be mentioned, even though the basic Hebrew words for this type of stone differs from the above applications of 'eben. The Hebrew words sagal (SRN 5619) and ragam (SRN 7275), though translated into the English word stone actually mean to lapidate and to stone a person to death.

Interestingly, the term stone, itself, is not found as a name of deity. But, this word coupled with other epithetical terms and genitive phrases form powerful substitutes for the name of deity. So we find the writers figuratively describing God and His attributes of great power, strength and protection for His people in terms of this material.

Purpose Of These Names:

Christ is the Stone or Rock. He is the precious hiding place for sure defense and protection. But He was rejected at His first coming and was a stumbling stone to His people, the Jews. To Israel at His second coming He will be the very capstone. To His church through the ages He is the foundation and chief corner Stone. To the unbeliever He is the crushing Stone.

16.7 STRENGTH OF ISRAEL:

This interesting OT genitive phrase is unique to 1Sa. 15:29, where Yahweh is identified as the Strength of Israel. But benefiting from this resource was conditional, for if Israel had or was ever to have a genuine strength relationship with God it could only be as the lifestyle of Israel became totally submitted to the LORD. But whether or not Israel would ever meet the requirements for such a walk with God, God is still the Strength of Israel; that is one of his names, waiting for Israel to call upon His attribute of strength. Since the phrase is a title of deity, further consideration will be given to its application.

In the OT the English word strength appears in 215 KJV passages, being translated from 36 different Hebrew words. Most of these applications either do not relate to deity or are adjectives or metaphors not considered direct appellations of God. The Hebrew term netsach (SRN 5331) is translated into no less than 12 different English words, including the word of interest, "strength." In the assortment of these dozen words we also find the term victory, which was used in David's prayer (1Ch. 29:11) to amplify the greatness of Yahweh.

One lexicon[141] suggests that this Hebrew word primarily means eminence, enduring, everlasting, perpetuity. Another lexicon[142] presents its initial English meanings as splendor and glory. So the 1Sa. 15:29 passage previously read "Strength

---

[141] Brown-Driver-Briggs-Gesenius, *The New Hebrew and English Lexicon*, Hendrickson Publishers, p. 664.

[142] Tregelles-Gesenius, *Hebrew and Chaldee Lexicon*, Baker Book House, Grand Rapids, p. 562.

of Israel," meaning Yahweh, can also be read "the Glory of Israel," and the phrase can more easily be seen as a title of deity. Some of these variations that appear in prominent Scripture versions are displayed in the following table:

Table 16.2

1Sa. 15:29 Scripture Variations

Version	1Sa. 15:29 Translation
KJV	the Strength of Israel
NKJV	the Strength of Israel
BECK	the Glory of Israel
JER	the glory of Israel
NAS	the Glory of Israel
NIV	the Glory of Israel
RSV	the Glory of Israel
MOF	the Splendour of Israel
NEB	the Splendour of Israel

In these nine scripture versions it can be seen that the English translation of the Hebrew word <u>netsach</u> as "strength" occurs twice. The translation into the English word "Glory" or "glory" occurs 5 times, and the English word "splendour" (Note: British spelling) is used twice. Why these variations? What is the meaning of the Hebrew word <u>netsach?</u>

First, examine the KJV OT's 215 verses that use the English word "strength." This English word can be translated from any of 37 Hebrew words, each of which have alternate renderings. For example, SRN 5797 is translated strength in Psa. 28:7-8, power in Psa. 63:2 and might in 1Ch. 13:8. SRN 5797 is one of 10 Hebrew words whose primary meaning is strength, power, etc. Hebrew is a very colorful language. For liveliness and variety, Hebrew twists and stretches other words to yield further synonyms. Fourteen of the 37 words translated "strength" come from this other category, which we can identify as words with specially derived meanings. We create new meanings for words often even in our modern world. Consider, for example, our slang expressions "cool" and "bad". In ancient Israel, at the crossroads of the three major continents, they were at least as creative in their use of their vocabulary as we are today. Even from a more conservative view of the flexibility of words, we know that most words can have secondary meanings that are derived from their primary meanings.

Coming back to SRN 5331, close consideration shows that in the KJV renderings of this word netsach, 23 times the English word forever appears and four times the term perpetual is used; strength and victory appear two times each. The words end and always are each used twice. We also find the English terms evermore, constantly, lasting, eternal and unceasing. Clearly strength is not the primary meaning of our word netsach.

By the time we are finished looking at SRN 5331, selected from 1Sa. 15:29, we find at least 12 possible meanings ranging through terms like splendor, always, constantly, evermore, perpetual, strength and victory.

So we ask the question, what is the meaning of the Hebrew word netsach? In this study it is sufficient to accept the consensus opinion that the fundamental meaning of the word is something like endless or eternal existence; glory and strength would both be secondary meanings of the word.

Now, examine the collection of verses listed in Table 16.2 using the word glory translated from the Hebrew noun netsach. This sense of the word does not occur in the KJV. However, in the NIV rendering of the 1Sa. 15:29 passage the Hebrew is translated "glory".[143] So the two versions of the 1Sa. 15:29 passage draw different meanings from a word that has a legitimate double nuance: eternal, forever, and endless on the one hand and eminence, glory or splendor on the other. Certainly for the phrase the netsach of Israel—applied as a metonym for the LORD—eminence, glory and strength are appropriate translations, and so the phrase is considered a name of God.

To Whom Does This Title Apply?

The genitive phrase, the Strength of Israel, the Glory of Israel or the Splendor of Israel is used as a name of God. The word strength, by itself, is not accepted as an appellation of deity.

---

[143] The NIV has been used as a comparison to the KJV. Other versions could be treated in a similar manner.

The Argument:

The title the Strength of Israel appears in one of the saddest stories in the Bible. In accordance with the requirements of the LORD Saul had been crowned king by Samuel. As king Saul was to obey God in certain detailed tasks, one of which was to completely destroy the wicked nation of Amalek. But Saul failed to obey the requirements of God, saving instead the life of Agag, the wicked king, and the spoil stuff from the conquest.

When he heard of the disobedience of Saul, the prophet Samuel searched out King Saul to tell him that because he had rejected the divine command Yahweh, the Strength of Israel, rejected Saul as king. Saul appears to be very penitent but it is too late—the disobedience had occurred. The prophet tells Saul, "The Strength of Israel will not lie nor repent, for he is not a man, that He should repent."

It was Yahweh, the LORD God, the One named the Strength of Israel, who acted, and we can understand this phrase as a name.

Purpose Of This Name:

Three of the attributes of God are observed in the consideration of this special title, the Strength of Israel. Strength in this derived sense is by implication lasting or durable; He is Israel's support for evermore, forever. Legitimately, some choose the meaning glory or eminence and arrive at the metonym the Glory of Israel. Similarly, others render the title the Splendor of Israel. These are nuances of a single word in the Hebrew, but in the English translations they sound different and far apart. Irrespective of the Scripture version under consideration (and hence the English word selection), remember that the LORD is from everlasting to everlasting. Strength is His very name.

16.8 STRONGHOLD:

The literature[144] suggests that the word stronghold is a title of deity, but there is a uniqueness about this word and its spelling that requires that care be exercised as to identification of the Scripture version involved in this title's appearance. For example, the word stronghold is not found at all in our primary study version, the KJV (1909-1917 edition). Rather the separated words strong and hold are used instead. This simply means that two words must be designated in the word or name search in place of the single word stronghold. If this is not done the computer search will fail to locate any term at all and, of course, any possible application of the word stronghold as a title of deity.

Consider a second example. A mixture of the single word stronghold and the two word variant is used in the KJV 1984 edition. In this mixture it happens that the word stronghold is used in the Nah. 1:7 passage where, in the earlier KJV edition, the title of deity appeared. So if the search is limited to the two word condition the deity title will not be found in this edition.

It may seem trivial to be concerned about these two cases, since the single word, stronghold, obviously is derived from the previously divided term. However, it becomes important when searching for this name or title of God whether by means of

---

[144] R. Purnell, *Knowing God by His Names*, Here's Life Publisher, p. 59, and C. J. Rolls, *The Name Above Every Name*, Loizeaux Brothers, Neptune, NJ, 1965, p. 208.

the available computer programs of today or merely the conventionally published Strong's Concordance.

The two examples just discussed will be examined further in connection with the following Name Variation chart. (Note: KJV translates seven different Hebrew words as strong hold. The other versions do a better job of distinguishing their meanings.)

Name Variations:

Ref.	KJV	NKJV	NIV	NAS	NEB	JER	BECK
2Sa. 24:7[145]	strong hold	stronghold	fortress	fortress	walled city	fortress	fortified
Hab, 1:10(same as 145 above)	strong hold	stronghold	fortified	fortress	fortress	fortresses	fortified
2Sa. 5:7[146]	strong hold	stronghold	fortress	stronghold	stronghold	fortress	fortress
Nah. 1:7[147]	strong hold	stronghold	refuge	stronghold	refuge	stronghold	fortress
Zec. 9:3[148]	strong hold	tower	stronghold	fortress	rampart	rampart	fortress
Isa. 31:9[149]	strong hold	stronghold	stronghold	rock	out (officers)	rock	out
Mic. 4:8[150]	strong hold	stronghold	stronghold	hill	hill	out	hill
Zec. 9:12[151]	strong hold	stronghold	fortress	stronghold	stronghold	out	fortified

(out = paraphrased out)

---

[145] The most commonly used word is mibtsar (SRN 4013) related to SRN 1225. Its basic meaning is fence or protective enclosure. It is commonly translated strong hold.
[146] m'tsudah (SRN 4686 with variant in SRN 4679) is translated strong place in Job 39:28 but strong hold elsewhere. One dictionary renders it "a place difficult to approach."

- ([145a]) Koehler-Baumgartner, Lexicon in Veteris Testament, Libros, Vol. 1.

[147] Ma'oz (SRN 4581) is normally translated fortress, stronghold or refuge.
[148] matsor (SRN 4692 with variants in SRN 4694 and SRN 6697) is a protective wall or rampart; it is translated Strong in Psalm 31:21 and Psalm 60:19 but strong hold elsewhere.
[149] (SRN 1225) is normally translated rock or crag.
[150] 'ophel (SRN 6076) is usually translated hill.
[151] bitstsarown (SRN 1225) can be translated either fortress or stronghold.

Column 1 lists the eight verses where the KJV 1909-1917 edition uses the two English words strong and hold. They are a compound expression consisting of the adjective strong and the noun hold. In this KJV edition the word stronghold does not appear. The English phrase translates a single Hebrew word in each case.

The translation variations are easily observable in the Name Variation Chart. In column 2, the KJV's rendering of the Hebrew original texts is given. The expression strong hold is a general, undefined equivalent of Hebrew words with specific meanings. (Strong hold in 2Sa. 24:7 and Hab. 1:10 are from the same Hebrew word). In column 3 the same seven Hebrew words from the previous column are translated into the English word stronghold 7 times, but once the NKJV substitutes the translation tower, which departs from the literal meaning of the Hebrew word in a direction none of the others follow.

Accepting as a figure of speech the phrase "the LORD is a strong hold" (Nah. 1:7, KJV 1909-1917) to indicate a title of deity, since a divine attribute is identified a grasp of the problem of title identification becomes clearer. The English words strong hold, stronghold, refuge and fortress are being used interchangeably in the various versions, so they all must be identified as titles of deity. The KJV and the NKJV have obscured the more specific titles. However, because of prominent use of a more general term, a case can be made for recognizing those other specific titles such as the Rock, the Fortress, the Rampart and the Hill in addition to the Stronghold (or the Strong Hold).

To Whom Does This Name Apply?

The words strong hold indicate Yahweh the LORD in the KJV 1909-1917 edition. Likewise, the word stronghold indicates Yahweh the LORD in the KJV 1984 edition. The NIV, used in this study as a support or commentary Scripture, presents eight passages displaying names of deity; six times the word stronghold indicates Yahweh the LORD and twice the word stronghold indicates Elohim as God.

For further discussion and word argument, consider the detail presented in the Chapter 16 APPENDIX.

16.9 SUN
16.10 SUN OF RIGHTEOUSNESS

The OT of the KJV 1909-1917 edition contains the English word sun 130 times (in 122 verses and 8 multiples); it represents six Hebrew root and cognate terms, making a separation of particular words and their Scripture location difficult. The word sun is used to indicate time (of day), a heavenly body (the sun), effects of the sun (warmth and light), and east-west direction, and it is the basis of an expression meaning openly, publicly or everywhere (under the sun). But in all these applications of the word sun, the literature[152] indicates that only twice the term sun is used to indicate deity (Psa. 84:11 and Mal. 4:2). Certainly confidence in the accuracy of another's identification of deity titles and their locations assists this study; however, encouragement to look up the literature sources is appropriate as always. To begin the examination of these two passages, a comparison of several Scripture versions has been incorporated into the following Name Variation Chart.

---

[152] J. A. Alexander, *Commentary on Psalms,* Kregel Pub. Grand Rapids, 1991, p. 366.
C. J. Rolls, *The Name Above Every Name,* Loiseaux Brothers Pub., Neptune NJ, 1965, pg. 244.
D. Purnell, *Knowing God By His Names*, Here's Life Pub., San Bernardino, CA, 1987, p. 59.
M. F. Unger, *The New Unger's Bible Dictionary*, Moody Press, Chicago, 1985, p. 1225.
R. L. Harris, ed., *Theological Wordbook of the OT, Vol. 2*, Moody Press, Chicago, 1980, p. 940.

Name Variation Chart:

Reference	Psa. 84:11	Mal. 4:2
KJV (1909-17 ed.)	sun	Sun of righteousness
KJV (1984 ed.)	sun	Sun of righteousness
NKJV	sun	Sun of Righteousness
NIV	sun	sun of righteousness
RSV	sun	sun of righteousness
NAS	sun	sun of righteousness
JER	battlement	sun of righteousness
NEB	battlement	sun of righteousness
BECK	Sun	Sun of Righteousness
MOF	sun	saving Sun

The consensus of eight Scripture versions as well as two different editions of the KJV indicate that the phrase in Psa. 84:11 predominantly reads, "the LORD God is a sun and shield." This is a metaphor meaning that Yahweh Elohim is represented as the sun or its attributes such as warmth, light, longevity and life itself, because without the sun there would not be life. The second part of this metaphorical statement, "and shield," indicates that the LORD is also the believer's protection and defense.

Care must be taken here to establish the difference between a simile and a metaphor. God does not tolerate sun worship such as the Egyptian cult of Ra. God does not want to be worshipped like that. God is not like the sun—a simile. Rather, God himself is the creator of the sun and the creator and sustainer of the very existence of His people. God goes on forever, but the sun is of limited duration. He does give warmth and light and life as does the sun. He is associated with the heavens as is the sun. Worship God, who has these attributes, but do not worship the astronomic sun.

It is interesting to note that the BECK version indicates the words Sun and Shield as titles of deity with capital letters for both of the two attributes.

Two of the versions elect to translate the metaphoric phrase to mean, "God is a battlement and shield." But who can complain, for surely God is our battlement, our pinnacle, the highest protection, our summit, our culmination.

Look again at the Name Variation Chart regarding the genitive phrase, the Sun of Righteousness. By application of antimereia—the exchange of parts of speech—we can write the Sun of Righteousness as Righteousness' Sun, which reminds us that Christ's righteousness is far brighter than our sun. It is interesting to note that about half of the versions examined render the component sun as a capitalized word, "the Sun," and that at least one version capitalizes both nouns in the phrase.

To Whom Do These Title Apply?

The majority of the examined versions use the metaphor the LORD God is a Sun, referring to Yahweh Elohim. There is no doubt that this title is applied to Him as Sun. On the other hand, the full genitive Sun of Righteousness indicates the Lord Jesus Christ.

The Argument:

Let us look at Psalm 84, which contains the first phrase of interest. The authorship of the Psalm is attributed to the Sons of Korah. But the content is so expressive of the experiences of David that many suppose that the Sons of Korah, who were Temple musicians, composed this psalm for David, the king himself. At any rate, the Psalmist writes of his longing for close communion with the Living God and His sanctuary. The "dwellings" relate to the earthly temple courts, the place in front of the temple building where God appeared in visible splendor. And if these earthly courts are viewed as lovely by the Israelite believer, how beautiful must be the Father's heavenly sanctuary, the eternal dwelling place of the family of God. The Psalmist also speaks of fellowship with the living God, anticipating the last days, when the true believing Israelite will be in His presence. But this is already the condition for the believers in Christ, His church. We enjoy fellowship with the Living God, who sees and hears and knows, and whose purposes will be accomplished. Happy are they that dwell in thy house in perfect fellowship with the King to continually praise Him forever.

The Psalmist then continues the prayer, addressing God in a series of names and titles that provide grounds for his petition; Hear my prayer, give ear, O God of hosts and of eternity, of protection, and covenant relation to Your people. The Psalmist proclaims, "For the LORD God is a sun and shield," a metaphoric phrase, expressing in David-like exclamation that God is the sun, the source of life and happiness, and the shield, representing protection and safety to all the believers who dwell in His house. Appropriately, He is given the appellations Sun and Shield.

In our Argument let us also pay attention to the appellation, "the Sun of Righteousness." The 122 passages (plus eight multiples) that have already been considered containing the word "sun" include the genitive phrase "the Sun of Righteousness," which is found in Mal. 4:2. It is special, as this compound phrase is a title used of the Lord Jesus Christ at His second coming, "But unto you that fear my name shall the Sun of Righteousness arise with healing in His wings." In Gen. 1:16 the writer initially speaks of the sun, saying, "And God made two great lights; the greater light to rule the day, and the lesser light to rule the night: He made the stars also." Here we have the Sun represented as a type of the Lord Jesus Christ. The moon is a type of the church of Jesus Christ reflecting the greater light. And there are stars, types of individual believers who shine as lights. Can there be any doubt that the Sun of Righteousness speaks of the righteousness of Christ shining as the greater light than the sun itself. Praise His name for this beautiful title.

Purpose of This Name:

This name is used to celebrate the providence of God. He is the sun, providing life, giving warmth and light. He is also the shield, offering safety and protection. Man experiences these well understood blessings. Reflection upon them and upon the divine attributes they represent provide some insight into God's names in Scripture. Then, regarding the genitive phrase the Sun of Righteousness, we are to understand that it is Christ spoken of here, particularly as seen at His second coming. To the lost that day will be dark, with great terror. But to all that fear His name His second coming will be a glorious and welcome sun-rising.

16.11 WONDERFUL:

Wonderful is an unusual appellation, and because of the alphabetical arrangement of this study, it is now the time to look closely at this word. Where does it come from? What does it mean? Is it a name of deity? The English word wonderful can be translated from two prime Hebrew roots. First, pala' (SRN 6381 and cognates), which translates into 19 separate, but related in meaning, English words—including the word wonderful. Second, the Hebrew word shammah (SRN 8047) meaning desolate or waste caused by some great disaster, usually as a result of divine Judgment. Strangely, this Hebrew word is also sometimes translated wonderful in the negative sense. For example, in the AV Jer. 5:30 reads, "A wonderful and horrible thing is committed in the land." The NAS translates this, "An appalling and horrible thing."

This study is especially concerned about the first root, pl', from which the cognant pele' (SRN 6382) is derived. Twelve times this word is used in the OT to express wonder or wonders, to describe something as wonderful or marvelous; and it is always used in a context relating to God's acts or words. Especially of interest is the application in Isa. 9:6, where the word "wonderful" relates to the wonder of wonders, the provision of the Messiah to mankind.

First, compare the Isaiah 9:6 passage in several Scripture translations and editions:

NAME VARIATIONS

Reference	Isaiah 9:6
KJV (1909-1917 ed.)	Wonderful (5 name series)
KJV (1984)	Wonderful (5 name series)
NKJV	Wonderful (5 name series)
NIV	Wonderful Counselor (4 names)
RSV	Wonderful Counselor (4 names)
NAS	Wonderful Counselor (4 names)
JER	Wonder-Counsellor (all names hyphenated)
NEB	in purpose wonderful (4 names)
MOF	"A wonder of a counsellor" (4 names)
BECK	Wonderful (5 names)

This list presents some interesting facts about the word "wonderful." The Scripture references have been limited to eight versions and two editions of the KJV. In these 10 translations it can be seen that four of them place the word Wonderful in a series of five names identifying the Lord Jesus. The other six translations consider the word wonderful as an adjective modifying the noun Counselor. However, in the margin the NIV does allow a choice between these two uses of the word wonderful. This is significant in the series of names as to whether the Lord is to be referred to with four double worded titles or with three such pairs of words plus the initial two separate words, Wonderful and Counselor.

Alternately, look at this in the manner of the JER translation. Here the series of four double words are maintained by hyphenation, thereby very closely coupling each set of double words.

The NEB has still another viewpoint. The word wonderful is placed in the phrase "in purpose wonderful," and that is what He shall be called. This implies that He is wonderful in all purposes, no doubt including counseling—but yet, not specifically indicating counseling efforts. It is interesting to notice that the discussed phrase, although said to be a name, is not set apart with capitals like a proper name.

In the various translations only two seem to have caught the interpretation that the series of names are not four or five individual appellations but rather, are the components of a fivefold single name or title. The RSV and MOF even set off the word series with quotation marks.

Finally, in this consideration, notice the spelling of the word Counselor is also a variable with some translations using the British, counsellor and others applying the Americanized word counselor. Spelling differences such as those again point out existing word search problems due to version variations.

To Whom Does This Name Apply?

Isaiah 9:6 speaks of the Child and the Son to be given at the advent of Jesus Christ. Eventually the government shall be upon His shoulder and His name shall be called "Wonderful Counselor, The Mighty God, The Everlasting Father, The Prince of Peace."

The Argument:

In Chapters 7 and 8 Isaiah presents a frightful description of the darkness and distress for apostate Israel that would be associated with the Assyrian invasion. Isaiah warns that there will be "...trouble and darkness, dimness of anguish; and they shall be driven to darkness." (AV Isa. 8:22.)

As one commentary suggests,[153] Isaiah is a book of contrast, and in the opening of Chapter 9 there is a change from low doom and gloom to high, brilliant hope. The light of Christ will bring a great reversal in the situation described in the previous chapter. Anger, defeat and famine will be replaced with joy, victory and abundance. Then the source of this light is finally identified: the glorious future predicted by Isaiah would come as a child, a son. The Son who is given is the eternal Son of God. He will also be a son of King David, and for this reason He will have the right to shoulder the responsibilities of government.

Scripture then proceeds to give the fourfold name by which this Son will be called. Notice that it is one name, not plural names, with a series of four double elements. First is presented "Wonderful Counselor," or more literally "a Wonder of a Counselor." Some argue that the two elements are to be separated into "Wonderful" and "Counselor". If biblical precedents are accepted—remembering the important clue in Jdg. 13:18, where we find the conversation between Manoah and the Angel of the

---

[153] H. M. Wolf, *Interpreting Isaiah*, Academie Books, Zondervan Publishing House, Grand Rapids, 1985, p. 96.

LORD (perhaps the preincarnate Christ), who said that His name is "secret" or "Wonderful,"—the appellation "Wonderful" is more easily separated from the name Counselor in Isaiah. In either case Christ will be the Counselor par excellence, not needing any other to give Him advice.

The other three elements of the fourfold name of Christ the Son are treated in alphabetical order elsewhere in this manuscript.[154]

The Purpose of the Name:

The OT presents certain specific names for deity that the LORD Himself emphasizes (Exo. 6:2 and 3, Jer. 33:2), and He also reveals names of the coming Messiah that are equally great (Isa. 7:14, Isa. 9:6, Jer. 23:5-6, Amos 4:13). His names are important, and they have been revealed in order that man might know Him and worship Him. The prophet Isaiah, especially, presented a series of appellations for the Messiah in verse 9:6 which set Him apart from all other men and ascribe to Him characteristics that are nothing short of divine.

---

[154] For the other three elements of this fourfold name, see "Mighty God" (Chapter 13), "Everlasting Father (Chapter 6) and "Prince of Peace" (Chapters 13,14).

16.12 <u>YAHWEH / YAH</u>:

The last name of deity to be considered in the alphabetical sequence of names and titles is Yahweh, along with its shortened form Yah (SRN 3050), which forms the ending of the familiar word hallelujah (praise the Lord). Other shortened forms of the Hebrew personal name of God Yahweh appear as component parts of personal names in the OT, that is, Yahu and Yo. However, these contractions do not occur as independent appellations. The name Yah is generally translated as "the LORD" in the KJV; it occurs only 507 times, mainly in poetic passages. The transliteration of Yah appears only once, spelled "JAH" (Psa. 68:4).

It might be appropriate to consider the name Yahweh and the contraction Yah together, because these two words frequently appear very close to each other, especially in the Hebrew poetic passages.[155] However, with both names being generally translated into English as "the LORD," it is most difficult to separate the two appellations in the English text of Scripture.[156] Because these two names of deity do coexist in our Bibles (Yahweh with SRN 3068 and Yah with SRN 3050), it is the intent to individually consider the two names. Since Yah has not been examined in prior chapters of this manuscript, a detailed consideration will be given to it here. The name Yahweh has been studied in detail in Chapter 10. In order to avoid duplication it is recommended that reference be made to that material. There is no dispute over the

---

[155] For example, consider Psa. 89:8; 104:35; 106:48.
[156] Ibid. #155.

proposition that both names are accepted names of deity, since Yah is a contraction of the only true personal name of God, Yahweh.

Additional detail, Scripture version comparison and word applications are to be found in APPENDIX to Chapter 16.

APPENDIX Chapter 1

Development of the El and Elohim Support Tables

The Bible Research Systems computer readout indicates that there are 227 verse applications in the OT using the word assigned the SRN 410. In this group there are 8 verses wherein the Hebrew word 'el is applied twice and one verse where there are three applications. This gives a total application of the word 'el 237 times. It is the intent of this appendix to identify the El compound combinations that are applied as names of God in this assortment of 237 possibilities. To achieve this purpose and capture the data, the tables of this appendix are presented.

This large group contains substantial variations in the use of the word 'el. We have already determined that 'el commonly stands alone without modifiers, applied as a generic name for the one true God of Israel. However, in the OT the word is also occasionally used to identify false or foreign gods.

The word 'el also appears many times with appropriate epithetical[157] embellishments wherein the writer desired to identify special attributes of God or, perhaps, to satisfy the wish to enhance the very name of God. These epithets modifying the word El usually produce a compound name with two or more separate parts; however, some of the English epithetical expressions require several words or

[157] Epithet: an adjective, noun or phrase used to characterize some person or thing.

even a short phrase to fully translate the simpler phrase in the Hebrew. For example, "El Elyon" translates in English to "most high God."

Then there are some situations where the word 'el is applied obliquely to persons other than God. For example, the word is translated "power" in Gen. 31:29; Mic. 2:1 and Pro. 3:27 with reference to men. In Job 41:25 and Psa. 89:6 the word 'el is translated into the English word "mighty" with reference to great men and to pagan gods, respectively.

Table A.1.1

In this study of the word 'el the 237 applications are assembled in Table A.1.1. The Scripture Reference is noted, the Epithetical Condition is shown, as is the English translation (Phrase or Compound Name). Lastly, a code number has been assigned to assist in the categorization of the entries.

These Code Numbers and their meanings are discussed below, including the application frequency in each group.

Code 1 Identifies the selected epithet-enhanced El words that form the El compound names and their passage locations. Eight verses contain two multiples[158] and one verse in the aggregate contains three applications of the word El. There are

[158] A multiple is a passage wherein the word El occurs two or more times in the verse, in a given passage.

APPENDIX Chapter 1

65 code 1 epithetically enhanced El words. (Note: the personal pronoun compound names are listed in Code 6).

Code 2 Identifies the applications of El (without epithet) where El is used as the generic name of the One True God of Israel. There are 108 El words considered to be generic names of God.

Code 3 Identifies the verses with application of compound names made up of Yahweh and El (LORD God). There are 9 compounds in this category.

Code 4 Identifies the verses wherein the word 'el is applied to false or foreign gods. There are 15 applications.

Code 5 Identifies the verses wherein the SRN 410 word was not translated into the English word god. there are 12 applications.

Code 6 Identifies the verses containing the word El enhanced with a personal pronoun in the El modifier. There are 28 applications.

It is obvious that Codes 2, 4, and 5 do not form compound names of the One True God of Israel. Code 3 verses contain compound names of God with the enhancing name, Yahweh. These names can be unusual in that the word El can have a double enhancement, with the name Yahweh preceding it, plus a follow-up epithet. When this occurs there is a double count in Table A.1.1 (this results in a "multi" for that particular verse.) Code 6 verses contain personal pronoun compound names. For this part of the study, they have been excluded from further discussion, since they materially increase the required work effort without yielding any significant contribution to the desired end result. This coding categorization eliminates consideration of all but Code 1 applications of the word El. As noted, however, there are many El compound names in categories code 3 and 6.

Table A.1.2

Table A.1.2. displays a summation of the Coding separation for the 237 possible 'el applications.

Table A.1.3

Table A.1.1 contains many duplications of Scripture passages, since this Table is a scan of the OT searching for epithetical compound names. To arrive at a consensus of the appearance of any given compound name, that name must first be identified in Table A.1.1 and then the duplicates combined in Table A.1.3. The epithets applied to all El names in this category, arranged in alphabetical order with verse references, are displayed. A simple tally of this information shows that there are 34 code 1 compound names.

Tables A.1.4 and A.1.5

All 34 El Compound names of God certainly deserve detailed consideration. However to simplify the presentation a limiting procedure has been applied wherein only those compounds with a frequency of more than four occurrences in the OT will be further discussed. These are referred to as the Prominent El Compound Names. They are displayed in Tables A.1.4. and A.1.5.

APPENDIX Chapter 1

Table A.1.1

Location of the Word 'el (SRN 410) by Verse

Reference	Conditions	Code	Phrase or Compound Name
Gen. 14:18	with epithet	1	most high God
Gen. 14:19	with epithet	1	most high God
Gen. 14:20	with epithet	1	most high God
Gen. 14:22	with epithet	1	most high God
Gen. 16:13	with epithet	6	God seest me
Gen. 17:1	with epithet	1	the Almighty God
Gen. 21:33	with epithet	1	the everlasting God
Gen. 28:3	with epithet	1	And God Almighty
Gen. 31:13	with epithet	6	God of Bethel
Gen. 31:29	not a name	5	(power) of my hand
Gen. 35:1	no epithet	2	unto God
Gen. 35:3	no epithet	2	unto God
Gen. 35:11	with epithet	1	I am God Almighty
Gen. 43:14	with epithet	1	And God Almighty
Gen. 48:3	with epithet	1	God Almighty
Gen. 49:25	with epithet	6	the God of thy father
Exo. 6:3	with epithet	1	the name of God Almighty
Exo. 15:2	with epithet	6	he is my God
Exo. 15:11	not a name	4	gods
Exo. 20:5	with epithet	1	a jealous God
Exo. 34:6	with epithet	3	LORD God
Exo. 34:14	with epithet	1+1	is a jealous God/other god (2x)
Num. 12:13	no epithet	2	O God
Num. 16:22	no epithet	2	O God

Table A.1.1. (Continued)

Reference	Conditions	Code	Phrase or Compound Name
Num. 23:8	no epithet	2	God
Num. 23:19	no epithet	2	God
Num. 23:22	no epithet	2	God
Num. 23:23	no epithet	2	God
Num. 24:4	no epithet	2	God
Num. 24:8	no epithet	2	God
Num. 24:16	no epithet	2	God
Num. 24:23	no epithet	2	God
Deu. 3:24	no epithet	2	God
Deu. 4:24	with epithet	1	a jealous God
Deu. 4:31	with epithet	1	a merciful God
Deu. 5:9	with epithet	1	a jealous God
Deu. 6:15	with epithet	1	a jealous God
Deu. 7:9	with epithet	1	the faithful God
Deu. 7:21	with epithet	1	a mighty God & terrible
Deu. 10:17	with epithet	1	a great God (a mighty & a terrible)
Deu. 28:32	not a name	5	might
Deu. 32:4	with epithet	1	a God of truth
Deu. 32:12	not a name	4	strange god
Deu. 32:18	no epithet	2	God
Deu. 32:21	no epithet	2	God
Deu. 33:26	personal	6	God of Jeshurun (Israel)
Jos. 3:10	with epithet	1	the living God
Jos. 22:22	Yahweh God	3+3	the LORD God of gods (2x)
Jos. 24:19	with epithet	1	a jealous God
Jdg. 9:46	not a name	4	the god berith
1Sa. 2:3	with epithet	1	God of knowledge
2Sa. 22:31	no epithet	2	God
2Sa. 22:32	no epithet	2	God

Table A.1.1. (Continued)

Reference	Conditions	Code	Phrase or Compound Name
2Sa. 22:33	personal	6	God is my strength & power
2Sa. 22:48	personal	6	God that avengeth me
2Sa. 23:5	no epithet	2	God
Neh. 1:5	with epithet	1	great and terrible God
Neh. 9:31	with epithet	1	gracious & merciful God
Neh. 9:32	with epithet	1	great, mighty & terrible God
Job 5:8	no epithet	2	God
Job 8:3	no epithet	2	God
Job 8:5	no epithet	2	God
Job 8:13	no epithet	2	God
Job 8:20	no epithet	2	God
Job 9:2	no epithet	2	God
Job 12:6	no epithet	2	God
Job 13:3	no epithet	2	God
Job 13:7	no epithet	2	God
Job 13:8	no epithet	2	God
Job 15:4	no epithet	2	God
Job 15:11	no epithet	2	God
Job 15:13	no epithet	2	God
Job 15:25	no epithet	2	God
Job 16:11	no epithet	2	God
Job 18:21	no epithet	2	God
Job 19:22	no epithet	2	God
Job 20:15	no epithet	2	God
Job 20:29	no epithet	2	God
Job 21:14	no epithet	2	God
Job 21:22	no epithet	2	God
Job 22:2	no epithet	2	God
Job 22:13	no epithet	2	God
Job 22:17	no epithet	2	God
Job 23:16	no epithet	2	God
Job 25:4	no epithet	2	God
Job 27:2	no epithet	2	God
Job 27:11	no epithet	2	God

Table A.1.1. (Continued)

Reference	Conditions	Code	Phrase or Compound Name
Job 27:13	no epithet	2	God
Job 31:14	no epithet	2	God
Job 31:23	no epithet	2	God
Job 31:28	with epithet	1	the God that is above
Job 32:13	no epithet	2	God
Job 33:4	with epithet	1	spirit of God
Job 33:6	not a name	2	God's
Job 33:14	no epithet	2	God
Job 33:29	no epithet	2	God
Job 34:5	no epithet	2	God
Job 34:10	no epithet	2	God
Job 34:12	no epithet	2	God
Job 34:23	no epithet	2	God
Job 34:31	no epithet	2	God
Job 34:37	no epithet	2	God
Job 35:2	no name	2	God's
Job 35:13	no epithet	2	God
Job 36:5	with epithet	1	God is mighty
Job 36:22	no epithet	2	God
Job 36:26	with epithet	1	God is great
Job 37:5	no epithet	2	God
Job 37:10	no epithet	2	God
Job 37:14	no epithet	2	God
Job 38:41	no epithet	2	God
Job 40:9	no epithet	2	God
Job 40:19	no epithet	2	God
Job 41:25	no name	5	mighty
Psa. 5:4	no epithet	2	God
Psa. 7:11	with epithet	1	God is angry
Psa. 10:11	no epithet	2	God hath forgotten
Psa. 10:12	no epithet	3	O LORD; O God
Psa. 16:1	no epithet	2	O God
Psa. 17:6	no epithet	2	O God
Psa. 18:2	personal	6	my God, my strength

APPENDIX Chapter 1

Table A.1.1. (Continued)

Reference	Conditions	Code	Phrase or Compound Name
Psa. 18:30	no epithet	2	God
Psa. 18:32	no epithet	2	God
Psa. 18:47	personal	6	God that avengeth me
Psa. 19:1	with epithet	1	the glory of God
Psa. 22:1	personal	6+6	My God, my God (2x)
Psa. 22:10	personal	6	my God
Psa. 29:3	with epithet	1	the God of glory
Psa. 31:5	with epithet	3	LORD God of truth
Psa. 36:6	not a name	5	great mountains
Psa. 42:2	with epithet	1	living God
Psa. 42:8	personal	6	God of my life
Psa. 42:9	personal	6	God my rock
Psa. 43:4	personal	6	God my exceeding joy
Psa. 50:1	with epithet	1	the mighty God
Psa. 52:1	with epithet	1	goodness of God
Psa. 52:5	no epithet	2	God
Psa. 55:19	no epithet	2	God
Psa. 57:2	with epithet	1	God that performeth
Psa. 63:1	personal	6	thou art my God
Psa. 68:19	with epithet	6	God of our salvation
Psa. 68:20	personal/worth epithet	6+1	our God/God of salvation(2x)
Psa. 68:24	personal	6	my God, my king
Psa. 68:35	with epithet	6	the God of Israel
Psa. 73:11	no epithet	2	God
Psa. 73:17	no epithet	2	God
Psa. 74:8	no epithet	2	God
Psa. 77:9	no epithet	2	God (forgotten)
Psa. 77:13	with epithet	1	great a God
Psa. 77:14	with epithet	1	God that does wonders
Psa. 78:7	no epithet	2	God
Psa. 78:8	no epithet	2	God
Psa. 78:18	no epithet	2	God
Psa. 78:19	no epithet	2	God

Table A.1.1. (Continued)

Reference	Conditions	Code	Phrase or Compound Name
Psa. 78:34	no epithet	2	God
Psa. 78:35	with epithet	1	the high God
Psa. 78:41	no epithet	2	God
Psa. 80:10	no name	5	goodly (cedars)
Psa. 81:9	no name	4+4	strange god/ strange god(2x)
Psa. 82:1	no name	5	the mighty
Psa. 83:1	no epithet	2	God
Psa. 84:2	with epithet	1	the living God
Psa. 85:8	with epithet	3	God the LORD
Psa. 86:15	with epithet	1	God full of compassion
Psa. 89:6	no name	5	mighty
Psa. 89:7	with epithet	1	God (to be feared)
Psa. 89:26	personal	6	my God & the rock of...
Psa. 90:2	no epithet	2	thou art God
Psa. 94:1	with epithet	3+1	LORD God to whom vengeance belongeth (2x)
Psa. 95:3	with epithet	1	a great God (& great King)
Psa. 99:8	with epithet	1	a God that forgavest
Psa. 102:24	personal	6	O my God
Psa. 104:21	no epithet	2	God
Psa. 106:14	no epithet	2	God
Psa. 106:21	personal	6	God their savior
Psa. 107:11	no epithet	2	God
Psa. 118:27	with epithet	3	God is the LORD
Psa. 118:28	personal	6	my God
Psa. 136:26	with epithet	1	God of heaven
Psa. 139:17	no epithet	2	God
Psa. 139:23	no epithet	2	God
Psa. 140:6	personal	6	Thou art my God
Psa. 146:5	personal	6	God of Jacob
Psa. 149:6	no epithet	2	God
Psa. 150:1	no epithet	2	God
Pro. 3:27	no name	5	power
Isa. 5:16	with epithet	1	God that is holy

Table A.1.1. (Continued)

Reference	Conditions	Code	Phrase or Compound Name
Isa. 8:10	no epithet	6	God is with us
Isa. 9:6	with epithet	1	the mighty God
Isa. 10:21	with epithet	1	the mighty God
Isa. 12:2	personal	6	God is my salvation
Isa. 14:13	no epithet	2	God
Isa. 31:3	no epithet	2	God
Isa. 40:18	no epithet	2	God
Isa. 42:5	with epithet	1	God the Lord
Isa. 43:10	no epithet	2	God
Isa. 43:12	no epithet	2	I am God
Isa. 44:10	no name/no epithet	2	Formed a god
Isa. 44:15	no name	4	a god
Isa. 44:17	no name	4+4	a god/my god (2x)
Isa. 45:14	no epithet	2	God
Isa. 45:15	with epithet	1	God that hidest thyself
Isa. 45:20	no name	4	a God
Isa. 45:21	with epithet	1	a just God (and a Savior)
Isa. 45:22	no epithet	2	I am God
Isa. 46:6	not a name	4	a god
Isa. 46:9	no epithet	2	I am God
Isa. 57:5	not a name	5	idols
Jer. 32:18	with epithet	1	the Great, (the Mighty God)
Jer. 51:56	with epithet	3	LORD God of recompenses
Lam. 3:41	with epithet	1	God in the heavens
Eze. 10:5	with epithet	1	Almighty God
Eze. 28:2	not a name	4+4	a god/God (2x)
Eze. 28:9	no epithet	2	no/God
Eze. 31:11	not a name	5	mighty one of the heathen
Eze. 32:21	not a name	5	strong
Dan. 9:4	with epithet	1	great and (dreadful God)
Dan. 11:36	no name/with epithet	4+1+4	god; God of gods (3x)
Hos. 1:10	with epithet	1	living Gods
Hos. 11:9	no epithet	2	I am God

Table A.1.1. (Continued)

Reference	Conditions	Code	Phrase or Compound Name
Jon. 4.2	with epithet	1	gracious God (and merciful)
Mic. 2:1	not a name	5	power
Mic. 7:18	with epithet	1	God that pardoneth
Nah. 1:2	with epithet	1	God is jealous
Mal. 1:9	no epithet	2	God
Mal. 2:10	with epithet	2	one God
Mal: 2:11	not a name	4	strange god

APPENDIX Chapter 1

Table A.1.2

Verse Coding Separation

Table A.1.2 displays a summation of the Coding separation for the 237 possible 'el applications.

Code	1	2	3	4	5	6	line entry	multi.	Total applications
Quantity	65	108	9	15	12	28	227	10	237

APPENDIX Chapter 1

Table A.1.3.
The Code 1 El Compound Names of God

Table A.1.3 displays the 34 code 1 compound names of God (El) after removal of duplicate verses.

Table A.1.3

The Code 1 El Compound Names of God

Qualifying Term or Epithet		Epithet Meaning	Reference
01	El that is above	on high, superior	Job 31:28
02	Almighty El	all powerful	Gen. 17:1; 28:3; 35:11; 43:14; 48:3; Exo. 6:3; Eze. 10:5
03	El is angry	indignant, enraged	Psa 7:11
04	El is full of compassion	merciful	Psa. 86:15
05	dreadful El	reverence, to fear	Dan. 9:4
06	everlasting El	eternal	Gen. 21:33
07	faithful El	trust, believe, true	Deu. 7:9
08	El to be feared	to awe, to fear	Psa. 89:7
09	El that forgives	forgive, pardon	Psa. 99:8
10	glory of El	splendor	Psa. 19:1; 29:3
11	God of gods	superior	Dan. 11:36
12	goodness of El	kindness, piety of El	Psa. 52:1
13	gracious El	kindness, mercy	Neh. 9:31; Jon. 4:2
14	great El	excellent	Deu. 10:17; Neh. 1:5; Neh. 9:32; Job 36:26; Psa. 77:13; 95:3; Jer. 32:18; Dan. 9:4
15	El of heaven	sovereign ruler	Psa. 136:26; Lam. 3:41
16	high El	the Supreme	Gen. 14:18, 19, 20, 22; Psa. 78:35
17	El that hidest self	conceal self	Isa. 45:15
18	El that is holy	sacred, set apart	Isa. 5:16

Table A.1.3 (Continued)

Qualifying Term or Epithet		Epithet Meaning	Reference
19	jealous El	righteous zeal	Exo. 20:5; 34:14; Deu. 4:24, 5:9, 6:15; Jos. 24:19; Nah. 1:2
20	a just El	righteous	Isa. 45:21
21	El of knowledge	understanding	1 Sa. 2:3
22	living El	sovereign, alive	Jos. 3:10; Psa. 42:2; 84:2; Hos. 1:10
23	merciful El	compassionate	Deu. 4:31; Neh. 9:31; Jon. 4:2
24	mighty El	exceeding	Deu. 7:21; Neh. 9:32; Job 36:5; Psa. 50:1; Isa. 9:6; 10:21; Jer. 32:18
25	El that pardoneth	forgives	Mic. 7:18
26	El that performeth	completes, ends	Psa. 57:2
27	El of recompenses	reward, requite	Jer. 51:56
28	El of salvation	safety, deliverance	Psa. 68:20
29	Spirit of El	Name of 3rd Person	Job 33:4
30	El of the spirits	supreme	Num. 16:22
31	terrible El	fear, awesome	Deu. 7:21; 10:17; Neh. 1:5, 9:32
32	El of truth	trustworthiness	Deu. 32:4; Psa. 31:5
33	El doest wonders	miracles	Psa. 77:14
34	El to whom vengeance belongs	revenge	Psa. 94:1

Table A.1.4

Selection of the Prominent Compound Names

Name	Prominence	7+	5	4
Almighty God	7	El Shaddai		
God of Glory	2			
Gracious God	2			
Great God	8	El Gadol		
God of Heaven	2			
(Most) High God	5		El Elyon	
Jealous God	7	El Qanna		
Living God	4			El Hai
Merciful God	3			
Mighty God	7	El Gabbor		
Terrible(awe) God	4			El Yare
God of Truth	2			
God of Vengeance	2			

Table A.1.5

Prominent El Compound Names that Appear 4 or More Times in the OT

English Name	Hebrew Name	References
Almighty God	El Shaddai	Gen. 17:1; 28:3; 35:11; 43:14; 48:3; Exo. 6:3; Eze. 10:5
Great God	El Gadol	Deu. 10:17; Neh. 1:5; Job 36:26; Psa. 77:13; 95:3; Jer. 32:18; Dan. 9:4
Jealous God	El Qanna	Exo. 20:5; 34:14; Deu. 4:24; 5:9; 6:15; Jos. 24:19; Nah. 1:2
Mighty God	El Gibbor	Deu. 7:21; Neh. 9:32; Job 36:5; Psa. 50:1; Isa. 9:6; 10:21; Jer. 32:18
Most High God	El Elyon	Gen. 14:18, 19, 20, 22; Psa. 78:35; Isa. 45:15
Living God	El Hai	Jos. 3:10; Psa. 42:2; 84:2; Hos. 1:10
Terrible (Awesome) God	El Yare	Deu. 7:21; 10:17; Neh. 1:5; 9:32

5.4 Anointed

The listings in Table A.5.1 include all 84 verse references found in the OT using the term "anointed". Careful reading of these verses indicates that there are only 10 passages relating to the application of the word in its highest sense, The Anointed, The Messiah of God. Contrary to the case where there is but a single verse entry and therefore a single argument for a name, it now becomes needful to examine all 10 verses individually with the intent to verify that the word "anointed" is indeed applied as a name of God in each case.

In Table A.5.1., the ten verses of special interest are underlined. They are further examined, detailed, and then listed in Table A.5.2. Included is information only hinted at in the Text Argument concerning the Application Conditions involving God's Character being Highlighted and the Need of man Met by the particular usage. The other usages of the word "anointed" listed in Table A.5.1 are not further developed or expanded upon.

APPENDIX Chapter 5

Table A.5.1

ANOINTED

The Word Anointed as applied in the Old Testament
(King James Version of Scripture)

Exo. 29:2	Exo. 29:29	Lev. 2:4	Lev. 4:3	Lev. 4:5
Lev. 4:16	Lev. 6:20	Lev. 6:22	Lev. 7:12	Lev. 7:36
Lev. 8:10	Lev. 8:11	Lev. 8:12	Num. 3:3	Num. 6:15
Num. 7:1	Num. 7:10	Num. 7:84	Num. 7:88	Num. 35:25
(1Sa. 2:10)	**(1Sa. 2:35)**	1Sa. 10:1	1Sa. 12:3	1Sa. 12:5
1Sa. 15:17	1Sa. 16:6	1Sa. 16:13	1Sa. 24:6	1Sa. 24:10
1Sa. 26:9	1Sa. 26:11	1Sa. 26:16	1Sa. 26:23	2Sa. 2:14
2Sa. 1:16	2Sa. 1:21	2Sa. 2:4	2Sa. 2:7	2Sa. 3:39
2Sa. 5:3	2Sa. 5:17	2Sa. 12:7	2Sa. 12:20	2Sa. 19:10
2Sa. 19:21	2Sa. 22:51	2Sa. 23:1	1Ki. 1:39	1Ki. 1:45
1Ki. 5:1	2Ki. 9:3	2Ki. 9:6	2Ki. 9:12	2Ki. 11:12
2Ki. 23:30	1Ch. 11:3	1Ch. 14:8	1Ch. 16:22	1Ch. 29:22
2Ch. 6:42	2Ch. 22:7	2Ch. 23:11	2Ch. 28:15	**(Psa. 2:2)**
(Psa. 18:50)	**(Psa. 20:6)**	**(Psa. 28:8)**	**(Psa. 45:7)**	Psa. 84:9
Psa. 89:20	**(Psa. 89:38)**	**(Psa. 89:51)**	Psa. 92:10	Psa. 105:15
(Psa. 132:10)	**(Psa. 132:17)**	Isa. 45:1	**(Isa. 61:1)**	Lam. 4:20
Eze. 16:9	Eze. 28:14	Hab. 3:13	Zec. 4:14	

Table A.5.2

The Anointed Or The Messiah Of God

Reference: (1)	1Sa. 2:10
Application Conditions:	Hannah's prayer contains the first reference in the OT to His King and His Anointed. (Prophecy.)
God's Character and Name Highlighted:	God is trusted to provide a king who is capable of completely delivering His people. King; implied Deliverer; Anointed or the Christ
Man's Need Met:	God provided in Samuel a prophet, priest, and judge, leader to save Israel from their enemies. God provided the Messiah as Saviour from sin to all people.
Reference: (2)	1Sa. 2:35
Application Conditions:	In the warning to Eli, Christ is referred to as Mine Anointed (Prophecy).
God's Character and Name Highlighted:	God will provide both a faithful priest and a worthy King in Messianic times
Man's Need Met:	God provided a faithful priest to bring mercy to Israel according to the LORD's will. However, the Messiah will be superior to this priest
Reference: (3)	Psa. 2:2
Application Condition:	Opposition to the LORD and His Anointed by rebellious nations: (Prophecy)
God's Character and Name Highlighted:	God's faithfulness to His anointed deliverer and His absolute power to conquer evil opposition are exalted in this passage.
Man's Need Met:	At the first advent of Jesus Christ, He came only to be rejected by His own. And there will be opposition to the very end of this age when His own will be rescued at His second coming.
Reference: (4)	Psa. 18:50
Application Condition:	The true Anointed One of God, Christ our Saviour, is shown in His suffering and deliverance from heaven above as well as His exaltation and coming kingdom. This constitutes the deeper,

	prophetic meaning of this great Messianic Psalm.[159]
God's Character and Name Highlighted	God is praised for the greatness of the deliverance He bring about through David, His anointed King and His steadfast love, for David is enhanced by His love for David's royal descendant, the Messiah.
Man's Need Met:	Seven things are mentioned which the LORD will be for those who trust Him: Strength, Rock, Fortress, Deliverer, Shield, Horn of Salvation and High Tower.

Reference: (5)	Psa. 20:6
Application Condition:	This Psalm is a prophetic praise of rejoicing that the LORD saves His Anointed, answers Him from heaven with mighty victories by His right hand.
God's Character and Name Highlighted:	Just as God has demonstrated His faithful commitment to delivering and prospering His servant David, so will he prove His faithfulness to the Messiah, David's descendant.
Man's Need Met:	Salvation and deliverance of His people through His resurrection, victory and His triumph over all forces of evil.

Reference: (6)	Psa. 28:8
Application Condition:	David's prayer in distress for Judgment upon the wicked is prophetic of the godly Israelite living at the close of this age, waiting for the promised deliverance from above. For indeed, the godly in Israel will, during the last days, turn to the LORD, the Rock, the rejected Stone.[160]
God's Character and Name Highlighted:	Messiah, Christ, has the power to save because His strength is abundantly provided by the Lord in heaven.
Man's Need Met:	David prays out of deep distress, an earnest prayer for deliverance and praise for the anticipated and expected deliverance. The "anointed one," the Messiah will meet the needs of man as the great deliverer of His waiting people in that day.

Reference: (7)	Psa. 45:7
Application	This Psalm gives a great prophetic picture of the Messiah, the

[159] Arno C. Gaebelein, *The Book of Psalms*, Van Kampen Press, Wheaton, 5/39, p. 81.
[160] Ibid., p. 132.

APPENDIX Chapter 5

Condition:	Lord Jesus Christ, as He appears in His Kingly glory at His second advent.
God's Character and Name Highlighted	The anointed King honors the One who sent him by loving righteousness and hating evil the way God does, and he is even called God in the preceding verse (v.6).
Man's Need Met	This is one of the Shoshannian or lilies Psalms, probably connected with the Passover Season. It reminds man of needed redemption out of bondage. The lily is the emblem of purity and simple gracefulness. This flower often grows out of mud without being contaminated by it. It is therefore a type of Him, who is the Lily of the Valley, the Lord Jesus Christ.
Reference: (8)	Psa. 89:38 and 51
Application Condition:	This Psalm is basically a lament prefaced by a lengthy introduction which consists of a hymn of praise and a description of the Davidic covenant. The first part of the Psalm celebrates the faithfulness and loving-kindness of God to David and looks forward to Him who is the Son of David, our Lord. The middle section notes that unworthy descendants of David have suffered God's punishment (vv. 38-45). The closing section reveals the conditions which precede that coming deliverance. Israel is unbelieving—they have rejected the sure mercies of David's line, for they have rejected the Messiah when He came to His own (V.51).[161]
God's Character and Name Highlighted:	The weaknesses and the failures of the royal line after David make the surpassing excellence and the everlasting dominion of the Messiah, God's anointed <u>par excellence</u>, all the more remarkable. God gets the glory!
Man's Need Met:	Apparent failure of the covenant is spoken of, but it will not always be so. The Day is coming when He who is the Son of David according to the flesh will occupy David's throne. Then He, the First-born, will become the highest of the Kings.
References: (9)	Psa. 132:10 and 17
God's Character and Name Highlighted:	The words "anointed one" in these two verses has drawn much discussion in the literature with less than agreement on the meaning. Because there are more than adequate examples of the application of the word "anointed" as a name of God

[161] Ibid., p. 339.

	elsewhere, no further examination of verses 10 and 17 is given, and the term "anointed one" is not considered as a name in these verses.
Reference: (10)	Isa. 61:1
Application Condition:	Isaiah paints a picture of the Messiah's mission as one of evangelism, healing, preaching, comforting and joy-giving. Jesus selected this portrait to describe Himself in the temple at Nazareth.
God's Character and Name Highlighted:	The wonderful, multi-faceted, comprehensive deliverance God promises is all revealed through this depiction of the Messiah (Prophet, Priest, King, Healer, Deliverer).
Man's Need Met:	As Isaiah was directed to proclaim liberty to the Jews in Babylonian capacity, so Christ was God's messenger to publish a joyful jubilee of liberty to a lost world through Himself.[162]

[162] Matthew Henry, *Commentary,* Zondervan Publishing House, Grand Rapids, 1961, p. 923.

APPENDIX Chapter 5

5.5 <u>Branch</u>

In the study of the term branch, it is early realized that the word is applied to many things, some related to horticulture, some relating to family branches or off-spring, and some pertaining to the very family of God. It is also pertinent to notice that the word can occur either in the singular or the plural. However, we are only interested here in the names of God, so the word branch must be in the singular, immediately removing some 45 references to branches. But it does leave a rather significant group of words or potential names of God to consider as referenced in Table A.5.3.

This Table's listings include the 29 references to the use of the term Branch found in the OT. Seven of these references seem to relate to the application of the word in its highest sense, even a name of Christ. These seven verses are set apart with underlines in Table A.5.3 and are further detailed.

Although the other 22 secondary uses of the word Branch are presented in Table A.5.3 they are not further detailed or expanded upon.

APPENDIX Chapter 5

Table A.5.3

THE WORD BRANCH IN THE OT

(The King James Version)

Exo. 25:33	Exo. 37:17	Exo. 37:19	Num. 13:23	Job 8:16	Job 14:7
Job 15:32	Job 18:16	Job 29:19	**Psa. 80:15**	Pro. 11:28	**Isa. 4:2**
Isa. 9:4	**Isa. 11:1**	Isa. 14:19	Isa. 17:9	Isa. 19:15	Isa. 25:5
Isa. 60:21	**Jer. 23:5**	**Jer. 33:15**	Eze. 8:17	Eze. 15:2	Eze. 17:3
Eze. 17:22	Dan. 11:7`	**Zec. 3:8**	**Zec. 6:12**	Mal. 4:1	

Regarding the seven occurrences of this term as a potential name of God appearing in Table A.5.3, we will organize these into a Table A.5.4 that identifies the passages of concern, details the phrase using the word "branch and the reason to accept or reject the word or phrase as a name of God.

APPENDIX Chapter 5

Table A.5.4.

THE WORD BRANCH APPLIED TO DEITY

(KJV)

Ref.	Title	Application
Psa. 80:15	the branch (or son)	The Messiah, Christ our Lord, the Son
Isa. 4:2	branch of the LORD	Christ in majesty at 2nd return
Isa. 11:1	a Branch	Christ's human nature & origin
Jer. 23:5	David's righteous Branch	Christ of David's dynasty will rule in righteousness
Jer. 33:15	Branch of righteousness	the same as verse above
Zec. 3:8	my servant the BRANCH	The humanity & humility of the Messiah highlighted
Zec. 6:12	whose name is THE BRANCH	The humility & lowliness of the Messiah named the BRANCH

All seven of the verses speak of the Anointed One, the Messiah, the Christ. Each one addresses a certain aspect of the Messiah's work. The Psalm 80 verse presents a highlight on the branch or the son of man whom God will make strong in that day. Isaiah 4 speaks of the "Branch of the LORD" to be made beautiful and glorious in that day. His full name "Branch of the LORD" is Christ the Messiah. The Jeremiah verses present the Messiah as David's "righteous Branch" or "Branch of righteousness." In that day, He will rule as Christ the King with judgment, justice and righteousness. In the Zechariah passages, the Messiah's humanity and humility as a servant are in view.

APPENDIX Chapter 5

(Note: It is in the Zechariah verses that the KJV highlights the name Branch with the oversized letters.)

Before we consider further details regarding the possibility of a verse containing a name of God, let us look at the Name Variation information contained in the Chapter 5.5 Text and in the expanded list in Table A.5.5. The comparison of word applications or variations in corresponding passages of different Scripture versions is a strong identification tool. This essentially uses each version as a commentary upon the others. This method of investigation is applied in Table A.5.5.

APPENDIX Chapter 5

Table A.5.5.

THE WORD "BRANCH" SCRIPTURE VERSION INTERCOMPARISON

Ref.	**BECK**	**JER**	**KJV**	**TLB**	**NAS**	**NEB**	**NIV**	**RSV**
Psa. 80:15	son	(out)	branch	son	son	son	son	(out)
Isa. 4:2	plant	branch	branch	(out)	Branch	plant	Branch	branch
Isa. 11:1	Branch	scion	Branch	Branch	branch	branch	Branch	branch
Jer. 23:5	Branch	Branch	Branch	Branch	Branch	Branch	Branch	Branch
Jer. 33:15	Branch	Branch	Branch	Son	Branch	Branch	Branch	Branch
Zec. 3:8	Branch	Branch	BRANCH	Branch	Branch	Branch	Branch	Branch
Zec. 6:12	Descendant	Branch	BRANCH	Branch	Branch	Branch	Branch	Branch

Examining Table A.5.5, it is seen that when the seven verses containing the word branch in the KJV, are compared to the companion verses in other versions, there are interesting variations. For example, comparing Psalm 80:15 indicates that sometimes the Hebrew phrase "and on the son you strengthened" is omitted at the end of verse 15. We find this happens in both the RSV and the JER versions with the result that the Hebrew word "ben", translatable by both the English words son or branch, is not translated in these versions. It would appear that the translators found enough duplication in verse 17 to allow this omission. We also observe the use of "son" in 5 versions of this verse and the translation of the Hebrew word "ben" into the English word "branch" in the KJV. These choices of words are at the discretion of the translators. The word branch can be supported with Genesis 49:22. The word son can be supported with verses such as Psalm 2:7; Isaiah 9:6; 1 Samuel 3:16 and others. Literal translation of the word as son seems proper, since it enjoys the stronger support.

In a second example of variation, examine the Isaiah 4:2 verse occurring in the 8 versions.[163] Five versions translate the Hebrew into the English word branch. Two versions elect to translate to the word plant, while the Living Bible paraphrases the word out of the passage.

The versions that translate ben with the English word 'plant' are simply resorting to a less specific figurative rendering of the Hebrew word—a sprout or a shoot or something that grows up like a plant. The English word branch is the more apt or likely figurative translation.

Perhaps of greater import is the capitalization used in rendering the word branch in some versions. The literature suggests that the first letter capitalization of the word Branch in both the NAS and the NIV versions indicates messianic identity. This seems reasonable with this verse, but it is contradicted by absence of capitalization in the NAS translation of the Isaiah 11:1 passage. If messianic identity is the reason for the first letter capitalization, then the NAS and other versions appear erratic in their application of capitalization.

---

[163] The eight scripture versions chosen for consideration in this study are but representative of much larger assembly of available versions. May the reader choose the group of versions that best satisfy his or her need.

APPENDIX Chapter 5

It should be noticed that the word branch in Zechariah 3:8 and 6:12, in the KJV version, has the word branch with all letters in large capital style. The significance of capitalization is apparent with many names and titles discussed throughout this manuscript. This especially involves first letter capitals of words, but it also includes the style which capitalizes an entire word that is mentioned above. Therefore a brief quote from the writings of E. W. Bullinger is relevant:[164]

> The use of large capital letters for certain words and phrases originated with the Authorized Version. None of the previous or 'former translators' have them.
>
> The revisers abandoned this practice but have not been consistent in the plan they substituted for it. In most of the cases they have used small capital letters instead of the large capital; but, in several cases, they have used large ordinary Roman type.
>
> The use of the large capitals by the translators of the AV are destitute of any authority and merely indicate the importance which they attached to such words and phrases.

Application of Capitalization to names and titles is of considerable importance. Care must be exercised in assigning meaning and significance to each capitalization.

---

[164] E. W. Bullinger, *Figures of Speech Used in the Bible,* Baker Book House, Grand Rapids. Orig. published 1989; republished 1968. 17th printing, Aug. 1993, p. 988.

APPENDIX Chapter 5

Purpose Of The Name

As a substitute for the name Messiah or Christ, "Branch" speaks to men about the Immanuel who will be fully manifested to restored and converted Israel after His return in divine glory. The earthly glory of Christ is spoken of as the exaltation of the Messiah, the seed of David according to the flesh, as King of kings and Lord of lords. The name Branch speaks of His reign as the promised Davidic Priest-King over all the earth in His dominion, that is yet to come. Man has always needed to be aware of these truths; but there is one more truth presented by the name Branch. This name presents the Messiah in His humiliation and obedience unto death for the sins of the people. So many men have not wanted to hear of this revelation but it is the greatest of all. Man needs to listen and hear!

APPENDIX Chapter 6

6.1 Deliverer

Text 6.1 discusses the first aspects of the name Deliverer. There we became acquainted with the two passages 2Sa. 22:2 and Psa. 18:2 and their containment of the word deliverer, together with other metaphors of importance. It was also stated that a display of additional applications of the word deliverer are presented in this Appendix. This information is supplementary since the Text information validates the word "Deliverer" as a name of God.

Let us first consider some **Bible Version Variations** for the five deity applications of the word deliverer in the OT.

Version	2Sa. 22:2	Psa. 18:2	Psa. 40:17	Psa. 70:5	Psa. 144:2
BECK	One who rescued	Rescuer	Deliverer	Deliverer	Haven
JER	deliverer	deliverer	saviour	saviour	saviour
KJV	deliverer	deliverer	deliverer	deliverer	deliverer
TLB	Savior	Savior	Savior	save me	deliverer
NAS	deliverer	deliverer	deliverer	deliverer	deliverer
NEB	champion	champion	salvation	salvation	refuge
NIV	deliverer	deliverer	deliverer	deliverer	deliverer
RSV	deliverer	deliverer	deliverer	deliverer	deliverer

The Hebrew word palat and its cognates may be translated into many English words with the resultant deviations displayed in the above Variation Chart. Indeed, if we count the detail, we arrive at the following English translations of this single Hebrew word: deliverer 25 times, savior 6, champion 2 and salvation 2. Then there are several translations of one each, such as Rescuer, Refuge and Haven. Perhaps one of the points of greatest interest, relating to this variation study, is the comparison of translations in the Beck version with the others. Beck treats each term in the series of words containing the word deliverer as a metaphor, carefully capitalizing each initial letter of the word in the series, including the term of interest, Deliverer. This seems reasonable since the metaphor simply indicates that the LORD is represented as the Deliverer. Other version styles seem to consider the metaphorical statements to be descriptive, with each containing a personal pronoun, thereby eliminating the capitalization.

This matter of capitalization is important, as it has the possibility of strong weighting in the matter of identification of names of God. The consideration of capitalization is not unique here. We have previously given some thought to the matter.[165]

Let us now compare Psa. 40:17 with Psa. 70:5.

compare:	with:
Psa. 40:17	Psa. 70:5
"the Lord (Adonai)..my God (Elohim)"	"Oh God (Elohim O LORD (Yahweh)"
help deliverer	help deliverer

---

[165] Refer to the *Text* of Chapter 5.7, "Creator," and the *Appendix*, of Chapt. 5.5, "Branch".

APPENDIX Chapter 6

Focusing on the metaphorical name of concern, "deliverer" we see that David continues to emphasize his strong feelings about his God. In Psa. 40:17 David addresses Him as The Lord (Adonai) and as God (Elohim), then he adds the epithets "my help and Deliverer." In Psa. 70:5 David addresses his God as Elohim and also Yahweh, again adding the epithets "my help and my Deliverer". These epithetical expressions in these two Psalms closely resemble those of the previous two songs (see Chapter 6 Text) again qualifying the word Deliverer as a name of God.

Now these two Psalms interrelate in a most interesting way. Psalm 70 is a close repetition of the last five verses of Psalm 40. There are variations in the repetition, to be sure, but in spite of this we can expect close duality in the two prayers. David seems to interchange the names Adonai and Elohim easily in Psa. 40; then he further expresses his feelings toward his God by applying the epithets "my help" and "my deliverer." We find in Psa. 70 that David interchanges the names Elohim and Yahweh quite easily and again expresses his strong feelings with additional epithets. From these two closely related Psalms it is easy to see again that the word "deliverer" is really not an original name but rather an epithetical or descriptive expression. However, since this assertion adds detail and description to the names Adonai, Elohim and Yahweh, the epithet is ultimately considered a name of God in itself.

Lastly, we will consider the fifth occurrence of the metaphorical name Deliverer. In Psalm 144:1-2 David writes, "the LORD my strength...my goodness...my fortress; my high tower and my deliverer and my shield."

This Psalm, probably written by David after his accession to the throne, acknowledges his dependence upon God. "Blessed be the LORD my strength (Rock)...my goodness, my fortress, my high tower and my deliverer." David again in this Psalm multiplies words upon words in an effort to express the satisfaction he has in God. Matthew Henry suggests the following thoughts: Earlier David had sheltered himself in the strong holds at En-gedi (1Sa. 23:29). He had more recently made himself master of the strong hold of Zion and he dwelt in this fort (2Sa. 5:7), but he depends not on these, for he says, LORD, thou art my fortress and my high tower, my shield, not only my fortress at home, but my shield abroad in the field of battle. Everywhere he went he carried his protection with him. David was born a shepherd, but God made him a soldier and a king, because he was a man of God.[166]

As in the other verses we have reviewed concerning the word deliverer, this word is used in a metaphor in connection with the name LORD. The LORD *is* my deliverer indicates that the deliverer is not <u>like</u> the LORD; rather, the phrase says that the LORD *is* or represents my Deliverer. The words LORD and Deliverer are equated, with the word *Deliverer* considered as a name of God.

---

[166] *Matthew Henry Commentary*, Zondervan Publishing House, Ed. 13, 1974, p. 727.

APPENDIX Chapter 6

Particular Aspect of God's Character Highlighted:

David provides a whole series of strong epithets in the metaphors describing certain of God's characteristics. Limiting our comments here to the name "Deliverer," we find that this highlights, on the one hand, God's desire of faithfulness and His ability to set free and save from evil and danger His own, on the other.

The Special Need of Man Met by the Revelation of this Aspect:

The revealing of this aspect of God's character by the Holy Spirit to David, and hence to the Scriptures, met a need of David and of all the people of God to express praise and joy to God Himself, the great Deliverer.

APPENDIX Chapter 6

6.2 Father

In the 541 appearances of the word father in the OT only 14 passages contain an application of the word father as a name of God. The first in the list has been discussed in the Chapter 6 Text. It is appropriate to include in this Appendix identification of the other 13 verses. This will be done with the **Name Variation Chart,** which will also allow variations in the word father to be observed.

Ref	BECK	JER	KJV	TLB	NAS	NEB	NIV	NKJV	RSV
Deu. 32:6	Father	father	father	Father	father	father	Father	Father	father
2Sa. 7:14	Father	father	father	father	father	father	father	Father	father
1Ch. 17:13	Father	father	father	father	father	father	father	Father	father
1Ch. 22:10	Father	father	father	father	father	father	father	Father	father
1Ch. 28:6	Father	father	father	father	father	father	father	Father	father
Psa. 89:26	Father	father	father	Father	Father	father	Father	Father	Father
Psa. 103:13	father	father	father	father	father	father	father	father	father
Isa. 9:6	Father	Father	Father	Father	Father	Father	Father	Father	Father
Isa. 63:16	Father	Father	father	Father	Father	father	Father	Father	Father
Isa. 64:8	Father	Father	father	Father	Father	father	Father	Father	Father
Jer. 3:19	Father	father	father	Father	Father	Father	Father	Father	Father
Jer. 31:9	Father	father	father	Father	father	father	father	Father	father
Mal. 1:6	Father	Father	father	Father	father	father	father	Father	father
Mal. 2:10	Father	Father	father	father	father	father	Father	Father	father

In order to simplify understanding of the particular application, let us first reduce these verses by isolating that portion of each that directly relates to a name of deity. Remember, a name must be established by Scripture in order to be accepted either as a primary or support name.

Deu. 32:6 Since we have discussed the Deu. 32:6 passage and the verification of the name Father in the Text, we will omit that verse here and proceed to the next entries in the Variation Chart.

2Sa. 7:14 Now we come to the first iteration of the Davidic Covenant, wherein the statement is made that Solomon will be as a son to the LORD and Yahweh will be his *Father*. this is not a title originating from man: The LORD is the one who titles Himself as *Father*, but there is more. The metaphor, "I will be his Father" is repeated three additional times as the Davidic Covenant is reiterated in **1Ch. 17:13, 1Ch. 22:10** and **1Ch. 28:6**. Can there be other than significant import in the repetition? Four times in connection with the building of the temple the LORD says He will be known as a *Father* to Solomon; and father would be His name.

Psa. 89:26 The LORD identifies Himself in this passage with several names that the Psalmist tells us David will use to address God: My *Father*, my God (El), and the Rock of my Salvation (i.e. Rock who saves me). Obviously the word *Father* is a name of God since it is used to address the LORD as God (El).

Psa. 103:13 Going on, we have these thoughts: In this verse a simile endeavors to express our Heavenly Father's compassion, even as infinite as He is, in all His attributes. Just as an earthly father has compassion and love toward his children, so the LORD has a father's compassion on those who hold Him in awe.

APPENDIX Chapter 6

The infinite compassion of the LORD as my *Heavenly Father*, which I certainly cannot grasp in its magnitude and depth, is expressed as being like that of an earthly father, which I can begin to understand. In this simile, the LORD is *Father* by implication but not by direct statement. (Note: It must be agreed that the time Father is applied to the LORD here only by simile implication and not by direct Scripture establishment, so this is a secondary identification but applicable as a name of God in this study.)

Isa. 9:6 There is no question in this passage but that The Mighty God (El) is also referred to as Everlasting *Father* (see the name Everlasting Father in Chapter 6.3).

Isa. 63:16 In this passage, there is no doubt that the LORD is referred to by name as *Father*, as Redeemer and LORD.

Isa. 64:8 Again in this verse, there is no doubt that the LORD is referred to by the name *Father*.

Jer. 3:19 In this passage the LORD is speaking, saying, "...Thou Israel shall call Me, *My Father*, and shall not turn away from Me."

Jer. 31:9 Again in this passage, the LORD is speaking. He says "I am a *Father* to Israel..." The LORD refers to Himself as *Father*.

Mal 1:6 The LORD speaking through Malachi says, "A son honors his father, a servant honors his master. I am your *Father* and Master, Yet you don't honor Me."

Although the relationship here is national and not personal, the Jews were correctly calling the LORD *Father* but failed to yield Him filial obedience.

<u>Mal. 2:10</u> Two views are readily possible in part (a) of this passage. (1) "Have we not all one *Father*?" referring to national Israel as off-spring of father Abraham. However, it seems more probable that (2) the writer is speaking not of Abraham but of God as their *Father*, in that He had chosen Israel as His son (Exo. 4:22, Jer. 31:9). The sense of this passage is that Israel has but one *Father* and one *creative God.* Therefore, following option (2), the verse simplifies to "Have we not all one *Father* and one *God*?"

APPENDIX Chapter 6

6.6 Fortress

There are seven verses that contain the word Fortress addressing deity in the OT. The first of these verses (2Sa. 22:2) was examined in the Text of Chapter 6.6 utilizing a Name Variation Chart to compare the word fortress in various Scripture versions. This chart is again displayed below omitting the duplication of the previous KJV presentation found in the name variation chart of Chapter 6.

NAME VARIATION In:

Version	Psa. 18:2	Psa. 31:3	Psa. 71:3	Psa. 91:2	Psa. 144:2	Jer. 16:19
BECK	Fortress	Fortress	Fortress	Fortress	Fortress	Fortress
JER	bastion	fortress	fortress	fortress	bastion	stronghold
KJV	fortress	fortress	fortress	fortress	fortress	fortress
TLB	fort	fortress	save-me	place of safety	fortress	Fortress
NAS	fortress	fortress	fortress	fortress	fortress	stronghold
NEB	fortress	stronghold	stronghold	safe retreat	fortress	stronghold
NIV	fortress	fortress	fortress	fortress	fortress	fortress
NKJV	fortress	fortress	fortress	fortress	fortress	fortress
RSV	fortress	fortress	fortress	fortress	fortress	stronghold

Consideration of the chart shows several interesting details. If we look first at the row information (horizontal entries), we see that only four of the nine rows translate the Hebrew word martsood (SRN 4686) into the English word fortress in all six passages. There are three more rows where the Hebrew word ma'oz (SRN 4581) as well as the previous word (SRN 4686) are translated stronghold. The dictionary points out that either of the two Hebrew words provides for the English meaning stronghold along with other synonyms. This simply indicates that either of the words fortress or stronghold are acceptable and that some of the various translations elected to use stronghold rather than fortress. The synonyms for the word fortress are broad enough to include the English terms bastion, safety, save me and safe retreat.

The word fortress is a name of God because it represents the name LORD in about 78% of the concerned metaphorical expressions—"the LORD is my fortress." One of the Scripture versions (Beck) capitalizes both nouns of the metaphor. Regarding the other versions it is assumed that similar capitalization would occur except for the style, which applies the negation of the second capital when there is a personal pronoun present.

Looking briefly at the vertical columns under each Scripture passage we see that even though the same Hebrew word is involved, the translation into English results in one or more word deviations per column from the widely accepted word fortress. This variation is related to translator style and choice, not to variations in the Hebrew.

The Special Need of Man Met by the Revelation of this Aspect of the Character of God:

The two Hebrew words of concern for fortress can be translated into English synonyms with meanings including castle, defense, fortified place, fortress, strength, bulwark, bastion and stronghold. In the case of our metaphorical expressions, such words suggest attributes of God that clearly point the way to Him who is our strength, our fortress and our stronghold.

APPENDIX Chapter 7

THE DEVELOPMENT OF THE COMPUTER LISTS

for

THE OF-(GENITIVE) NAMES OF GOD STUDY

Chapter 7 contains a number of computer lists detailing the methodology used to produce the data supporting the of-(genitive) study. It is the author's intent to separate in Appendix format these lists since they may be only of limited interest.

APPENDIX Chapter 7

There are four tables of data supporting the argument. In the OT there are at least 52 valid of-(genitive) names of God in the form, "God of__". These tables are presented in their entirety to provide in-depth detail on the of-(genitive) names of God.

Table A.7.1

The Basic 436 "Of-(Genitive)" Name Reference List

The Computer Concordance[167] yielded a list of 420 Scripture references containing possible of-(genitive) names of God when commanded to print out the list "God of__". Careful physical reading and counting of the 420 entry reference list indicate that it is actually composed of 377 verses each with but a single name usage or application, 23 multiple verses containing 54 name applications (a multiple verse contains two or more genitive name applications), and four mixed passages containing five applications. (A mixed passage contains at least one correct name application as well as one or more computer error phrases). The summation of this assembly produced a total of 377+54+5=436 "name applications" in the 420 verses. In addition there are 22 genitive phrases in the 420 passages that must be classed as "computer errors" (a computer error results when the computer misreads a "God of__" phrase, such as Lev. 22:25, "God of any of these" as a name.

---

[167] *Word Processor Program*, Bible Research Systems, Copyright 1982, 1990, Austin, TX.

Table A.7.1 (Continued)

The 420 References of the Form "God of__"

Gen. 9:26	Gen. 24:3	Gen. 24:7	Gen. 24:12	Gen. 24:27	Gen. 24:42
Gen. 24:48	Gen. 26:24	Gen. 28:13	Gen. 31:15	Gen. 31:13	Gen. 31:29
Gen. 31:42	Gen. 31:53	Gen. 32:9	Gen. 43:23	Gen. 46:1	Gen. 46:3
Gen. 49:24	Gen. 49:25	Gen. 50:17	Exo. 3:6	Exo. 3:13	Exo. 3:15
Exo. 3:16	Exo. 3:18	Exo. 4:5	Exo. 5:1	Exo. 5:3	Exo. 7:16
Exo. 9:1	Exo. 9:13	Exo. 10:3	Exo. 18:4	Exo. 24:10	Exo. 32:27
Exo. 34:23	Lev. 22:25	Num. 16:9	Num. 16:22	Num. 27:16	Deu. 1:11
Deu. 1:21	Deu. 4:1	Deu. 6:3	Deu. 10:17	Deu. 12:1	Deu. 16:2
Deu. 26:7	Deu. 27:3	Deu. 27:6	Deu. 29:25	Deu. 32:4	Deu. 33:26
Jos. 7:13	Jos. 7:19	Jos. 7:20	Jos. 8:30	Jos. 9:18	Jos. 9:19
Jos. 10:40	Jos. 10:42	Jos. 13:14	Jos. 13:33	Jos. 14:14	Jos. 18:3
Jos. 22:16	Jos. 22:22	Jos. 22:24	Jos. 24:2	Jos. 24:23	Jdg. 2:12
Jdg. 4:6	Jdg. 5:3	Jdg. 5:5	Jdg. 6:8	Jdg. 11:21	Jdg. 11:23
Jdg. 21:3	Rth. 2:12	1Sa. 1:17	1Sa. 2:3	1Sa. 2:30	1Sa. 5:7
1Sa. 5:8	1Sa. 5:10	1Sa. 5:11	1Sa. 6:3	1Sa. 6:5	1Sa. 10:18
1Sa. 14:41	1Sa. 17:45	1Sa. 20:12	1Sa. 23:10	1Sa. 23:11	1Sa. 25:32
1Sa. 25:34	2Sa. 5:10	2Sa. 7:27	2Sa. 12:7	2Sa. 22:3	2Sa. 22:47
2Sa. 23:1	2Sa. 23:3	2Sa. 24:24	1Ki. 1:30	1Ki. 1:36	1Ki. 1:48
1Ki. 8:15	1Ki. 8:17	1Ki. 8:20	1Ki. 8:23	1Ki. 8:25	1Ki. 8:26
1Ki. 11:9	1Ki. 11:31	1Ki. 11:33	1Ki. 14:7	1Ki. 14:13	1Ki.15:30
1Ki. 16:13	1Ki. 16:26	1Ki. 16:33	1Ki. 17:1	1Ki. 17:14	1Ki. 18:36
1Ki. 19:10	1Ki. 19:14	1Ki. 20:22	1Ki. 22:53	2Ki. 1:2	1Ki. 1:3
2Ki. 1:6	2Ki. 1:16	2Ki. 2:14	2Ki. 9:6	2Ki. 10:31	2Ki. 14:25

Table A.7.1 (Continued)

2Ki. 17:26	2Ki. 17:27	2Ki. 18:5	2Ki. 19:15	2Ki. 19:20	2Ki. 20:5
2Ki. 21:12	2Ki. 21:22	2Ki. 22:15	2Ki. 22:18	1Ch. 4:10	1Ch. 5:25
1Ch. 5:26	1Ch. 12:17	1Ch. 15:12	1Ch. 15:14	1Ch. 16:4	1Ch. 16:35
1Ch. 16:36	1Ch. 17:24	1Ch. 22:6	1Ch. 23:25	1Ch. 24:19	1Ch. 28:4
1Ch. 28:9	1Ch. 29:7	1Ch. 29:10	1Ch. 29:18	1Ch. 29:20	2Ch. 2:12
2 Ch. 6:4	2 Ch. 6:7	2 Ch. 6:10	2 Ch. 6:14	2 Ch. 6:16	2 Ch. 6:17
2Ch. 7:22	2Ch. 11:16	2Ch. 13:5	2Ch. 13:12	2Ch. 13:18	2Ch. 14:4
2Ch. 15:4	2Ch. 15:12	2Ch. 15:13	2Ch. 17:4	2Ch. 19:4	2Ch. 20:6
2Ch. 20:19	2Ch. 20:33	2Ch. 21:10	2Ch. 21:12	2Ch. 24:18	2Ch. 24:24
2Ch. 28:6	2Ch. 28:9	2Ch. 28:25	2Ch. 29:5	2Ch. 29:7	2Ch. 29:10
2Ch. 30:1	2Ch. 30:5	2Ch. 30:6	2Ch. 30:7	2Ch. 30:19	2Ch. 30:22
2Ch. 32:15	2Ch. 32:17	2Ch. 32:19	2Ch. 33:7	2Ch. 33:12	2Ch. 33:16
2Ch. 33:18	2Ch. 34:3	2Ch. 34:23	2Ch. 34:26	2Ch. 34:32	2Ch. 34:33
2Ch. 36:13	2Ch. 36:15	2Ch. 36:23	Ezr. 1:2	Ezr. 1:3	Ezr. 3:2
Ezr. 4:1	Ezr. 4:3	Ezr. 5:1	Ezr. 5:11	Ezr. 5:12	Ezr. 6:9
Ezr. 6:10	Ezr. 6:14	Ezr. 6:21	Ezr. 6:22	Ezr. 7:6	Ezr. 7:12
Ezr. 7:15	Ezr. 7:19	Ezr. 7:21	Ezr. 7:23	Ezr. 7:27	Ezr. 8:28
Ezr. 8:35	Ezr. 9:4	Ezr. 9:15	Ezr. 10:11	Neh. 1:4	Neh. 1:5
Neh. 2:4	Neh. 2:20	Psa. 4:1	Psa. 18:46	Psa. 20:1	Psa. 24:5
Psa. 25:5	Psa. 27:9	Psa. 29:3	Psa. 31:5	Psa. 41:13	Psa. 42:8
Psa. 43:2	Psa. 46:7	Psa. 46:11	Psa. 47:9	Psa. 51:14	Psa. 59:5
Psa. 59:10	Psa. 59:17	Psa. 65:5	Psa. 68:8	Psa. 68:19	Psa. 68:20
Psa. 68:35	Psa. 69:6	Psa. 72:18	Psa. 75:9	Psa. 76:6	Psa. 79:9
Psa. 80:4	Psa. 80:7	Psa. 80:14	Psa. 80:19	Psa. 81:1	Psa. 81:4
Psa. 84:8	Psa. 85:4	Psa. 88:1	Psa. 89:8	Psa. 94:7	Psa. 106:48

Table A.7.a (Continued)

Psa. 109:1	Psa. 114:7	Psa. 132:2	Psa. 132:5	Psa. 136:2	Psa. 136:26
Psa. 146:5	Psa. 2:3	Psa. 3:15	Psa. 10:23	Psa. 10:24	Psa. 17:6
Isa. 17:10	Isa. 21:10	Isa. 21:17	Isa. 22:5	Isa. 22:12	Isa. 22:14
Isa. 22:15	Isa. 24:15	Isa. 28:22	Isa. 29:23	Isa. 30:18	Isa. 37:16
Isa. 37:21	Isa. 38:5	Isa. 41:17	Isa. 45:3	Isa. 45:15	Isa. 48:1
Isa. 48:2	Isa. 52:12	Isa. 54:5	Isa. 65:16	Jer. 2:19	Jer. 5:14
Jer. 7:3	Jer. 7:21	Jer. 9:15	Jer. 11:3	Jer. 13:12	Jer. 15:16
Jer. 16:9	Jer. 19:3	Jer. 19:15	Jer. 21:4	Jer. 23:2	Jer. 23:36
Jer. 24:5	Jer. 25:15	Jer. 25:27	Jer. 27:4	Jer. 27:21	Jer. 28:2
Jer. 28:14	Jer. 29:4	Jer. 29:8	Jer. 29:21	Jer. 29:25	Jer. 30:2
Jer. 31:1	Jer. 31:23	Jer. 32:14	Jer. 32:15	Jer. 32:27	Jer. 32:36
Jer. 33:4	Jer. 34:2	Jer. 34:13	Jer. 35:13	Jer. 35:17	Jer. 35:18
Jer. 35:19	Jer. 37:7	Jer. 38:17	Jer. 39:16	Jer. 42:9	Jer. 42:1
Jer. 42:18	Jer. 43:10	Jer. 44:2	Jer. 44:7	Jer. 44:11	Jer. 44:25
Jer. 45:2	Jer. 46:10	Jer. 46:25	Jer. 48:1	Jer. 49:5	Jer. 50:18
Jer. 50:25	Jer. 50:31	Jer. 51:5	Jer. 51:33	Jer. 51:56	Eze. 8:4
Eze. 9:3	Eze. 10:19	Eze. 10:20	Eze. 11:22	Eze. 12:19	Eze. 43:2
Eze. 44:2	Dan. 2:18	Dan. 2:19	Dan. 2:23	Dan. 2:37	Dan. 2:44
Dan. 2:47	Dan. 3:28	Dan. 3:29	Dan. 6:26	Dan. 11:36	Dan. 11:37
Dan. 11:38	Hos. 12:5	Amo. 3:13	Amo. 4:13	Amo. 5:14	Amo. 5:15
Amo. 5:16	Amo. 5:27	Amo. 6:8	Amo. 6:14	Amo. 9:5	Jon. 1:9
Mic. 4:2	Mic. 7:7	Hab. 3:18	Zep. 2:9	Mal. 2:16	Mal. 2:17

APPENDIX Chapter 7

Table A.7.2

The Selection of the 52 *true* Of-(genitive) names of God

The *true* of-(genitive) names are arrived at by reading, rereading and rereading again the 436 application names contained in the 420 verses for the correct of-(genitive) selection. It was at this point that the 22 non-applicable prepositional combinations and the 54 multiple passages were identified. Certain other restrictions were also imposed such as the application count for 1Ki. 18:36, 1Ch. 29:18 and 2Ch. 30:6. These passages include the common phrase "God of Abraham, Isaac and Israel." Although three names are intimated, only one application was counted for each verse.

This selection produced 52 names, which were arranged into the four Groups displayed in Tables A.7.2.a, b, c, and d. Exhibited there are the Selected Name, the Initial Verse Location, the Number of Applications of this name in the OT, and the Hebrew Name translated into the English word God. Group identification was assigned depending on the Group content. An index of the application verse locations for each Group member is presented in Tables A.7.3a, b, c, and d.

APPENDIX Chapter 7

Table A.7.2a

"Personal Names" - Group 1

Name	**Initial Ref.**	**Quantity**	**God (Heb. Name)**
1. God of Abraham	Gen. 26:24	16	Elohim
2. God of Daniel	Dan. 6:26	1	Elah
3. God of David	2Ki. 20:5	4	Elohim
4. God Elijah	2Ki. 2:14	1	Elohim
5. God of Hezekiah	2Ch. 32:17	1	Elohim
6. God of Isaac	Gen. 28:13	4	Elohim
7. God of Jacob	Gen. 49:24	20	El
8. God of Nahor	Gen. 31:53	1	Elohim
9. God of Shadrach	Dan. 3:28	2	Elohim
God of Meshach			Elohim
God of Abednego			Elohim
10. God of Shem	Gen. 9:26	1	Elohim
11. God of my Life	Psa. 42:8	1	El

(Note): Shadrach, Meshach and Abednego counted as one name

APPENDIX Chapter 7

Table A.7.3a

Index

"Personal Names" Application Verses

God of Abraham					**16 References**
Gen. 24:12	Gen. 24:27	Gen. 34:42	Gen. 24:48	Gen. 26:24	Gen. 28:13
Gen. 31:42	Gen. 31:53	Exo. 3:6	Exo. 3:15	Exo. 3:16	Exo. 4:5
1Ki. 18:36	1Ch. 29:18	2Ch. 30:6	Psa. 47:9		
God of Daniel					**1 Reference**
Dan. 6:26					
God of David					**4 References**
2Ki. 20:5	2Ch. 21:12	2Ch. 34:3	Isa. 38:5		
God of Elijah					**1 Reference**
2Ki. 2:14					
God of Hezekiah					**1 Reference**
2Ch. 32:17					
God of Isaac					**4 References**
Gen. 28:13	Exo. 3:6	Exo. 3:15	Exo. 4:5		
God of Jacob					**20 References**
Gen. 49:24	Exo. 3:6	Exo. 3:15	Exo. 4:5	2Sa. 23:1	Psa. 20:1
Psa. 46:7	Psa. 46:11	Psa. 75:9	Psa. 76:6	Psa. 81:1	Psa. 81:4
Psa. 84:8	Psa. 94:7	Psa. 114:7	Psa. 132:2	Psa. 132:5	Psa. 146:5
Isa. 2:3	Mic. 4:2				

Table A.7.3a (Continued)

God of Nahor **1 Reference**

Gen. 31:53

God of Shadrach **2 References**

God of Meshach

God of Abednego

Dan. 3:28 Dan. 3:29

God of Shem **1 Reference**

Gen. 9:26

God of My Life **1 Reference**

Psa. 42:8

APPENDIX Chapter 7

Thoughts on the members of Group A.7.2a

"Personal Names"

These eleven names of God all have a single and outstanding interrelationship characteristic—Sphere.[168] This life style is expressed in the activities of each person. They all have a very close relationship to El or Elohim; He is their God. Of course, God actually belongs to no one; however, so close is this relationship that He is referred to as the God of Abraham, of Daniel, of Isaac, and of Nahor, and these possessive expressions stand as His name. It is easily determined that the extent of this life style experience varied in the lives of the eleven individuals associated with God in this way. Yet Scripture records that there was a sphere of relationship in each case to such an extent that a name was established.

[168] Sphere: to have, range, or an extent of action, existence, knowledge, experience, influence of one person to another: the walk of life or life style.

APPENDIX Chapter 7

Table A.7.2b

"Groups of people" - Group 2

Name	Initial Ref.	Quantity	God (Heb. Name)
1. God of All Flesh	Jer. 32:27	1	El
2. God of Armies of Israel	1Sa. 17:45	1	Elohim
3. God of Israel	Exo. 5:1	201	Elohim
4. God of Jeshuran	Deu. 33:26	1	El
5. God of His Father	Gen. 46:1	8	Elohim
6. God of My Father	Gen. 31:5	6	Elohim
7. God of Our Father	Deu. 26:7	4	Elohim
8. God of Their Father	Gen. 31:53	21	Elohim
9. God of Thy Father	Gen. 46:3	9	El
10. God of Your Father	Exo. 3:13	13	Elohim
11. God of The Hebrews	Exo. 3:18	6	Elohim
12. God of Hosts	2Sa. 5:10	40	Elohim
13. God of The Inhabitants of Jerusalem	Eze. 12:19	1	Adonai
14. God of My lord	1Ki. 1:36	1	Elohim
15. God of The Spirits of All Flesh	Num. 16:22	2	El

APPENDIX Chapter 7

Table A.7.3b

Index

"Groups of People" Application Verses

*Note: Verse 1 Sa. 5:8 has the name God of Israel entered 3 times

Table A.7.3b (Continued)

Isa. 37:16	Isa. 37:21	Isa. 41:17	Isa. 45:3	Isa. 45:15	Isa. 48:1	Isa. 48:2
Isa. 52:12	Jer. 7:3	Jer. 7:21	Jer. 9:15	Jer. 11:13	Jer. 13:12	Jer. 16:9
Jer. 19:3	Jer. 19:15	Jer. 21:4	Jer. 23:12	Jer. 24:5	Jer. 25:15	Jer. 25:27
Jer. 27:4	Jer. 27:21	Jer. 28:2	Jer. 28:14	Jer. 29:4	Jer. 29:8	Jer. 29:21
Jer. 29:25	Jer. 30:2	Jer. 31:23	Jer. 32:14	Jer. 32:15	Jer. 32:36	Jer. 33:4
Jer. 34:2	Jer. 34:13	Jer. 35:13	Jer. 35:17	Jer. 35:18	Jer. 35:19	Jer. 37:7
Jer. 38:17	Jer. 39:16	Jer. 42:9	Jer. 42:15	Jer. 42:18	Jer. 43:10	Jer. 44:2
Jer. 44:7	Jer. 44:11	Jer. 44:25	Jer. 45:2	Jer. 46:25	Jer. 48:1	Jer. 50:18
Jer. 51:33	Eze. 8.4	Eze. 9:3	Eze. 10:19	Eze. 10:20	Eze. 11:22	Eze. 43:2
Eze. 44:2	Zep. 2:9	Mal. 2:16				
God of Jeshuran					**1 Reference**	
Deu. 33:26						
God of His Father					**8 References**	
Gen. 46:1	2Ki. 21:22	2Ch. 17:4	2Ch. 21:10	2Ch. 28:25	2Ch. 30:19	2Ch. 33:12
Dan. 11:37						
God of My Father					**6 References**	
Gen. 31:5	Gen. 31:42	Gen. 32:9*	Exo. 18:4	Dan. 2:23		
God of Our Father					**4 References**	
Deu. 26:7	1Ch. 12:17	2Ch. 20:6	Ezr. 7:27			
God of Their Father					**21 References**	
Gen. 31:53	Exo. 4:5	Deu. 29:25	Jdg. 2:12	1Ch. 5:25	1Ch. 29:20	2Ch. 7:22
2Ch. 11:16	2Ch. 13:18	2Ch. 14:4	2Ch. 15:12	2Ch. 19:4	2Ch. 20:33	2Ch. 24:18
2Ch. 24:24	2Ch. 28:6	2Ch. 30:7	2Ch. 30:22	2Ch. 34:32	2Ch. 34:33	2Ch. 26:15

*Note: Gen. 32:9 contains a 2 x multiple.

Table A.7.3b (Continued)

God of Thy Father					**9 References**	
Gen. 46:3	Gen. 49:25	Gen. 50:17	Exo. 3:6	Deu. 1:21	Deu. 6:3	Deu. 12:1
Deu. 27:3	1Ch. 28:9					
God of Your Father					**13 References**	
Gen. 31:29	Gen. 43:23	Exo. 3:13	Exo. 3:15	Exo. 3:16	Deu. 1:11	Deu. 4:1
Jos. 18:3	2Ch. 13:12	2Ch. 28:9	2Ch. 29:5	Ezr. 8:28	Ezr. 10:11	
God of The Hebrews					**6 References**	
Exo. 3:18	Exo. 5:3	Exo. 7:16	Exo. 9:1	Exo. 9:13	Exo. 10:3	
God of Hosts					**40 References**	
2Sa. 5:10	1Ki. 19:10	1Ki. 19:14	Psa. 59:5	Psa. 69:6	Psa. 80:4	Psa. 80:7
Psa. 80:14	Psa. 80:19	Psa. 84:8	Psa. 89:8	Isa. 3:15	Isa. 10:23	Isa. 10:24
Isa. 22:5	Isa. 22:12	Isa. 22:14	Isa. 22:15	Isa. 28:22	Jer. 2:19	Jer. 5:14
Jer. 15:16	Jer. 35:17	Jer. 38:17	Jer. 44:7	Jer. 46:10*	Jer. 49:5	Jer. 50:25
Jer. 50:31	Hos. 12:5	Amo. 3:13	Amo. 4:13	Amo. 5:14	Amo. 5:15	Amo. 5:16
Amo. 5:27	Amo. 6:8	Amo. 6:14	Amo. 9:5			
God of The Inhabitants of Jerusalem					**1 Reference**	
Eze. 12:19						
God of My Lord					**1 Reference**	
1Ki. 1:36						
God of The Spirits of All Flesh					**2 References**	
Num. 16:22	Num. 27:16					

*Note: Jer. 46:10 contains a 2x multiple

APPENDIX Chapter 7

Thoughts on the members of Group A.7.2b

"Groups of People"

Table A.7.2b is an assemblage of 15 additional names of God with variations from the simple possessive personal name case of the previous table. This listing is referred to as the "Peoples" Group since each name relates God to either a group of people (i.e., God of the Hebrews or God of Israel) or to progenitors (I.e., God of their father or God of his father). Table A.7.2b again presents all names in the attributive of-(genitive case), but some are in the appositive and some contain double possessive genitives.

In contrast to the entries in Table A.7.2a the uniqueness of some of the Table A.7.2b names requires individual consideration. First, application of metonymy in modern Bible versions tends to produce some changes in the meaning from the AV. Secondly, the name "God of the father(s)," requires special attention due to its prominence in the Scriptures. There is also the variation in the group size from one or a few, as in the father references, to the very comprehensive "for all mankind". Lastly, the exceptional name "God of my lord" needs special scrutiny. Then let us examine these names but, for convenience, not necessarily in the order given in the Table.

Let us consider the names "the God of all flesh" and "the God of the spirits of all flesh". Two variations from the simple possessive genitive occur here. First, metonymic application in the more current versions of Scripture, such as the NIV and

Beck, has yielded "the God of all mankind" and "the God of the spirits of all mankind". In the sense that God is "the" God of mankind {This is true. He has made all flesh and the spirits of all mankind}, since there is no God but this God. However, in the possessive sense, He is not "the" God of mankind, for there is no sphere of God belonging to or in association with vast numbers of human beings who have turned away from this God. Secondly, these two names are in the appositive genitive wherein the noun God is simply explained by the following phrase; He is the God of all mankind, that's who He is.

The name "the God of the Armies of Israel" is unusual. Actually, in the containing text, a prior possessive name exists. The AV reads, "...the LORD of hosts, the God of the armies of Israel..." (1Sa. 17:45). This statement is certainly true, since God is the LORD of hosts—that is His name (Amo. 4:13; 5:27). He belongs to this vast heavenly group. He is in their sphere of operation. Yet the Armies of Israel, also, according to David, claimed that God belonged to them. He was their God even though their faith was weak. This is simply an expression of a double possessive genitive involving these two groups.

The God of Hosts is a possessive genitive name appearing 40 times in the OT Scriptures. The hosts are generally understood as heavenly and primarily angels. There is some argument that heavenly bodies or stars, completely in the sphere of God, may be involved. In either case the name gathers into itself the idea of all divine or heavenly power as possessed by God for the needs of His peoples. However, Unger's comment should not be missed; he writes,[169] "...the tribes of Israel, who were led by God out of Egypt, are also called 'the hosts of the LORD' (Exo. 7:4; 12:41). As in heaven the angels and stars form the host of God, so on earth the sons of Israel are His hosts". Here His people operated with God in their sphere of daily communion as He delivered them out of Egyptian bondage. The LORD is frequently identified by means of the possessive genitive case in the OT where, for example, His name is called "the LORD (Yahweh) God of hosts". Even more often, His name the Lord GOD of hosts, Adonai Yahweh, appears. There can be no doubt that His name is "God of hosts".[170]

Examine how the name "the God of the Hebrews." This name, in the possessive genitive, occurs only 6 times in the OT, exclusively in connection with the dialogues in which God gave to Moses directions for persuading Pharaoh to let the Hebrews go. The name could well be expressed in the 's-(genitive) as "The Hebrew's God," for so He was. There was great sphere of relationship between the Hebrew people and God as they awaited deliverance from their Egyptian task masters.

Another unique name in this list is "the God of the inhabitants of Jerusalem". Actually the AV text reads, the Lord GOD (Adonai Yahweh) of the inhabitants of

---

[169] Unger, Merrill, F., *The New Unger's Bible Dictionary*, Chicago, Moody Press, 1988, p. 592.
[170] The LORD (Yahweh), unmistakably states His name is "The God of hosts" in Amo. 5:27.

Jerusalem, and the land of Israel. This title appears but once in the OT (Eze. 12:19), where God refers to Himself with a double possessive genitive expression, the Adonai Yahweh of the people living in Jerusalem on Israel's soil. Probably this extended title can be considered more as a description of who God is than as a statement of possession, since these people of the city of Jerusalem and the land were very weak in faith and obedience at that time. Still this name belongs in the of-(genitive) class relating to groups of people.

A large group of the possessive of-(genitive) People-Group names express relationships with "the fathers" by adding personal pronouns to the divine name, for example the God of our/your Father. There are 71 applications of this title of God in the OT utilizing six different personal pronouns. Perhaps some will not agree that this possessive of-(genitive) expression is even a name of God. Yet this compound of words is no different than the many other names in this extensive series. The various versions of Scripture do not capitalize the phrase "of the fathers"[171]: only the words God or LORD God (where both names appear) are capitalized.

Before we look more closely at this name, consider the word father as applied in the OT. This term can mean several things depending on the context and usage. It can signify an earthly father per se. For example, "Solomon sat upon the throne of

---

[171] The phrase "of the father(s)" does not appear in the OT of the AV. However, this expression is used to represent the cluster of names, each actually with its own personal pronoun (i.e., my father, your father, his father, etc.).

David his father..." (1Ki. 2:12). Or the word father may be applied to progenitors several generations removed. For example, "Asa did that which was right in the eyes of the LORD, as did David his father" (1Ki. 15:11). Asa spoke of David his father yet the lineage was David>Solomon>Rehoboam>Abijam>Asa. Actually, David was Asa's great-great-grandfather. But look at one more case that is even more unusual. In 2Ki. 14:3, Amaziah who "...was right in the sight of the LORD, yet not like David his father: he did according to all the things as Joash his father did." Joash was the actual father of Amaziah. David was certainly in his lineage, but that was some nine generations earlier. Yet both Joash and David are referred to as Amaziah's father in the same verse. So father may be either a close or a more distant relative. The word father may also be in the plural (fathers), meaning forefathers of the same lineage.

To return to the phrase "of the father(s)," Gen. 46:1 reads in the of-(genitive), "...the God of his father Isaac," which could be alternately written with the s-genitive form, "his father's God." Yet in the various Scripture versions considered, the s-genitive case is not found; it is consistently written in the of-(genitive). God belongs to "his father"...that is, God belongs to the sphere of operation of the father(s). Or more explicitly, God is in the sphere of "his father(s) or in the way of life of "his father(s)".

Now, who are the father(s)? They were those God following, God committed and God fearing progenitors of the individual referencing this name. Indeed there is no surprise in finding the father(s) to be the very persons specifically named in the

Personal Names Group of Table A.7.2a. They may be one or many generations removed from the applying person, but they are the great, godly leaders and patriarchs.

It has been observed that the phrase "of the father(s)" is commonly employed in the OT Scriptures as a part of the name of God. This is interesting, because the name God (or LORD God) certainly is most adequate in itself. Yet the author elects to embellish the primary name with an of-(genitive) phrase to relate God to godly progenitors. Why is this done? It is suggested that the reason is simply to relate God to well known people with Godly values of other days. For example, Abraham had a widely known and well understood relationship with God. God was central in his sphere of everyday life. Everyone knew this great fact, so they called upon and referred to this God, the God of Abraham, as the God of the fathers of Israel.

As the final comments upon Table A.7.2a, consider the name "the LORD God of my lord the king". (1Ki. 1:36 AV.) This expression, though rather lengthy, does indeed meet all the requirements for a possessive of-(genitive) name. In this verse, the phrase my lord the king refers to David. The expression then becomes like one we have seen before, "the God of David".

Table A.7.2c

"Locations and Places - Group 3

Name	Initial Ref.	Quantity	God (Heb. Name)
1. God of Bethel	Gen. 31:13	1	El
2. God of the Earth	Gen. 24:3	1	Elohim
3. God of Heaven	Gen. 24:3	21	Elohim
4. God of Heaven and Earth	Ezr. 5:11	1	Eloah
5. God of Jerusalem	2Ch. 32:19	2	Elohim
6. God of the Land	2Ki. 17:26	3	Elohim
7. God of the Whole Earth	Isa. 54:5	1	Elohim

Table A.7.3c
Index

"Location and Places" Application Verses

God of Bethel						**1 Reference**
Gen. 31:13						
God of the Earth						**1 Reference**
Gen. 24:3						
God of Heaven						**21 References**
Gen. 24:3	Gen. 24:7	2Ch. 36:23	Ezr. 1:2	Ezr. 5:11	Ezr. 5:12	Ezr. 6:9
Ezr. 6:10	Ezr. 7:12	Ezr. 7:21	Ezr. 7:23	Neh. 1:4	Neh. 1:5	Neh. 2:4
Neh. 2:20	Psa. 136:26	Dan. 2:18	Dan. 2:19	Dan. 2:37	Dan. 2:44	Jon. 1:9
God of Heaven and Earth						**1 Reference**
Ezr. 5:11						
God of Jerusalem						**2 References**
2Ch. 32:19	Ezr. 7:19					
God of the Land						**2 References**
2Ki. 17:26*	2Ki. 17:27					
God of the Whole Earth						**1 Reference**
Isa. 54:5						

*This verse contains a 2x multiple

APPENDIX Chapter 7

Thoughts on the members of Group A.7.2c

"Location and Places Names"

The names God of Bethel and God of Heaven have been considered in this chapter's text. However, in conjunction with that information let us now look at the other names in Group 3.

The name the God of Jerusalem was introduced by the Chroniclers (2Ch. 32:19). The record shows that the heathen Assyrian king, Sennacherib, was invading Judah with the intent to soon lay siege to Jerusalem. As that attack drew near officers of the insurgents slandered the LORD, taunting Hezekiah and his people in the city that this "God of Jerusalem" was just like all the other gods of the people of the world that human hands have made. He would not or could not rescue or save them. But remember that Hezekiah included the very God being taunted in his sphere of operation. This God belonged to Hezekiah, who knew that his God would fight his battles. Scripture says that Hezekiah and Judah took this matter to the LORD in prayer with immediate results. The heathen army found out that Israel's God was much more than just a man-made deity, for the LORD sent an angel who destroyed all the leaders and fighting men of the Assyrian horde. Hezekiah and the people of Jerusalem were delivered from Sennacherib's taunting army. The LORD proved that indeed this name was correct. He was the God of Jerusalem.

There is another interesting example of ownership or belonging, involving the only other use of the name the God of Jerusalem in the OT (Ezr. 7:19). Ezra, a Jewish priest of considerable reputation before the court of Artaxerxes, King of Persia, was directed by God to lead a group of the exiled Jews back to Jerusalem from Babylonia. It is perfectly clear that God was in the operating sphere of Ezra. Yet it is now Ezra but the heathen King Artaxerxes who uses this name to identify God. Ezra indicates in his praise to the LORD that God had placed in the king's mind the intention to allow the return. Now it is doubtful that King Artaxarxes knew God beyond the acknowledgment that He was the God of Ezra. Still the king states that the God of Israel lives in Jerusalem and that the temple of God in Jerusalem shall receive gold and silver gifts from the king and the officials of Persia. Furthermore, Ezra is to receive government funds to buy animals for the altar sacrifices in the temple of God in Jerusalem. The king then states that the sacred utensils given to Ezra by the king shall be presented before "the God of Jerusalem". All this was written in a formal letter by the King to Ezra. How amazing! This heathen king who knew little about the Jewish God in Jerusalem identifies Him so very correctly as the God of Jerusalem. That is, the people of Jerusalem had God in their sphere of operation, something Artaxerxes knew about but didn't understand.

Now consider the name "the God of the Land". Shalmaneser, King of Assyria besieged and conquered Samaria and carried Israel away into Assyrian captivity. This judgment resulted as a consequence of Israel's sin. (2 Kings 17:7-23.) Following the removal of the Israelite people, Assyria imported other people from various countries to inhabit the land. These gentile settlers didn't worship the LORD, and He sent lions among them so that some of the people were killed. The inhabitants told Shalmaneser that the people of the nations which had been imported and placed in the cities of Samaria did not know the manner of "the God of the Land". Scripture then reiterates that lions, sent by God, killed some of the people, because they knew not the manner of "the God of the Land". The Assyrian King commanded that an exiled Jewish priest be reinstalled at Bethel to teach the imported peoples the manner of "the God of the Land".

Three times the name the God of the land occurs in two verses (2Ki. 17:26, 27). One might think that this name cannot relate to the Jewish people, for God had removed most of them from the land for their sin. Yet let us remember that some 1200 years earlier the God of Abraham covenanted to give to the patriarch and his offspring this very land. Now, even though the Israelite nation was gone, God was still mindful of the land as "the God of the Land". One day the God of Abraham—the covenant God of Israel, the personal God to His people, the God of this land—will restore His people to this land, and "the God of the land" will be the God of His people in the land.

Finally, let us consider the title "the God of the whole earth." The name "the God of the earth" (Gen. 24:3) has already received review as part of the title, "The God of heaven and God of the earth". There is no question but that God is the possessor of the heavens. Neither should there be doubt that the whole earth is His, for He manifests Himself as the God of the whole earth everywhere, ruling and overruling in the affairs of man. For example, in Syria and Egypt, in Israel and Judah, at the Red Sea and during the great liberations of the Judges period, God was in charge. Isaiah expressed who He was in this way: "For thy maker is thine husband; the LORD of hosts is His name; and thy Redeemer the Holy One of Israel; the God of the whole earth shall He be called" (Isaiah 54:5.)

Table A.7.2d

"Characteristics" - Group 4

Name	Initial Ref.	Quantity	God (Heb. Name)
1. God of Glory	Psa. 29:3	1	El
2. God of gods	Deu. 10:17	5	Elohim
3. God of The Hills	1Ki. 20:28	1	Elohim
4. God of Judgment	Isa. 30:18	2	Elah
5. God of Knowledge	1Sa. 2:3	1	Elohim
6. God of My Mercy	Psa. 59:10	2	Elohim
7. God of My Praise	Psa. 109:1	1	Elohim
8. God of Recompenses	Jer. 51:56	1	El
9. God of My Righteousness	Psa. 4:1	1	Elohim
10. God of My Rock	2Sa. 22:3	1	Elohim
11. God of The Rock of My Salvation	2Sa. 22:47	1	Elohim
12. God of Salvation	Psa. 68:20	1	El
13. God of His Salvation	Psa. 24:5	1	Elohim
14. God of My Salvation	Psa. 18:46	7	Elohim
15. God of Our Salvation	1Ch. 16:35	5	Elohim
16. God of Thy Salvation	Isa. 17:10	1	Elohim
17. God of My Strength	Psa. 43:2	1	Elohim
18. God of Truth	Deu. 32:4	4	El
19. God of The Valleys	1Ki. 20:28	1	Elohim

Table A.7.3d

Index

"Characteristics" Application Verses

God of Glory	**1 Reference**
Psa. 29:3	
God of Gods	**5 References**
Deu. 10:17 Jos. 22:22 Psa. 136:2 Dan. 2:47 Dan. 11:36	
God of the Hills	**1 References**
1Ki. 20:28	
God of Judgment	**2 References**
Isa. 30:18 Mal. 2:17	
God of Knowledge	**1 Reference**
1Sa. 2:3	
God of My Mercy	**2 References**
Psa. 59:10 Psa. 59:17	
God of My Praise	**1 References**
Psa. 109:1	
God of Recompenses	**1 Reference**
Jer. 51:56	

Table A.7.3d (Continued)

Index

"Characteristics" Application Verses

God of My Righteousness					**1 Reference**
Psa. 4:1					
God of My Rock					**1 Reference**
2Sa. 22:3					
God of The Rock of My Salvation					**1 Reference**
2Sa. 22:47					
God of Salvation					**1 References**
Psa. 68:20					
God of His Salvation					**1 Reference**
Psa. 24:5					
God of My Salvation					**7 Reference**
Psa. 18:46	Psa. 25:5	Psa. 27:9	Psa. 51:14	Psa. 88:1	
Hab. 3:18	Mic. 7:7				
God of Our Salvation					**5 References**
1Ch. 16:35	Psa. 65:5	Psa. 68:19	Psa. 79:9	Psa. 85:4	
God of Thy Salvation					**1 References**
Isa. 17:10					

Table A.7.3d (Continued)
Index
"Characteristics" Application Verses

God of My Strength **1 Reference**

Psa. 43:2

God of Truth **3 References**

Deu. 32:4 Psa. 31:5 Isa. 65:16*

God of The Valleys **1 Reference**

1Ki. 20:28

*Contains a 2x multiple

APPENDIX Chapter 7

Thoughts on the members of Group A.7.2.d

"Characteristics"

This listing, called the Characteristics Table, is an assemblage of those of-(genitive) names that are predominantly employed in the OT to express (or even explain), certain of the specific attributes of God. With only a single exception the entries all fall in the appositional category of genitives, wherein the writer places a term or prepositional expression beside the word God so that the second term focuses attention on a characteristic of God (sometimes El and other times Elohim). For example, He is the God of Judgment (Isa. 30:18) or the God of Truth (Deu. 32:4). Certainly these are appropriate names, because God is referred to as a judge in numerous passages (Deu. 32:4; Psa. 9:8), and all His ways are truth (Psa. 25:10). Or again, consider the typical statement, God is My Rock (2Sa. 22:3). The Scripture writers frequently use the metaphor Rock to represent God (Deu. 32:4; Psa. 18:2; 62:7, Isa. 17:10) as the strength of His people. These examples and many others point out that these of-(genitive) names present distinguishing attributes of God that are also spoken of in other places in the Scripture in other than the genitive case.

The God of Glory is an unusual name that can be easily confused with a mere reference to the theophanic glory of God (or God's glory). But His name, the God of Glory is much more meaningful for what is glory? This word when used of God is particularly appropriate for describing the moral uniqueness and grandeur of God as

Lord of the universe. Any endeavor to specifically qualify or quantify the use of the word glory produces an endless series of descriptive adjectives. He is the God of all this. How can He ever be adequately described.

The name the God of gods, as was stated, is an exception in this listing of appositive genitive names. This special variety of the partitive genitive denotes the whole supernatural realm of which only a part, the God of Israel alone is taken to express a genitive of graduation.

APPENDIX Chapter 7

Table A.7.4

A Chronological Index of

"The Computer Error Verses"

In the search for the of-(genitive) names of God the computer was programmed to select all possible of-(genitive) phrases of the form "God of—". However, it early became evident that a significant phrase population of the form "God of—" are not names at all, but rather "look-a-likes" to the computer. These are intermingled with the searched names. These imposter phrases, often caused by punctuation problems, have been identified and are presented in Table A.7.4, "The Computer Error Verses."

Lev. 22:25

"Neither from a stranger's hand shall ye offer bread of your **God of any of these**; because their corruption is in them, and blemishes be in them: they shall not be accepted for you."

Deu. 16:2

"Thou shalt therefore sacrifice the passover unto the LORD thy **God of the flock and the herd**, in the place which the LORD shall choose to place His name there."

Deu. 27:6

"Thou shalt build the altar of the LORD thy **God of whole stones**: and thou shalt offer burnt-offerings thereon upon the LORD thy God."

Table A.7.4 (Continued)

"The Computer Error Verses:

Jdg. 2:12

"And they forsook the LORD God of their fathers, which brought them out of the land of Egypt, and followed other **gods, of**[172] **the gods of** [173] **the people** that were round about them, and bowed themselves unto them, and provoked the LORD to anger."

2Sa. 24:24

"And the king said unto Arauah, Nay, but I will surely buy it of thee at a price: neither will I offer burnt-offerings unto the LORD my **God of that which doth cost me nothing**. So David bought the threshing floor and the oxen for fifty shekels of silver."

1Ki. 11:33

"Because that they have forsaken me, and have worshipped Astoreth the goddess of the Zidonians, Chemosh the **god of**[174] **the Moabites**, and Milcom the **god of**[175] **the children** of Ammon, and have not walked in my ways, to do that which is right in mine eyes, and to keep my statutes and my judgments, as did David his father."

2Ki. 1:2

"And Ahaziah fell down through a lattice in his upper chamber that was in Samaria, and

---

[172] Jdg. 2:12 contains 2 errors as shown.
[173] Ibid. fn. 172.
[174] 1Ki. Contains 2 errors as shown.
[175] Ibid. fn. 174.

was sick: and he sent messengers, and said unto them, Go, enquire of Baal-zebub the **god of Ekron** whether I shall recover of this disease."

2Ki. 1:3

"But the angel of the LORD said to Elijah the Tishbite, Arise, go up to meet the messengers of the king of Samaria, and say unto them, Is it not because there is not a God in Israel, that ye go to enquire of Baal-zebub the **god of Ekron?**"

2Ki. 1:6

"And they said unto him, There came a man up to meet us, and said unto us, Go, turn again unto the king that sent you, and say unto him, Thus saith the LORD, is it not because there is not a god in Israel, that thou sendest to enquire of Baal-zebub the **God of Ekron?**"

2Ki. 1:16

"And he said unto him, Thus saith the LORD, Forasmuch as thou hast sent messengers to enquire of Baal-zebub the **god of Ekron**, is it not because there is no God in Israel to enquire of his word? therefore thou shalt not come down off that bed on which thou art gone up, but shalt surely die."

1Ch. 5:25

"And they transgressed against the God of their fathers, and went a whoring after the **gods of the people** of the land, whom God destroyed before them."

APPENDIX Chapter 7

1Ch. 29:7

"And gave for the service of the house of **God of gold** five thousand talents and ten thousand drams, and of silver ten thousand talents, and of brass eighteen thousand talents, and one hundred thousand talents of iron."

2Ch. 32:15

"Now therefore let not Hezekiah deceive you, nor persuade you on this manner, neither yet believe him" for **no god of any nation** or kingdom was able to deliver his people out of mine hand, and out of the hand of my fathers: how much less shall your God deliver you out of mine hand."

2Ch. 32:17

"He wrote also letters to rail on the LORD God of Israel, and to speak against him, saying, As the **gods of the nations** of other lands have not delivered their people out of mine hand, so shall the God of Hezekiah deliver his people out of mine hand."

2Ch. 32:19

"And they spake against the God of Jerusalem, as against the **gods of the people** of the earth, which were the work of the hands of man."

2Ch. 33:7

"And he set a carved image, the idol which he has made, in the house of **God, of which God** has said to David and to Solomon his son, In this house, and in Jerusalem, which I have chosen before all the tribes of Israel, will I put my name for ever."

APPENDIX Chapter 7

Jer. 23:36

"And the burden of the LORD shall ye mention no more: for every man's word shall be his burden; for ye have perverted the words of the living **God, of the LORD** of hosts our God."

Jer. 31:1

"At the same time, saith the LORD, will I be the **God of all the families** of Israel, and they shall be my people."

Jer. 51:5

"For Israel hath not been forsaken, nor Judah of his **God, of the LORD** of hosts, though their land was filled with sin against the Holy One of Israel."

Dan. 11:38

"But in his estate shall he honour the **God of forces** and a god whom his fathers knew not shall be honour with gold, and silver, and with previous stones, and pleasant things."

APPENDIX Chapter 8

8.1 Governor Among The Nations

Psalm 22 speaks in prophetic testimony of the Lord Jesus Christ under two conditions. The first 21 verses describe in detail the terrible suffering Jesus endured while on the cross. Then verses 22 through 31 present the glory of Christ Jesus following His resurrection and beyond to the day when all nations accept Him as Lord and pay Him the homage that is due Him.

Since the name of God of concern here is in the second part of the Psalm, only the verses from 22 to the song's end will be examined in detail. The KJV of the Scripture, as in all other places of the study, will be used as the guide document and as usual, other versions will be compared to this guide. In following this procedure it becomes immediately apparent that significant variations exist between the versions. Furthermore, the problem of who is being addressed in these verses becomes evident because of the abundant use of personal pronouns.

To begin with, let us examine the ten prophetic verses of concern, inserting proper names in place of the AV personal pronouns relating to deity. Appropriate explanatory paraphrase will also be added to justify and/or clarify the perspective of the pronoun substitution.

Psalm 22:22. I (Jesus Christ) will declare thy name (God) unto My (Jesus') brethren: in the midst of the congregation will I (Jesus Christ) praise Thee (our God and our Father).

Beginning in the 22nd verse, the Spirit of Christ in David declares the Glory that should follow His resurrection. Here Jesus Christ makes known the name of God to His brethren, Jesus' disciples, the redeemed ones who are indwelt by His Spirit, those who Jesus has brought to God. Jesus praises God in the midst of the congregation, the church.[176]

Psalm 22:23 Ye that fear the LORD, praise Him (Jesus Christ), all ye the seed of Jacob, glorify Him (Jesus Christ) and fear Him (Jesus Christ), all ye the seed of Israel.

But even more than that, the very seed of Jacob and all the seed of Israel, these people who once rejected Jesus, will now bow and worship Jesus in His presence. This acceptance of Jesus and His salvation by the seed of Jacob will not occur until Jesus returns to the earth in great power and glory. What a glory will be His, when all the seed of Israel will worship and adore Him and He comes at last in all His glory as the King of the Jews and Governor of the nations.

Psalm 22:24 For He (Jesus Christ) hath not despised nor abhorred the affliction of the afflicted; neither hath He (God) hid His (God's) face from Him (Jesus Christ); but when He (Jesus Christ) cried unto Him (God), He (God) heard.

---

[176] Arno C. Gaebelein, *The Book Of Psalms*, Van Kampen Press, Wheaton, C.R. 1939, p. 107.

The people realize and acknowledge that God's face is not hidden from Jesus Christ. Jesus was heard on the cross, for God raised Jesus from the dead and gave Him great glory.[177]

Psalm 22:25 My (Jesus Christ's) praise shall be of Thee (God) in the great congregation: I (Jesus Christ) will pay My (Jesus Christ's) vows before them that fear Him (God).

The great congregation refers to that great Kingdom that is to come. In this Kingdom Jesus receives great glory, praises the Name of God and rules in righteousness, when the whole earth, even all the families of the nations, worship Jesus as they turn to the LORD.[178]

<u>Psalm 22:26</u> The meek shall eat and be satisfied: they shall praise the LORD that seek Him (Jesus Christ): your heart shall live for ever.

Lev. 7:11-20 speaks of the Peace offering, where a feast was spread. In the Leviticus passage the invitation to the poor to partake of what was left over is not given. But through Jesus, who went into the jaws of death, who has fulfilled every offering (they foreshadowed His own redemptive work) and paid His vows, a feast is spread to which the humble can come and be satisfied.[179]

---

[177] Ibid., p. 108.
[178] Ibid., p. 109. Also see Psalm 109:30.
[179] Ibid., p. 110.

Another has put it this way, "Those shall praise the Lord that seek Him, because through Christ they are sure of finding Him, in the hopes of which they have reason to praise Him even while they are seeking Him. The souls that are devoted to him shall be forever happy with Him.[180]

Psalm 22:27 All the ends of the world shall remember and turn unto the LORD and all the kindred of the nations shall worship before thee (Jesus Christ).

They shall remember the steps toward true conversion, including, first, serious reflection or introspection and then a turning unto Him.

Psalm 22:28 For the kingdom is the LORD's: and he (Jesus Christ) is the governor among the nations.

The church of Christ and, with it, the Kingdom and God among men should extend to all the corners of the earth. The Kingdom of nature is the LORD's and His providence rules among the nations. The Kingdom of grace is the Lord Jesus Christ's, and He, as Mediator, is appointed governor among the nations. The head over all things to His church.[181]

The kingdoms of this earth will belong to the LORD, and in that Kingdom Jesus Christ will rule in righteousness among the nations.

---

[180] Matthew Henry, *Commentary*, Zondervan Pub. House, Grand Rapids, 13th ed., 1974, p. 600.
[181] Ibid., p. 600.

Psalm 22:29 All they that be fat upon the earth shall eat and worship: all they that go down to the dust shall bow before him (Jesus Christ): and none can keep alive his own soul.

High and low, rich and poor, bond and free meet in Christ. Seeing that we cannot keep alive our own souls, it is our wisdom by obedient faith, to commit our souls to Jesus Christ, who is able to save them and keep them alive for ever.[182]

Psalm 22:30 A seed shall serve him (Jesus Christ); it shall be accounted to the Lord for a generation.

The church, the remnant, shall serve Jesus Christ. And He, Jesus Christ, will be the same to them that He was to their progenitors. His church shall serve Him (Jesus Christ) and shall provide satisfactory reasons, explanations and descriptions of Him to those that are yet to come.

Psalm 22:31 They shall come, and shall declare His (Jesus Christ's) righteousness unto a people that shall be born, that He (Jesus Christ) hath done this.

This church shall declare to the yet unborn in the nations, the righteousness of God in Jesus Christ.

---

[182] Ibid., p. 600.

APPENDIX Chapter 8

Christ Jesus and His work are the great subject and theme of this Psalm. Therefore, every opportunity is taken to call out the name of Jesus Christ (or a substitute pronoun) as He relates to His purpose.

Particular Aspect Of God's Character Highlighted:

Both the LORD and Jesus Christ are seen in the given verse. The kingdom of nature is the LORD's, and His providence rules among the nations. The kingdom of grace is the Lord Jesus Christ's, and He, as Mediator, is appointed "Governor Among The Nations," the head over all things to His church. It is the work of Jesus to bring God and His people together. He is the governor, mediating between the people and God. And one day Jesus will be recognized for who he is, Son of God, Governor, Ruler and King.

The Special Need Of Man Met By The Revelation Of This Aspect Of His Character:

Man needs repeated reminders of just who Jesus is. Today, sitting at the right hand of the Father, He mediates between God and man. In that day Jesus will rule as Governor Among The Nations.

APPENDIX Chapter 9

9.1 HOLY

The computer concordance indicates that there are 430 occurrences of the term "holy" in the O.T.[183] translated from various Hebrew words as shown in Table A.9.1.

Table A.9.1

Hebrew Words Translated Into The English Word Holy

Occurrence	Hebrew (Word SRN / Meaning)	
5	chaciyd (SRN 2623)	kind, pious, godly, holy (one), saint
3	miqdash (SRN 4720)	a consecrated thing, holy place
102	qadowsh (SRN 6918)	sacred, God, an angel, a saint, holy (One), a sanctuary
7	qaddiysh (SRN 6922)	holy (One), saint
7	qadash (SRN 6942)	Pri. Root, to be clean consecrate, hallow, to be or keep holy, sanctify
301	qodesh (SRN 6944)	a sacred place or thing, consecrated, holy thing
5	With SRN Unassigned.	Two of these have been identified, MAQDISHIYM, QADASHIYM. See (Neh. 12:47; Eze. 20:40)

[183] The 430 occurrences are contained in 375 verses, 324 single applications per verse, 48 verses with two applications per verse, two verses with three applications per verse and one verse with four (324+ 96+6+4 = 430).

APPENDIX Chapter 9

It can be seen that 6 Hebrew words (with SRN identifications) plus 5 other occurrences (with no SRN I.D.) are all translated into a form of the English word "holy." It is to be noted that these same Hebrew words are also translated into other English words such as sanctuary, halloed, chapel, etc., in verses other than the ones of concern here, namely those containing the word holy. The existing challenge is to determine whether or not the English word holy is applied in the OT as a stand alone name of deity.

For example, by asking the computer to look in detail at SRN 2633 it has been determined that this Hebrew word, chaciyd, is translated into the English words saints, merciful, godly and good in addition to the word holy, as demonstrated in the following tabulation:

Deu. 33:8	holy one	meaning high priest	not a name of deity
Psa. 16:10	the Holy One	meaning Jesus Christ	the Holy One is a name
Psa. 86:2	holy	meaning God fearing	not a divine name
Psa. 89:19	the holy one	meaning faithful servants	holy one is not a name
Psa. 145:17	holy	meaning gracious/kind	not a divine name

In summary, the Hebrew word chaciyd (SRN 2623) can be translated into English as the name "the Holy One" and is considered a name of deity.[184] The other

[184] The single Hebrew word translates into the English words The Holy One, which are not a searched for stand alone.

four cases involving the word holy do not produce either stand alone or compound names of deity.

The application of chaciyd Psa. 145:17 in classed as an adjective describing attributes of the LORD, who is holy, gracious and kind in all His works. Therefore, holy is not perceived as a name of deity there. This adjective relationship will soon be encountered again.

Repeating this investigative process on the second Hebrew word, "miqdash" (SRN 4720, Table A.9.1), reveals that it has been translated into English words relating to a consecrated thing or place. So the Hebrew when rendered into English produces such verbs as dedicate, consecrate and a comparative, holier. The SRN 4720 word is translated into the English word holy in only three OT verses (Psa. 68:35; Eze. 21:2; and Eze. 45:4), and none of these terms are names of deity.

Looking at the third Hebrew word "qadowsh or qadosh." (SRN 6918), we find that it has been translated into the English words Holy, the Holy One, the Holy One of Israel and the Holy One of Jacob. In addition this Hebrew word has been translated into several other related terms, such as Saint and Saints.[185] In the OT this word (SRN 6918) is translated into modifiers of the word holy 61 times, the compound expression the Holy One appears 9 times, the phrase the Holy One of Israel 31 times and the

---

[185] Quadosh is translated into the word "saint" three times and into "saints" nine times. These are not applicable to this study at this time.

phrase the Holy One of Jacob only once. Careful attention will now be given to these English translations in order to extract those which are names of deity.

Let us consider the usage of the word holy or Holy. Sixty-one cases apply the word to the nation, the place of worship, groups of people, single individuals and certain special places or locations, none of which are names of deity. There is, in addition, a group of 18 uses of Holy that single out that characteristic and extremely important attribute of God but are not to be considered a name.

These 18 verses that contain the English word holy, translated from the Hebrew word qadowsh or qadosh (SRN 6918), are identified in the following Table:

Table A.9.2

The English Word Holy Translated From The Hebrew SRN 6918

Reference		**Word holy Usage**
1. Lev. 11:44	"I am holy"	Adjective
2. Lev. 11:45	"I am holy"	Adjective
3. Lev. 19:2	"I...am holy"	Adjective
4. Lev. 20:26	"I...am holy"	Adjective
5. Lev. 21:8	"I...am holy"	Adjective
6. Jos. 24:19	"He is a holy God"	Adjective
7. 1Sa. 2:2	"holy as the LORD"	Adjective
8. 1Sa. 6:20	"holy LORD God"	Adjective
9. Psa. 22:3	"thou art holy"	Adjective
10. Psa. 99:3	"name is holy"	Adjective
11. Psa. 99:5	"for He is holy"	Adjective

Table A.9.2 (Continued)

12. Psa. 99:9	"our God is holy"	Adjective
13. Psa. 111:9	"holy...is His name"	Adjective
14. Pro. 9:10	"knowledge of the holy"	*Noun
15. Pro. 30:3	"knowledge of the holy"	*Noun
16. Isa. 5:16	"God that is holy"	Adjective
17. Isa. 6:3	"Holy, holy, holy is the LORD"	Adjective
18. Isa. 57:15	"whose name is holy"	*Noun/Adjective

*Highlighted Applications

In this listing the word holy appears in fifteen different Scripture verses used as an adjective modifying the noun "God." These verses simply exclaim the truth that the LORD or the LORD God is holy, or set apart and far above all else. This is one of His major attributes, and certainly none of His characteristics are more important. However, even though the word holy appears to serve as an adjective in most of the above occasions, remember that a name of deity also generally defines a characteristic, quality or attribute of God. From this perspective, since holiness is a characteristic of God, it follows that holy is a name of God.

This adjective argument is reasonably satisfying except for the above three highlighted applications. Consider these in the following manner. The Hebrew word qadosh (SRN 6918) has been translated into only six English words or phrases (see Table A.9.1). Two of these are Holy (holy) and the Holy One. Upon examining in detail

APPENDIX Chapter 9

Pro. 9:10, the first highlighted word reads in the KJV[186], "The fear of the LORD is the beginning of wisdom: and the knowledge of the holy is understanding." Looking at other Bible versions of this Proverb, the following is observed:

Beck (1976 Ed.)	the Holy One
Jer (1966 Ed.)	the Holy One
KJV (1984 Ed.)	the Holy
KJV (1909-1917 Ed.)	the Holy
NKJV (1967 Ed.)	the Holy One
TLB (1973 Ed.)	God
NAS (1975 Ed.)	the Holy One
NEB (1976 Ed.)	the Holy One
NIV (1978 Ed.)	the Holy One
NRSV (1991 Ed.)	the Holy One

Scrutiny of the above Scripture information indicates that there is not a complete consensus of agreement on the word holy (SRN 6918). Seven of the versions agree with the "Holy One." The KJV (2 Editions) and The Living Bible apply different terms. It is also interesting to note that the NKJV (1967 Ed.) has updated to Holy One but a new

[186] Scofield, Ed., 1909/1917; Collins & Co. Ed., 1959 and others.

edition of the KJV (1984 Ed) has not. It appears that the Editor/Publisher popular vote is to translate it as the Holy One. Accepting this as correct, the author immediately selects "the Holy One" as a name of God and excludes the word Holy as a divine name.[187]

But there is more to this argument. The Hebrew word in question is plural in form (q'doshiym), like the word Elohim. If the word was singular it might be an adjective. The plural form is referred to by some gramarians as an honorific plural. In this forum the word functions like a noun, not an adjective.

Now look in the KJV (Pro. 30:3) at "I neither learned wisdom, nor have the knowledge of the holy." Even though the term holy is from the same Hebrew word that was used in Prov. 9:10 it is prudent to check again several Scripture versions/translations for variations of the word "holy."[188]

---

[187] The retention of the Holy rather than the Holy One in the KJV occurs as a possible continuation of an earlier error.
[188] Bruce Waltke actually includes this verse (Prov. 9:10) as an example of this usage. For him the proper translation can only be "the Holy One." See his Biblical Hebrew Syntax, Eisenbrauns, 1990, pp. 122-123.

Beck (1976 Ed.)	the Holy One
Jer (1966 Ed.)	*the Holy Ones (plural of majesty)
KJV (1984 Ed.)	the Holy
KJV (1909-1917 Ed.)	the holy
NKJV (1967 Ed.)	the Holy One
TLB (1973 Ed.)	God
NAS (1975 Ed.)	the Holy One
NEB (1976 Ed.)	the Holy One
NIV (1978 Ed.)	the Holy One
RSV (1991 Ed.)	the Holy One

*Highlighted applications

Once more the expected variations between versions are observed with a single additional change in the Jerusalem version. The final result of the study of this is word in Pro. 30:3 is that the word "holy" is again used in the KJV (1909-1917 Ed.) as a name of deity; English usage requires that it be rendered as a compound name, the Holy One, which is found in most of the recent English translations.

A third possible application of the word Holy as a divine name translated from the Hebrew qadosh appears in the Scripture verse Isa. 57:15. In the KJV (1909-

1917 Ed.), this reads in part as follows: "For thus saith the high and lofty One that inhabiteth eternity, whose name is Holy..." The Scripture versions previously examined indicate the following English variations of the word Holy in this verse:

Beck (1976 Ed.)	holy
Jer (1966 Ed.)	holy
KJV (1984 Ed.)	Holy
KJV (1909-1917 Ed.)	Holy
NKJV (1967 Ed.)	Holy
TLB (1973 Ed.)	the Holy One
NAS (1975 Ed.)	Holy
NEB (1976 Ed.)	holy
NIV (1978 Ed.)	holy
RSV (1991 Ed.)	Holy

The previously observed variations and lack of agreement as to application or meaning of the word holy again occurs. This time the Hebrew word is in singular form. It appears that the rival possibilities of accepting the word as either a noun or an adjective compete here on almost equal terms. The noun agreement sees a metaphor wherein God's name is Holy, that is, He is known by this identifier. The adjective argument applies the word holy in a simple descriptive statement, that is another way of saying that He has a holy name. We, in this study, accept the word to mean Holy, a noun. It is a stand alone name of deity.

The summary of all this detail reveals that in only three cases is the word Holy considered a noun and a stand alone name of God. This is important in that not only is the word "holy" commonly used in compound names, as we shall subsequently see, it is also a stand alone name in its own right.

Looking back again to Table A.9.1, we find that the fourth Hebrew word is translated into the two words holy and saints. This is the word qaddiysh (SRN 6922). It is found in Scripture only in that portion of the Book of Daniel that is written in Aramaic.[189] It may be of more than academic interest to observe that qaddiysh is translated into the English word holy seven times[190], four of which speak of holy gods. But these are not verses talking about the Holy Spirit of God; no, the pantheon of heathen gods is spoken about by the king, who also includes in his thinking all that he knows of the true God of Daniel. Obviously, these writings to not contain names of our God. These three uses of the word holy relate to the "watchers" or holy ones. These

---

[189] Daniel 2:4 through 7:28 was written in Aramaic, the international language of that period. International commerce and diplomacy used that language in a way that is similar to the international use of English today.

[190] Qaddiysh is also translated into the English word saints six times in the Aramaic portion of the book of Daniel but this is of no significance in this study.

seem to be supernatural messengers, perhaps angels; once again, the facts do not suggest that they are divine names.

Table A.9.1 lists a fifth Hebrew word, the verb qadash (SRN 6942), that is sometimes translated to be holy. Qadash is a primary root word expressing the idea of being pure or devoted to God, and as such, it has been translated into a multiplicity of English words. Phrases like to be clean, to make clean, to make oneself clean, to pronounce clean, to hallow, to dedicate, to sanctify, to purify, to be consecrated, to be holy are all derived from this root. Indeed, some 19 different English words in 173 places in the OT have been discovered as direct translations from qadash, and there may be others. Among this assortment, the English word "holy" appears six times.[191] However, in none of these applications is qadash translated to mean or indicate a name of god.

Reverting back to Table A.9.1 once more presents the Hebrew word qodesh (SRN 6944) for consideration. This Hebrew word is a noun derived from the primary root word qadash (SRN 6942). Qodesh has been translated into nine different English words, which are distributed throughout the OT. Scriptures in 384 verses.[192] Of these,

---

[191] Qadash is translated using the English word "holy" in the following verses: Exo. 20:8; 30:29; Lev. 6:18, 27; Isa. 30:29; and in Hag. 2:12.

[192] The Hebrew word qodesh has been translated into the following English words: Holy, Holiness, Most Holy, Hallowed, Saints, Sanctuary, Consecrated and Dedicated.

235 verses contain the word holy at least once; these are concentrated upon for examination as possible containers of deity names.

Leviticus, Psalms and Ezekiel all contain at least one verse worthy of attention as we seek to determine whether this word "holy" might be considered merely as adjective or a name.[193] For example, in Lev. 20:3 the KJV text reads, "I will set my face against that man, and will cut him off from among his people, because he hath given of his seed to Molech, to defile my sanctuary and to profane my holy name." In the phrase "to profane my holy name," consider this proposal. "My holy name" refers to the LORD. Therefore, "my holy name" is an identifier of the LORD and the phrase becomes a name of deity.

Look at Psa. 106:47 for another example of this prospective name. "Save us, O LORD our God, and gather us from among the heathen, to give thanks unto thy holy name, and to triumph in thy praise." The phrase "thy holy name" is an identifier of the LORD our God and is therefore a name of deity. There are several verses of this type in the OT, and they are interesting to consider and wonder about. Actually, all of these unusual applications are probably intended to be simple descriptive statements. "My holy name" means my sacred or set apart name; likewise, "thy holy name" is intended to be read, your sacred or set apart name. However, it makes for interesting thinking.

---

[193] Lev. 20:3; 22:2; 32; Psa. 103:1; 105:3; 106:47 and 145:21; Eze. 39:7.

APPENDIX Chapter 9

For this manuscript, the word "holy" as translated from the Hebrew word qodesh (SRN 6944) will not be considered to be a name of deity in spite of the argument given above.

It should be mentioned in passing that Holy, as in Holy Spirit or Holy One, translated from qodesh or qadesh, is applied in several other verses and will be given careful consideration at the proper time.

All of the Hebrew words of Table A.9.1 have been considered with regard to the application of the single word Holy (holy) as a possible name of deity. Interestingly enough the 430 occurrences of Holy (holy) translated from the six Hebrew words produce only three prospective examples in the newer KJV (1984 Ed.) and two examples in the older (1909-17 Ed.). In the other tabulated Scripture versions, the possible name "holy" gives way to the more modern and preferred usage of the compound name "the Holy One."

APPENDIX Chapter 9

9.2 HOLY ONE

The computer indicates there are 45 applications of the words, the holy one. All are translated from one or more of the three Hebrew words SRN 2623, 6918 or 6922 which are identified in Table A.9.1. In addition to the 45 listed under this rendering there are other English translations of this word with their own examples. For instance, the Hebrew word chaciyd (SRN 2623) is translated into "saints" 19 times, into "merciful" three times, into "godly" three times, into "holy" two times, into "holy one" three times and into "good" once. In Deu. 33:8 we find the compound word "holy one," but applied to a priest. Obviously this is not a name of God.

Examining a second use SRN 2623 found in Psa. 89:19, the translation holy one is present, but it relates to faithful ones or faithful servants or godly ones. Some Scripture translations even suggest that this term applies to Samuel and Nathan. Once again, we are not arriving at a name of God.

However, looking at the third application of the term. "holy one," found in Psa. 16:10, the consensus of opinion in the literature identifies this Holy One to be Jesus Christ; here, of course, we have a name of God. Interestingly enough, these three applications are the only translations of the Hebrew word chaciyd into the English term "holy one."

Now look at the Hebrew word qaddiysh (SRN 6922). This word is translated into the English "holy one" in only two places, both of them in that portion of Daniel written in

Aramaic (Dan. 2:4-7:28). In neither of the applications is holy one considered to be a name of God.

At this point it is appropriate to pause and take a brief inventory of the two Hebrew words that have been considered. The word chaciyd (SRN 2623) is translated once as the name of God, "Holy One." The word qaddiysh (SRN 6922) is not found as the name of God, "Holy One."

Proceeding now to the third Hebrew word qadosh SRN 6918), we find that eight times the English compound term "Holy One" is translated from qadosh as a name of God. These eight are separated from a usage population including the Holy One of Israel, the Holy One of Jacob and the stand alone name, the Holy One. It should be noticed that even though the more complex expressions contain the words the Holy One as a part of their make up, these complex compounds, yet to be considered, require additional words to form a name of God. Of course the simpler expression Holy One is found as a name of God. This expansion of the basic name "holy" into the compound name "the Holy One" and then into "the Holy One of Israel" is interesting, but is not unique in the OT. Such expansions will be observed with many other names in this study.

The following Table A.9.3 displays the arrangement and locations of the words that are translated holy one.

Table A. 9.3

Holy One Locations

No. & Reference	2623	4720	6918	6922	6942	6944
01 Deu. 33:8	4					
02 2Ki. 19:22			2			
03 Job 6:10			1			
04 Psa. 16:10	3					
05 Psa. 71:22			2			
06 Psa. 78:41			2			
07 Psa. 89:18			2			
08 Psa. 89:19	4					
09 Isa. 1:4			2			
10 Isa. 5:19			2			
11 Isa. 5:24			2			
12 Isa. 10:17			1			
13 Isa. 10:20			2			
14 Isa. 12:6			2			
15 Isa. 17:7			2			
16 Isa. 29:19			2			
17 Isa. 29:23			5			
18 Isa. 30:11			2			
19 Isa. 30:12			2			
20 Isa. 30:15			2			

Table A.9.3 (Continued)

Holy One Locations

No. & Reference	2623	4720	6918	6922	6942	6944
21 Isa. 31:1			2			
22 Isa. 37:23			2			
23 Isa. 40:25			1			
24 Isa. 41:14			2			
25 Isa. 41:16			2			
26 Isa. 41:20			2			
27 Isa. 43:3			2			
28 Isa. 43:14			2			
29 Isa. 43:15			1			
30 Isa. 45:11			2			
31 Isa. 47:4			2			
32 Isa. 48:17			2			
33 Isa. 49:7			2 + 1			
34 Isa. 54:5			2			
35 Isa. 55:5			2			
36 Isa. 60:9			2			
37 Isa. 60:14			2			
38 Jer. 50:29			2			
39 Jer. 51:5			2			
40 Eze. 39:7			6			
41 Dan. 4:13			7			
42 Dan. 4:23				7		
43 Hos. 11:9			1			
44 Hab. 1:12			1			
45 Hab. 3:3			1			

APPENDIX Chapter 9

Identification Coding for Table A.9.3

1. Holy One
2. the Holy One of Israel
3. holy one (a Priest)
4. The Holy One of Jacob
5. the Holy One in Israel
6. holy one (a Watcher), a servant of the Most High, possibly an Angel

Table A.9.3 exhibits 45 applications of the compound expression holy one. In addition there is one multiple (Listing No. 33 or Isa. 49:7) wherein the names the Holy One of Israel and the Holy One both appear. This makes the Table display a total of 46 entries including the Holy One 9 times and the compound name, the Holy One of Israel 31 times. In addition, holy one (Priest) appears twice, holy one (Watcher) appears twice, the Holy One of Jacob appears once and the name the Holy One is Israel appears once.

The Particular Aspect of God's Character highlighted.

The name of God "the Holy One" highlights God's unique and essential characteristic or attribute of separateness in the sense that He is the One set apart from and above all other known things in the universe; He is the Creator set apart from the creation. Furthermore, He is the One separate from all sin and evil, the One who is separated by His infinite and absolute perfection.

APPENDIX Chapter 9

The Special Need of Man Met by the Revelation of this Aspect of God's Character.

In observing the use of this name of God, "the Holy One," it is obvious that other synonyms for God could have been appropriately applied. However, the Holy Spirit seems to select this name to remind the readers of Scripture, as well as the writers, that God is who He is, the all Powerful, the Supreme and Set Apart One, who is nevertheless willing and longing to be involved in the affairs of men and women in order to teach them of the necessity of holiness in their relationship toward God and, ultimately, to make them conform to His holiness through the redemptive plan He revealed through His prophets.

APPENDIX Chapter 10

10.3 KING

The study of the term "king" presents interesting applications of a word that usually implies sovereign direction, control or leadership by a male ruler. The word king may be in compound with other adjectives or epithets in order to be more precise, in identification or the word may exist as a stand alone identifier. This means that the word, with or without other modifiers, is obviously a name, title or appellation of deity. The term king, when used as a stand alone, is presented in the application sentence structure in a manner intended to clearly identify characteristics, privilege, distinction, claim or right to kingship.

In the considerations of the term "king" we will look first at the single stand alone word. Then we will examine the compound applications wherein the word king must be present in the compound phrase in order to produce the title or name.[194]

Then word "king" is very prominent in the OT. The concordance indicates there are 1677 verses that contain the term king one or more times. The vast majority of these are rulers not of interest in this study, since we are concerned only with those occurrences that use the word king in a manner that applies it to deity. However, there

[194] The names King of Glory, King of Heaven, King of Israel, King of Jacob, King of Nations and King over all the world have arbitrarily been removed from this discussion of the name "King." Each of the compounds have been placed in an adjoining independent and separate section.

are 26 such verses in the AV where deity and the word king interrelate. These are listed below in Table A.10.1 for further consideration.

Table A.10.1

Listing Of The "King" Passages That Apply To Deity

No.	Verse	Application Phrase	Type of Usage
01	Psa. 2:6	My King (Messiah)	stand alone
02	Psa. 5:2	my King & my God	stand alone with Per. Pron.
03	Psa. 10:16	the Lord is King	stand alone
04	Psa. 29:10	enthroned as King	stand alone
05	Psa. 44:4	my King & my God	stand alone with Per. Pron.
06	Psa. 45:1	the King (Messiah)	stand alone
07	Psa. 45:11	the King	stand alone for "the" King
08	Psa 47:6	to God & to King	stand alone couplet
09	Psa. 48:2	the great King	stand alone with adj.
10	Psa. 68:24	my God, My King	stand alone
11	Psa. 74:12	God is my King	stand alone metaphor
12	Psa. 84:3	LORD, my King	stand alone with Per. Pron
13	Psa. 95:3	LORD is a great God and a great King	stand alone
14	Psa. 98:6	the LORD, the King	stand alone
15	Psa. 145:1	my God, the King	stand alone
16	Isa. 6:5	the King, the LORD	stand alone
17	Isa. 33:17	see the King (Messiah)	stand alone
18	Isa. 33:22	the LORD is our King	metaphor
19	Isa. 43:15	the LORD, your King	stand alone

Table A.10.1 (Continued)

20	Jer. 10:10	everlasting King	stand alone
21	Jer. 46:18	King, LORD of hosts	stand alone
22	Jer. 48:15	King, LORD of hosts	stand alone
23	Jer. 51:57	King, LORD of hosts	stand alone
24	Zec. 14:16	King, LORD of hosts	stand alone
25	Zed. 14:17	King, LORD of hosts	stand alone
26	Mal. 1:14	King, LORD of hosts	stand alone

As an example of the application of the information in Table A.10.1 let us select at random line item Number 3, Psa. 10:16, for detailed consideration. This is viewed as a "stand alone," name.

Psa. 10:16. "The LORD is King for ever and ever: the heathen are perished out of his land." First, look at the phrase, "the LORD is King". This is a statement wherein the LORD is recognized as actually being sovereign. The people could well relate to this expression, for an earthly king who was now ruling in their land, exercising all of the many kingship qualities, responsibilities and obligations was understood by the people. But in addition to a localized reign, as on earth, this King is the LORD with all power and all might, not just for the present but for ever and ever.

Consider now, a second example, line item number 16.

Isa. 6:5 "Then said I, Woe is me! for I am undone, because I am a man of unclean lips, and I dwell in the midst of a people of unclean lips: for mine eyes have seen the King, the LORD of hosts." Again, especially consider the phrase "the King, the LORD of hosts." In this case the name of the King and hence His epithetical identity is given. He is King. Wherever the name "the LORD of hosts" occurs, the discussion is about "the King."

Let us look at one more example, line item number 2.

Psa. 5:2 "Hearken unto the voice of my cry, my King and my God: for unto thee will I pray." In this prayer for guidance David characteristically addresses his one God with two of His names, Elohim and King, in a phrase equating the names, thereby allowing other readers to think of God as King wherever the name God is encountered.

The Particular Aspect of God's Character Highlighted:

"God is highlighted as King" whether He is referred to as God, Yahweh, the Lord of hosts or Elohim. He made the earth and all that is contained therein and has every right to be called "the King." He is the rightful, sovereign ruler and will, in the course of time, rule over all. At that time, contrary to now, all His subjects will be willing and happy people, rejoicing and worshipping the King who is God.

The Special Need Of Man Met By The Revelation Of This Aspect Of His Character.

Man is inherently rebellious and defiant of outside authority over his actions and deeds. Man says, "I will rule my own heart and life," refusing to allow his Maker to have His rightful place as King of the heart. All men would be in this state except for the work of Christ in the hearts of the children of God and the witnessing of the indwelling Holy Spirit that Jesus is King. The child of God knows that Jesus is King but needs constant reminding of this true fact. The person outside of God who does not accept who the real King is, even more, must have repeated directions toward the King.

12.2 LORD

As the Text discussion has shown YHWH=Yahweh is sometimes transliterated directly into English documents even though it is normally translated into the word LORD. Is that important? Isn't it true that to say LORD is to imply Yahweh and to say Yahweh is to say GOD and to say GOD is to say Yahweh? It is not possible to appreciate the character of GOD without giving careful attention to its details. So, to be consistent with the intent of this manuscript, some little effort will be expended to discuss the character of Yahweh. This will be done by excerpting appropriate comments from the writing of Nathan Stone.[195]

At the start it should be mentioned that Yahweh has no beginning, for He is absolutely self-existent and continuous, possessing essential life forever. He is Savior, for Isaiah writes (43:10-11) that besides Yahweh the LORD there is no Savior. Yahweh, the proper name, discloses the person of the true and living God of Israel. He is especially the God of revelation and redemption to His creatures, who are able to apprehend and appreciate the infinite. Elohim is the general name of God concerned with the creation and preservation of the universe, that is, His works. But as Yahweh He is the God of revelation in the expression of Himself in His essential moral and spiritual attributes. Elohim assumes a love towards all creation. Yahweh reveals the

---

[195] Nathan Stone, *Names of God*, Moody Press, Chicago, C.R., 1944, p. 18-29.

enjoyment His love as conditioned upon conforming to His moral and spiritual requirements. He gives His people these obligations with warnings of punishment for disobedience. In the OT perhaps the two greatest attributes associated with the name Yahweh are righteousness and holiness. A righteous Yahweh, whose holiness is violated and outraged, must condemn unrighteousness and punish it. So it is Yahweh who pronounces judgment and metes out punishment. But as Yahweh, God is also love. When the nation Israel forsook the LORD and served the elohims of the peoples about them, the anger of Yahweh brought grievous punishment upon them. But the same Yahweh loves His own, and He can not give them up; He will not forsake the fallen man, for He loves and He redeems. True, His Spirit continues to strive with man, but as Yahweh He manifests Himself in covenants and acts of deliverance and redemption. Perhaps the character of God, as contained in the name Yahweh, can best be glimpsed in Exodus 34:5-7, "And the LORD descended in the cloud, and stood with him there, and proclaimed the name of the LORD. And the LORD passed by before him, and proclaimed, The LORD, The LORD God, merciful and gracious, long-suffering, and abundant in goodness and truth."

APPENDIX Chapter 12

12.5 The Compounds

As we begin to study the compound names in the LORD/Lord/lord series, let us remember that a compound of LORD or Lord may increase the intensity of the name, that either the name LORD or Lord can stand alone, and that the compounds are always names of God applied for a particular purpose. However, we must be careful of the name lord, because on occasion lord applies not to man but to God.

We will organize the assortment of compound names into groups. This will allow easier name comparison. For example, we will compare the compound "LORD God of hosts" with "Lord GOD of hosts." What are the differences in these similar names? Do specific compound names in one group, for example, names that are based on LORD, always have corresponding compound names with each of the other principle names (Lord and lord)?

First let us review the names in Table 12.1, noting that this list is primarily composed of compound names with LORD. However, since some consideration has already been given to this list it is a good place to begin our compound study, expanding into the other names when desirable. The listings in Table 12.1 are rearranged and supplemented, as necessary for the convenience of the Group consideration approach.

APPENDIX Chapter 12

Group 1

First we establish Group 1 by appropriate expansion of Table A.12.1 and selection of the first 6 members of that Table for the first Group study. This approach produces the following:

Table A.12.1 with Expansion and Reorganization

Name	**Ref.**	**Comments**
LORD God (Yahweh Elohim)	Gen. 2:4	
Lord GOD (Adonai Yahweh)	Gen. 15:2	
LORD of hosts	1Sa. 1:3	
Lord of hosts	special	
LORD God of hosts	2Sa. 5:10	
Lord GOD of hosts	Psa. 69:6	
LORD Who Heals	Exo. 15:26	Rophe
LORD Who Sanctifies	Lev. 20:8	M'Kaddesh
LORD OUR RIGHTEOUSNESS	Jer. 23:6	Tskidkenu
LORD Our Shepherd	Eze. 34:15	Rohi
LORD is Present (literally there)	Eze. 48:35	Shammah
LORD will Provide	Gen. 22:14	Jehovah-jireh
LORD Our Banner	Exo. 17:15	Jehovah-nissi
LORD is Peace	Jdg. 6:24	Jehovah-shalom

APPENDIX Chapter 12

The first six listed names are selected and identified as Group 1. Now we will compare these members in a limited number (5) of Scripture versions. To assist in the examination the SRN identifications are also given in the Name column. The results are displayed in Table A.12.2.

Table A.12.2

Group 1

(LORD God vs. Lord GOD)

Name	Initial Ref.	KJV.	NIV.	JER.	NAS.	NEB.
LORD God 3068 430	Gen. 2:4	the LORD God	LORD God	Yahweh God	LORD God	THE LORD GOD
Lord GOD 136 3068	Gen. 15:2	Lord GOD	Sovereign LORD	Lord Yahweh	Lord GOD	Lord GOD
LORD of 3068 hosts	1Sa. 1:3	LORD of hosts	LORD Almighty	Yahweh Saboath	LORD of hosts	LORD of Hosts
Lord of 136 hosts	none (special)					
LORD God 3068 430 of hosts	2Sa. 5:10	LORD God of hosts	LORD God Almighty	Yahweh, God of Saboath	LORD God of hosts	the LORD the God of
Lord GOD 136 3068 of hosts	Psa. 69:6	Lord GOD of hosts	LORD Almighty	Yahweh Saboath	Lord GOD of hosts	Lord GOD of Hosts

Consider the first member of Group 1, "the LORD God." This initial compound name is introduced in Gen. 2:4. The compound appears in this form in 3 of the 5 compared /Scripture versions of Table A.12.2. The Jerusalem Bible characteristically transliterates the name the LORD as the Tetragrammaton Yahweh. This gives us Yahweh God for the compound. The NEB fully translates the compound name as THE LORD GOD.

Now look at the second member of this group, Lord GOD. Here again three of the five versions agree on name format. Again the Jerusalem Bible continues to use the transliteration, Yahweh, instead of the English word LORD, while the NIV translates "Sovereign LORD."

Carefully consider these two compound names. Why do we find the name "LORD" (Yahweh) "God" (Elohim), yet a few chapters further, in Genesis 15:2, we encounter the compound "Lord" (Adonai) "GOD" (Yahweh)?

God (Elohim) made the earth and all that it contains. Every herb and tree, all the beasts in the fields, the foul of the air, the fish of the deep and all things that creep upon the earth—all these that have life God fashioned. Then the LORD God formed man in His own image out of the dust of the earth and breathed into his nostrils the breath of life; and man became a living soul. Before the creation of man it was the (generic) triune God, Elohim, who created everything, and all was good. But at the creation of man it was the LORD God, Yahweh Elohim who was involved. Elohim is known for His unconditional love, which He offers to repentant sinners as a benefit of a[196] covenant relationship. But there is another aspect here. With the arrival of man on the scene, Yahweh in His holiness, truth and righteousness provides immediate commands for man, and man is placed under God's law with its "Thou shalt" and "Thou shalt not." Elohim provided unconditional love, but Yahweh provided limiting conditions with a warning and a threat that disobedience must surely bring judgment. Both of these aspects of the God-head are continually intermingled, yet always with a purpose to bring out something distinctive in our God, the knowledge of which adds to His people's strength or gladness.

Now look again at the second compound name in Group 1, "Lord GOD." Lord is translated from the Hebrew word adōnay. When used among men, the related term adōn relates to the servant and his master, the wife to her husband or the relationship of one who is superior to another more inferior. When 'adōnāy is used, addressing deity, the concept of Master remains, with the idea of man's relationship of dependence upon God paramount. Then the English translation becomes "O Lord" or "My Lord", always applying only to deity. The application of the compound expression, "Lord LORD" (Adonai Yahweh), while maintaining the special meaning of each component of the name, will be found to emphasize the Adonai rather than the Yahweh character of deity.

---

196 Note: Ancient Judaism derived the opposite interpretation from the same data. Yahweh was associated with mercy, and Elohim was associated with judgment. While these findings probably resulted

Each of the two compounds are considered distinct and separate names, with each being distinctively applied in the Scriptures.

We will now consider the compounds relating to the word "hosts." This term has previously been studied (see Chapter 7). Therefore only a brief summary will be presented here. Hosts are generally understood to be heavenly and primarily angelic; however, there is some argument that heavenly bodies, such as the stars, might be included. The term carries the idea of divine or heavenly power as exercised by God for the needs of His people, particularly as the elect have experienced corporate or national failure and grief because of sin and disobedience. Hosts (or "the" hosts) occurs as an epithet in such expressions as LORD of hosts or God of hosts. As such the phrase is a possessive genitive, designating God as the Supreme Head and Commander of all heavenly forces (1Ki. 22:19).

It is the intent now to present the argument that the remaining four expressions in Table A.12.1 containing the term host are all names of God.

Argument:

The words LORD and Lord have previously been considered in this manuscript, and the reasons have been presented that validate them as names of God. Adding the title God to the name LORD produces the first compound name, LORD God (Heb.

---

from smoothing of the data (to borrow a statistical notion), there is good reason to agree with that interpretation.

Yahweh Elohim), which speaks of two of the major qualities of God: First, as Elohim, we are assured of His unconditional love by virtue of His relationship to His people. Secondly, with Yahweh, we are reminded of the limiting conditions of reward and penalty connected with judgment for sin and disobedience. This compound name is first observed in Gen. 2:4.

Then by further augmenting the compound name LORD God with the genitive expression "of Hosts," the name "LORD God of Hosts" is produced. Initially this compound name occurs in 2Sa. 5:10.

Now consider the third compound name in our argument, "Lord GOD" (note the reversal of application of upper and lower case letters). The word Lord and GOD are respectively translated from the Hebrew words 'adōnāy and Yahweh in that order. As has been seen earlier, the term Lord implies total dependence of the servant upon God the Master and, in return, complete obedience of the servant to the Master. GOD in this expression is a substitution for Yahweh, the only self-proclaimed personal name of God in Israel's faith. This substitution was intended to avoid an awkward duplication since the Jews usually replaced the name Yahweh with 'adōnāy, which is already present in this compound name, readers of the Hebrew scriptures found themselves referring to God as Adonay Adonay. In the Septuagint, the Greek translation of the OT, more than 50 verses have this doublet, Lord Lord (see, for example, Eze. 12:10; 14:6). Before the translators finished their project they began substituting God for the second Adonay (see, for example, Eze. 43:18 and Amos 1:8). That substitution was much more acceptable to religious Jews. Not to be outdone in the Jewish homeland and in the dispersed Jewish communities in Mesopotamia, where an Aramaic paraphrase of the OT was regularly read in the synagogues, rather than accept the rendering Lord Lord they regularly made written substitutions for both halves of the name, writing instead Yahweh Elohim. Of course, then they uttered this name they said Adonay Elohim instead. Over 200 examples of this practice are preserved on these Aramaic translations, the Targums. We should not be surprised that these ancient traditions have been honored and imitated by the translators of our English bibles.

Here again we can add the genitive "of hosts" and produce Lord GOD of hosts, the fourth compound name in our argument.

Now let us hurry on to complete Group one. We find that the compound names the LORD our Maker and LORD Most High included in the set. Both of these names have been detailed in Chapters 1 and 2. Further consideration is not necessary here.

Group 1, as listed in Table 12.1, deals with the name LORD and the supplemental English words to produce the first five compound divine names, which are found in the lifestyle listing of Christian growth. The details of these names are found in Chapter 3, Tables 3.1 and 3.2.

APPENDIX Chapter 12

The application of the word Jehovah (YHWH erroneously) is transliterated in combination with select Hebrew words, produces three more compound names of God. These are listed below for convenience, since they are discussed in Chapter 3.

Finally, let us mention the four additional applications of the word Jehovah. These should be observed in conjunction with the Jehovah transliteration list in order to carefully account for all of the seven names of Jehovah that appear in the AV of the OT.

The five names of God relating to Christian character growth are:

the LORD Who Heals

the LORD Our Righteousness

the LORD Who Sanctifies

the LORD Who is Present

LORD our Shepherd

The three Names from Hebrew in transliteration are:

Jehovah jireh	LORD will Provide
Jehovah nissi	LORD Our Banner
Jehovah shalom	LORD is Peace

The locations of the four additional Jehovah Words are:

Exo. 6:3, Psa. 83:18, Isa. 12:2; 26:4.

Group 2

Additional "LORD" Compound Considerations:

LORD: (SRN 3068) Names:

In comparison to the relative large quantity of names in the Group 1 aggregation, the Group 2 list, relating to "LORD," are few and easy to substantiate. These are shown below:

Name	Ref.	Comments
the LORD, the God of heaven	Gen. 24:3; Jonah 1:9	
the LORD God of heaven	Gen. 24:7; 2Ch. 36:23	
	Ezr. 1:2; Neh. 1:5	
the LORD God of Israel	Exo. 5:1	(there are 107 ref.)
the LORD, the God of heaven and the God of the Earth		Gen. 24:3

There are three names, almost phrases, that describe certain characteristics of the LORD. He is "the God of heaven," or with even more expansion, "the LORD, the God of heaven, and the God of the earth." These three genitive phrases each speak of the LORD in His possessive relationship to heaven and earth. Those present in heaven are now in complete accord and sphere with this One who is their Sovereign and their God, this one who is known as the LORD of heaven and earth. Of course, the LORD is possessively related to earth as well as to heaven. It is His now and forever, but only in God's time scale will his full possession be observable.

The fourth name in this series, "the LORD God of Israel," appears 107 times in the AV of the Old Testament. He is the LORD, Yahweh, the only true God of Israel. He is also, Elohim, the God of unconditional love to his creatures. This phrase, the LORD God of Israel is appropriate to express a name of the Supreme One who indeed is the LORD God of Israel.

Group 3

Special Compound Names With "LORD"

LORD (pronoun) God (i.e.: pronouns my, our, thy, your, their, his.)

The listed possessive pronouns are used to produce compound names of God in almost 600 cases in the AV of the OT.

Let us examine, for example, the name the LORD my God. LORD speaks of Yahweh, the One with divine self existence; Yahweh is the name of the only true God, in Israel's faith, and the One who loves but must mete out judgment to the disobedient and sinner, because He is Righteous, True and Holy.

The term God (or Elohim) speaks of the fullness of divine power. The name Elohim (God), with pronominal suffix, frequently occurs with Yahweh (LORD) to form a compound name of God. For example, the name "the LORD my God" is formed in this manner and is significantly frequent in the OT. Other possessive pronouns that form names of God are illustrated in the Table A.12.3.

Table A.12.3

The "LORD" (pronoun) God" Compound Names

Pronoun	**Applications**	**Formed Compound Name**
his	29 times	the LORD his God
my	38 times	LORD my God
our	94 times	LORD our God
their	38 times	the LORD their God
thy	253 times	the LORD thy God
your	143 times	the LORD your God

595 total applications in AV

While we are examining the pronominal suffix names of God, let us observe the special case occurring in Deu. 28:58 in the AV: "If thou wilt not observe to do all the words of this law that are written in this book, that thou mayest fear this glorious and fearful name, THE LORD THY GOD...." There is neither reason nor authority for capitalization of this name in the AV. It seems that translators through the years added this embellishment, because they felt the importance of the statement. The full capitalization of this name of God is unique. However, phrase or word capitalization for obscure reasons is not unique in the AV (Ref. Chap. 12 Text, page 190).

APPENDIX Chapter 12

During the search for compounds with the name LORD we find an unusual metaphor stated twice in the AV of the OT (Exo. 15:2, Psa. 118:14, "The LORD is my strength and song...."). Yahweh is represented as "strength" in a manner similar to the metaphor "The LORD is my Shepherd." Shepherd is a representation of the LORD. It is He who tends His people and does more for them than any earthly shepherd.

So the LORD is my Strength and Song is appropriate where strength carries the meaning of praise, majesty and security. And song implies praise with or without accompanying music. This phrase is interesting even though the metaphor is not counted as a name of God.

Group 4

Additional "Lord" Compound Considerations

Lord (SRN 113) Names:

Most of the genitive compound names of God in the form "Lord of__" or "Lord (pronoun) God," where deity is addressed, have been previously considered. However, there remain 5 names to be examined, as shown below:

Name	Ref.	Comments
the Lord of the whole earth	Psa. 97:5	English translation from adon
the Lord of all the earth	Jos. 3:11	Also from adon
the Lord of lords	Deu. 10:17	Honorific plural of adon
O Lord my God	Psa. 38:15	From adonay
the Lord our God	Dan. 9:9	From adonay

APPENDIX Chapter 12

First, consider the two phrases, the Lord of the whole earth and the Lord of all the earth. In the KJV, these two phrases are nearly the same. In the NIV version the two phrases are rendered exactly alike. The phrases simply state that the Lord or Master is the Owner of all the earth. Whereas He enjoys only a limited recognition of His sovereignty in this world today, there is coming a day when His ownership in scope and reality will be universally acknowledged. Some consider these phrases to be merely descriptive. However, these acclamations of the greatness of God ascribe to Him such supreme authority over the universe in such concise expressions that they become virtual names of God and are so counted in this manuscript.

Consider the name Lord of lords (Deu. 10:17; Psa. 136:1-3). Observe the contexts in which this name appears. In both passages He is called God of gods and Lord of lords. We are not interested in the referenced group of gods or lords. Rather these honorific titles serve to exalt the one and only God and Lord. In function the names "God of gods" and "Lord of lords" are the equivalent of "the LORD your God...a mighty God and a terrible..." (Deu. 7:21).

Then consider the two pronominal phrases, O Lord my God and O Lord our God. When we looked at the possessive pronouns combined with LORD (Yahweh) we observed that six different pronouns were involved in delineating the divine relationships with men. But with the name Lord ('aḏōnāy), we find only the first person singular and first person plural pronouns involved and with very limited applications in the AV ("my" used in Psa. 38:15; 86:12 and "our" is applied in Dan. 9:9, 15). Based upon our earlier observations, there is no question that Lord (Adonay) God is a name of deity. We simply identify who is acknowledging His lordship ("my" and "our"). This completes our study of these compound phrases as names of God.

Finally, Chapter 12 is completed with Table A.12.4, a Summary of The Names of God Validated In Chapter 12.

Table A.12.4

Summation of the LORD/Lord/lord name of God from Chapter 12

01	LORD God		17	LORD God of Israel
02	Lord God		18	LORD, THE God of heaven and the God of earth
03	LORD of hosts		19	LORD my God
04	Lord of hosts		20	LORD our God
05	LORD God of hosts		21	LORD thy God
06	Lord GOD of hosts		22	LORD your God
07	LORD Who Heals		23	LORD their God
08	LORD Our Righteousness		24	LORD his God
09	LORD Who Sanctifies		25	Lord of the whole earth
10	LORD is Present			
11	LORD Our Shepherd		26	Lord of lords
12	LORD will Provide		27	Lord my God
13	LORD Our Banner		28	Lord our God
14	LORD is Peace			
15	LORD, the God of heaven			
16	LORD God of heaven			

Examination of this Table indicates that all of its line items are new to in-depth consideration in this chapter except elements 7 through 14, the names of God highlighted in the Study of Christian Character Growth. These have been previously considered in Chapter 3. Therefore, there are 20 names of God unique to this chapter.

APPENDIX Chapter 13

13.1 Maker

The English translation of the word "maker" may come from one of several forms of the Hebrew words 'asah, pa'al, or yatsar, in each case coming into the English as a possessive pronoun compound name. For example, in Job 32:22, all considered Scripture versions agree that the writer is speaking about God, man's maker. However, the single Hebrew word 'asah translates into the English as "the One who makes me" or simply, the possessive adjective, "my Maker." But who is my Maker? This passage implies that God is the Maker but does not explicitly identify Him as the Maker. Therefore, based on this verse alone, Maker is not considered a name of God.

But consider another instance; in Job 35:10 the writers in the KJV, NIV, Jerusalem and Moffatt versions translate the Hebrew 'asah into the direct identifier, "God my Maker." The same Hebrew word is translated by Beck into the phrase "God who made me." In the former versions God is explicitly identified by the participle 'osay and that is one of His names. In Beck's case, "God who made me," acknowledges God's creative work but does not call Him by His name, "my Maker." Further version comparisons can be made; however, the evidence in this verse is that "my Maker" is a name of God.

Consider one more example: In Psa. 95:6, the KJV and the NIV modify the name LORD with the epithet "our Maker," demonstrating that the word Maker is a primary name of God. The Jerusalem version uses "Yahweh" and the augmented participle "our Maker." The same Hebrew word is translated by Beck as "the LORD who made us," and Moffatt translates into merely "who made us." Again, with care we can see that God is specifically entitled Maker in the earlier English versions. In the later versions the word Maker is not specifically used.

In summary consider the 16 OT verses of general interest applying the word maker as shown in Table A.13.1. There are eight variations with simpler possessive pronouns like "his" or "my" Maker, without identifying who Maker is, in contrast to the more specific epithetical identities of God as Maker, like "God my Maker," the LORD our Maker," "the LORD thy Maker" and "the LORD the Maker thereof." Since we have succeeded in establishing that the word Maker is a name of God, the passage identifications using the term Maker as an epithet for God will be shown only for further interest and study.

One other observation is to be made. The older Scripture versions, such as the KJV, seem to be very reserved in the matter of capitalization of proper nouns, omitting the capitals randomly. The newer versions apply the capital letters to the proper nouns much more carefully and completely.

APPENDIX Chapter 13

Table A.13.1

The Word "Maker"

REF.	KJV	NIV	JERU	Beck	MOFFATT
Job 4:17	his maker	his Maker	his Maker	his Maker	his Maker
Job 32:22	my maker	my Maker	my creator	my Maker	my Maker
Job 35:10	God my maker	God my Maker	God, my Maker	God who made me	God my Maker
Job 36:3	my Maker	my Maker	my Maker	Him who made me	my Creator
Psa. 95:6	LORD our maker	LORD our Maker	Yahweh our maker	LORD who made us	who made us
Pro. 14:31	his Maker	their Maker	his creator	his Maker	his Maker
Pro. 17:5	his Maker	their Maker	his creator	your Maker	his Maker
Pro. 22:2	LORD is maker	LORD is Maker	Yahweh has made	LORD made both	Eternal made
Isa. 17:7	his Maker-Holy One	their Maker-Holy	One creator-Holy	his Maker-Holy One`	Maker-Majesty
Isa. 22:11	the maker their of	One who made	the Maker	One doing this	him who brings
Isa. 45:9	his Maker	his Maker	who fashioned it	His Maker	his Maker
Isa. 45:11	LORD his Maker	its Maker	he who fashions	Creator of	Israel's Maker
Isa. 51:13	LORD thy maker	LORD your Maker	Yahweh who made	LORD who made you	One who made
Isa. 54:5	Maker is LORD	Maker is LORD	your creator	He who made you	Owner is Maker
Jer. 33:2	LORD the maker	he who made earth	Yahweh who made	LORD who made	Eternal made
Hos. 8:14	his Maker	his Maker	his Maker	his Maker	his Maker

APPENDIX Chapter 13

We will first identify the passages that apply the word Maker as part of a phrase relating the term Maker to deity. It is the intent to show that these applications directly relate the word Maker to God in a manner allowing no doubt that the "Maker" is God. Of course, it is only necessary to vindicate the word Maker once as a name of God. We have located these eight applications:

No.	**Ref**	**Phrase**	**Comment**
01	Job 35:10	"God my Maker"	Maker is an epithetical participle modifying the word God
02	Psa. 95:6	"LORD our Maker"	Similar to number 01
03	Pro. 22:2	"LORD is the Maker"	Maker is an indicator of the preeminence of the LORD
04	Isa. 17:7	"look to his Maker eyes shall respect the Holy One"	poetic couplet closely relating Maker and God
05	Isa. 45:11	"the LORD, the Holy One, his Maker"	Israel's Maker is the Holy One, the LORD
06	Isa. 51:13	"the LORD thy Maker"	Similar to number 01
07	Isa. 54:5	"thy Maker is thine husband the LORD of hosts is His name..."	thy Maker is the LORD of hosts (LORD Almighty)
08	Jer. 33:2	"LORD the Maker thereof"	Similar to number 01

Now let us identify the simple possessive pronoun passages in which the deity of the Maker is only implied: Job 4:17; Job 32:22; Job 36:3; Pro. 14:31; Pro. 17:5; Isa. 22:11; Isa. 45:9 and Hos. 8:14.

APPENDIX Chapter 13

Particular Aspect Of God's Character Highlighted

God is the Maker or Creator of all with special attention to His supreme achievement, mankind.

The Special Need Of Man Met By The Revelation Of This Aspect Of His Character

God is the One who forms; He is the Maker and Creator of all. Man needs desperately to remember his place and God's place.

13.5	**Mighty God**
13.6	**Mighty One**
13.7	**Mighty One Of Israel**
13.8	**Mighty God Of Jacob**
13.9	**Mighty One Of Jacob**

The English word mighty can be translated from some 38 different Hebrew words that appear at least once among the 240 verses in the OT that the computer has identified. Some of the verses contain the word twice, making a total of 248 appearances.

Now what of these verses? We are interested in finding applications of the word mighty that produce a name of God. To accomplish this we must first examine the usage of the rather large assortment of the 38 Hebrew words translatable into the English word "mighty." We must be prepared to be involved in the consideration of only compound names, since the adjective mighty, by itself, is never used as a name of deity. The approach to finding the compound names or phrases simply involves the careful physical reading of the 240 verses and the listing of the likely candidates that may contain names of deity. Five categories of compound words or phrases have been discovered. These are presented in Table A.13.2. the verses in each category will be individually examined for possible names of deity.

APPENDIX Chapter 13

Table A.13.2

The Compound Names and Phrases Applying the Word "Mighty"

Reference Verse	Summary of Application
Mighty God	There are 13 compounds in this category
Mighty One	Only a single application was discovered in this category
Mighty One of Israel	Two compound phrases have been identified in this group
Mighty God of Jacob	Three compound phrases are in this category
Mighty One of Jacob	Two compound phrases are in this category

First let us look at the initial category. Thirteen times the word combination "Mighty God" appears. Table A.13.3 identifies these verses, their locations and the particular "mighty" phrase of interest.

Table A.13.3

The 13 Category One Applications of "Mighty God"

Reference	**Phrase Of Concern**
Deu. 7:21	...for the LORD thy God is among you, a mighty God and terrible
Deu. 10:17	...Lord of lords, a great God, a mighty, and a terrible...
1Sa. 4:8	...hand of these mighty Gods? These are the Gods...
Neh. 9:32	Now therefore, our God, the great, the mighty, and the terrible...
Job 36:5	Behold, God is mighty, and despiseth not any: he is mighty...
Psa. 24:8	...The LORD strong and mighty, the LORD mighty in battle
Psa. 50:1	The mighty God, even the LORD, hath spoken...
Isa. 9:6	...and His name shall be called...the mighty God...
Isa. 10:21	...even the remnant of Jacob, unto the mighty God
Jer. 20:11	But the LORD is with me as a mighty terrible one...
Jer. 32:18	...the Great, the Mighty God, the LORD of hosts, is his name.
Hab. 1:12	...and, O mighty God...
Zep. 3:17	The LORD thy God in the midst of thee is mighty...

The Deu. 7:21 passage is saying that the true God of Israel is the greatest in all senses of the word. Mighty is an epithetical adjective and cannot be verified as being applied as part of a compound name. The next four verses are similar to this example, with the word mighty being used as an adjective modifying the word God.

That Isa. 9:6 contains a name of God is quite clear: "and His name shall be called...the Mighty God."

Isa. 10:21 and Jer. 20:11 both contain adjectives that further describe deity. In the first case mighty is an epithet enriching the name God. In the second case mighty is applied more loosely as an adjective. Neither application produces a compound name.

Jer. 32:18 contains an interesting array of adjective describing the great authority of Israel's divine judge. The verse can be read, "the Great, the Mighty God, the LORD of hosts is his name." Since the last phrase is designated as His name, we are discouraged from regarding the preceding three terms as containing a name of God.

Hab. 1:12 and Zep. 3:17 both contain limiting adjectives that further describe God as having the attribute of being mighty. He is not only God, He is the Mighty God.

In summary, the 13 verses contain the compound name "Mighty God" only once. However, this is sufficient to accept this compound as a name of deity.

Now consider the second category, "Mighty One." displayed in Table A.13.4

APPENDIX Chapter 13

Table A.13.4

The Single Application of Category Two "Mighty One"

Reference	Phrase Of Concern
Isa. 10:34	...Lebanon shall fall by a mighty one.

This passage has interesting variations in interpretation. Some argue that the verse is literal and that some pruning is being discussed. ""The LORD of hosts cleaves the trees with a flash of lightning. The tallest are hewn down, the lofty laid low, the heart of the forest is felled with the axe, and Lebanon with its noble trees has fallen." (NEB.) But more realistic is the viewpoint that the verse is figurative, that the LORD of hosts intends to destroy the armies of Assyria, both men and officers, the small and the great. He, the Mighty One, will cut down the enemy as a woodsman's axe cuts down the forest of trees in Lebanon. He, the LORD of hosts, the Mighty One—here we have a name of God, the Mighty One.

Now let us consider the third category, where we see the more complex phrase, "the Mighty One of Israel." The appropriate verses, locations and the phrases of interest are displayed in Table A.13.5.

APPENDIX Chapter 13

Table A.13.5

The Applications Of The Third Category "Mighty One Of Israel"

Reference	Phrase Of Concern
Isa. 1:24	Therefore saith the Lord, the LORD of hosts, the Mighty One of Israel
Isa. 30:29	...come into the mountain of the LORD, to the Mighty One of Israel

In both of these verses the phrase "Mighty One of Israel" is accepted as a compound name of God. Each appearance of the name is in the poetry of Isaiah, and both of them are of genitive construction, indicating the close relationship of the LORD to Israel. It is interesting to note that the English combination of words, "Mighty One," in the two verses, are translated from different Hebrew root words. In the Isa. 1:24 passage, the root word is 'abiyr (SRN 46), translated mighty or strong, but when spoken of God it translates to Mighty One or Mighty God. In the Isa. 30:29 passage, the root word tsur (SRN 6697) is used, which literally means stone or rock and then, figuratively, refuge. The KJV follows a somewhat obscure Jewish tradition when it substitutes "the Mighty" for "the Rock." The first passage (Isa. 1:24) is sufficient in itself, however, to establish this title as a valid name of God.

The two names of God—Mighty God of Jacob and Mighty One of Jacob—will be examined together. The Table A.13.6 identifies the verse location and the particular phrases of interest.

Table A.13.6

Applications Of "Mighty God/One Of Jacob" in Categories 4 and 5

Reference	**Phrase of Concern in "Mighty *God* of Jacob"**
Gen. 49:24	...made strong by the hands of the "Mighty *God* of Jacob"
Psa. 132:2	...sware unto the LORD, and vowed unto the mighty *God* of Jacob
Psa. 132:5	...an habitation for the mighty *God* of Jacob
	Phrase of Concern in "Mighty One of Jacob"
Isa. 49:26	...I the LORD am thy Savior & Redeemer, the mighty One of Jacob
Isa. 60:16	...I the LORD am thy Saviour & Redeemer, the mighty One of Jacob

Upon examining the English expression, the mighty God of the Category 4 applications, the word mighty appears to be an adjective qualifying our idea of not just God but He is the mighty God of Jacob. But that is misleading. The Hebrew 'abiyr (SRN 46) has been translated into the English compound expression Mighty God, but "God" is not in the Hebrew text. Mighty is not serving as an adjective. Rather, Mighty should be translated with the English compound term the Mighty One—it is a noun in Hebrew. When we see Mighty God of Jacob in English, translated from the Hebrew 'abiyr, we should substitute the English composite name the Mighty One of Jacob as a name of God. In the Category 4 applications, this Mighty God is closely related to Jacob (Israel) rather than Abraham or Isaac. This connection which often troubled Jacob opens up new dimensions of God's faithfulness and grace for us to appreciate.

Looking at the Category 5 applications, we can carry through the argument of mighty God (Heb. 'abiyr) or mighty One with full assurance because of the additional self-description of the LORD as Savior and Redeemer (compare Gen. 48:15-16).

The summation of all this indicates that the five compound expressions are to be accepted as names of God.

Particular Aspect Of God's Character Highlighted

The Lord is repeatedly referred to as the Mighty God or the Mighty One. In these names, we are reminded of His characteristic power, strength, greatness and might which He uses to achieve His goals and fulfill His plan to save and redeem those who trust in Him.

The Special Need Of Man Met By The Revelation Of This Aspect Of His Character

Cyclically through the ages, as even today, man has forgotten the greatness and power of Our Mighty God. Man needs to be continually reminded of just who God is and the tremendous power that is His. Man needs to look at the name, "the Mighty God," and think!

APPENDIX Chapter 15

15.1 Redeemer

The redeemer (the go'el) is the kinsman who will rescue and provide support to members of his family who may be in need. Now we need to carefully notice that the word of import is redeemer, not redeem, or redeems, or redeemed, or redemption or any of other related words. It is the Hebrew word go'el, translated redeemer, that we are considering. This is important because ordinarily the redeemer is a man who is intervening on behalf of a family member. But, as mentioned, in some 18 passages the word Redeemer is often applied to God because of His redemptive acts.

VERSION VARIATIONS:

As has been done when considering other names, let us first examine the consistency of the use of the word Redeemer in select versions of the Scripture. The question is, in the 18 appearances what do the various versions say? Is the word Redeemer always used? Is either the word Redeemer or any of its synonyms considered a name of God? Table A.15.1 presents the variations in the selected versions with comments about the variations and their significance.

APPENDIX Chapter 15

Table A.15.1

Summary Of Appearances Of The WORD Redeemer

Ref.	KJV	NIV	JER	Beck	MOFF	TLB
Job 19:25	redeemer	Redeemer	Avenger	Redeemer	champion	Redeemer
Psa. 19:14	redeemer	Redeemer	Redeemer	Redeemer	saviour	Redeemer
Psa. 78:35	redeemer	Redeemer	redeemer	Redeemer	preserver	Savior
Pro. 23:11	redeemer	Defender	avenges	Redeemer	Champion	Redeemer
Isa. 41:14	redeemer	Redeemer	redeemer	redeemed	champion	Redeemer
Isa. 43:14	redeemer	Redeemer	redeemer	redeems	deliverer	Redeemer
Isa. 44:6	redeemer	Redeemer	redeemer	Redeemer	deliverer	Redeemer
Isa. 44:24	redeemer	Redeemer	redeemer	redeems	redeemer	Redeemer
Isa. 47:4	redeemer	Redeemer	redeemer	Redeemer	Deliverer	Redeemer
Isa. 48:17	Redeemer	Redeemer	redeemer	redeems	deliverer	Redeemer
Isa. 49:7	Redeemer	Redeemer	redeemer	redeems	deliverer	Redeemer
Isa. 49:26	Redeemer	Redeemer	redeemer	redeeming	(out)*	Redeemer
Isa. 54:5	Redeemer	Redeemer	redeemer	redeems	redeemer	Redeemer
Isa. 54:8	Redeemer	Redeemer	redeemer	redeems	redeemer	Redeemer
Isa. 59:20	Redeemer	Redeemer	Redeemer	Redeemer	deliverance	Redeemer
Isa. 60:16	Redeemer	Redeemer	redeemer	saves	deliverer	Redeemer
Isa. 63:16	redeemer	Redeemer	Redeemer	Redeemer	deliverer	Redeemer
Jer. 50:34	Redeemer	Redeemer	redeemer	Redeemer	champion	Redeemer

*paraphrased out

Upon examining the version columns of Table A.15.1 it can be seen that the KJV[197] (column 2) applies the Hebrew word go'el, translated redeemer consistently in all 18 passages. However, capitalization of the word when applied to or substituted for deity is a variable. For example, In Psa. 19:14, in the phrase "O LORD, my strength, and redeemer," the words strength and redeemer seem to be metaphors used to characterize the ways the Lord protects and rescues His people. (The KJV term "strength" is itself a figurative translation of the Hebrew, which literally reads "my rock." The KJV is following a rather obscure Jewish tradition of substituting figurative or abstract words for words like "rock" when they are used to describe God. The Jewish Targum—a paraphrase—on the Psalms makes the very same substitution here that the KJV does.) However, the "strength," or even "rock," can well be considered a metaphoric title, while the word redeemer is a more straightforward epithetical title. If this is accepted, then both of these words refer to deity and should be capitalized. This sort of argument is applicable in most cases in the KJV, making it a legitimate question as to whether "redeemer" is an adjective or a metaphor or an epithetical title. Unmistakable, however, in eight passages the word redeemer is definitely used as an appellation of God.

In the Isa. 48:17 passage the word redeemer appears to be applied as a title along with the phrase, "the Holy One of Israel." In this case the name Yahweh or LORD and the additional titles have been capitalized. It is interesting to note that the NKJV version changes the initial lower case letter in the word redeemer to capitals in many passages. Comparison of the KJV, NKJV and the NIV indicate that all titles

---

[197] KJV, Copyright 1909, 1917 and renewed 1937, 1945.

involving Redeemer should be capitalized. Certainly the word "Redeemer" is demonstrated to be a title of deity in many passages in the KJV.

The third column lists the Hebrew word go'el as it is translated in the NIV. Here the title Redeemer is consistently capitalized, because it represents a title of deity. There is an interesting translation change in the Pro. 23:11 passage in the NIV. The Hebrew phrase "one redeeming them" is translated into the English words "their Defender" rather than "their Redeemer." The context is concerned with the deceptive movement of ancient land boundary markers. "Don't do this, for their Defender is strong."[198]

The fourth column lists the Hebrew word go'el as it is translated in the Jerusalem Bible in the verses in question. Here the word redeemer appears to be applied as an adjective more times than as a title. This would indicate that in these cases the word redeemer is not considered to be a title of deity. However, in Psa. 19:14, Isa. 59:20 and Isa. 63:16 the term is considered a title of the LORD. This version of Scripture also advances the idea of an avenger in Pro. 23:11 and Job 19:25. In Job the idea of an Avenger, even God Himself, is presented in Job's thinking. In the Proverbs verse the word "avenges" describes the action expected against anyone who deceptively moves property boundary markers.

---

[198] The prime root, to redeem, according to the Hebrew law of kinship, carried with it the idea of taking up the cause of avenging, defending, redeeming, championing, etc., thereby producing the variations in translation of the Hebrew word go'el.

The fifth column presents the translation of the Hebrew go'el as found in the Beck Scripture version. It should be remembered that the Hebrew word ga'al or its cognates produce a series of closely related English words, like redeems, redeemed, redeeming, redemption and the title of the LORD—Redeemer. Three in this group of related words are found in the Beck translation.

Column six displays the translation of the Hebrew word go'el as found in the Moffatt version of Scripture. Deliberate employment of synonyms appear to prevail in this interpretation so that the title of the LORD, Redeemer, appears only three times in the 18 passages. This version presents the word go'el in six different English words in the group of 18 passages. It is interesting to observe that in Isa. 49:26 the English word redeemer (or its synonym) has been lost completely.

Column 7 lists the translation of the Hebrew word go'el as it appears in the Living Bible paraphrased version of the Scripture. Throughout the 18 passages in question a high degree of consistency is evident in its translation of the Hebrew into the English word "Redeemer" as a title of the LORD. Only in the Psa. 78:35 passage is the word Redeemer replaced with the word Savior.

The information from Table A.15.1 again visually demonstrates the difficulty in establishing the identity and location of certain names and titles of God in the Scriptures. It can be seen that a given title in one version is not presented as a title in another version; often we find that even the words used in the translations vary radically. To help solve this problem a specific version should be designated as the basic Scripture for the given study, as, for example, the KJV has been chosen accordingly in this manuscript. This allows all other versions to be applied as support commentaries. However, difficulties certainly arise when the different versions presume to substitute editorial changes for a literal rendering of the Hebrew text.

To Whom Does This Name Apply?

The word "Redeemer" is applied as an epithet and/or a metonym for the name Yahweh or LORD.

The Argument:

Phrases in 18 passages have been located in various books of the OT that contain the Hebrew word go'el, translated redeemer. It will now be our intent to examine the application of the terms Redeemer and Redeemer of Israel with special considerations being given to the questions (1) are these words really names or titles of deity, and (2) what is the evidence for resolution of the first question?

In Psa. 19:14 "O LORD, my strength, and my redeemer"

The word strength[199] is an alternate word that expresses in a generalized way characteristics of the LORD associated with the more graphic metaphor rock or

[199] Note: neither the words strength nor redeemer are capitalized in the 1909-'17 KJV.

fortress. These synonyms, particularly in David's time, became epithets for Yahweh. The word redeemer is also classed as a general metaphor wherein attributes and actions of the LORD are compared to the protection and deliverance accessible to the Israelite under the Jewish kinsman redeemer law (Lev. 25:47-48). But, to be even more specific, the descriptive word redeemer in Jewish culture became a term closely associated with Yahweh and certainly an epithet.

In modern updates of the KJV such as the 1984 printing, and even the NKJV, these words remain without capitalization. However, in such Bible versions as the NIV, Jerusalem and Beck, both words have been capitalized.

For the purposes of this manuscript the word Redeemer is an epithetical name of God and should be capitalized.

Psa. 78:35 "God was their rock, and the High God their redeemer."

In this Psalm, Israel's sin is rehearsed before the people. It is pointed out that God, referred to as the Redeemer, though wroth with their sins, still loves His people.

The word redeemer in this passage is applied in a manner similar to what we found in Psa. 19:14. The word Redeemer is classified here as a general metaphor as God and the kinsman Redeemer are compared. Here again, the word Redeemer has become very closely associated with God and is considered an epithetical name of God.

It can be observed that even the more modern KJV printings do not capitalize the word redeemer. Both the NIV and the Beck capitalize the word, but the Jerusalem does not.

It can be easily understood that this inconsistent capitalization of proper nouns prevents the norms of capitalization from being applied as an aid in determining the status of a noun.

Pro. 23:11 "For their redeemer is mighty; he shall plead..."

This Proverb warns those who are tempted to defraud the fatherless concerning the retribution to be expected from God, who is referred to as their Redeemer. God is mighty, and He Himself will plead their cause, especially in the matter of landmark removal and property ownership falsification.

The word redeemer in this passage is a metaphorical name of Yahweh. He is mighty and will plead their case. The 1984 printing of the KJV, the NKJV and the Beck versions all capitalize the title Redeemer. The NIV translates the Hebrew word go'el into the English word Defender, complete with capitalization.

The Other Table A.15.1 Entries:

In addition to the examples of the Hebrew word go'el so far presented in this argument the term is frequently used in the OT, especially in the Isaiah and Jeremiah passages displayed in Table A.15.1. All the verses occurring in this table refer to Yahweh as the Redeemer, involving a personal relationship with God. In each case these are titles of God wherein the word Redeemer is used metaphorically for Yahweh. The 1984 printing of the KJV (with the exception of Isa. 43:14), the NKJV and the NIV treat the word as a title of deity. In this manuscript the diverse renderings in the various versions are noted, the evidence supports the conclusion that the word is accounted a title of Yahweh.

In summary, this presented argument assigns the word Redeemer in each of these verses either to the category of a divine title or to that of an appropriate epithet for deity.

15.1.1 Redeemer of Israel.

Now briefly consider the unique compound title, "the Redeemer of Israel", found in the Isaiah 49:7 passage. This phrase can be written "Israel's Redeemer," which helps us see the intended meaning. But if the phrase is written as "The LORD, the Redeemer and Holy One of Israel," it can be seen that Redeemer of Israel and Holy One are both subordinate phrases describing the LORD. Each in its own right could stand as a name of God. Of course, regardless of the translation format used all elements of the compound must be present to form a distinct name of God.

15.1.2 The Names Rock, Rock of Israel and Refuge

Before studying the name treated next in Chapter 15 it is appropriate to consider some especially interesting names associated with the name Redeemer in Psa. 19:14; 78:35 and other passages.

APPENDIX Chapter 15

First, look again at the phrase in Psa. 19:14, "my strength and my redeemer." "The word "strength" is not actually found in those verses. The words are literally my Rock and my Redeemer. God is known as Rock as well as Redeemer. These belong to Him as names. However, Jewish tradition often substitutes the general immaterial or even abstract concept of strength for the specific (or concrete, or) material object that is used here metaphorically.

Now look again at the phrase in Psa. 78:35, "...God was their Rock and the high God their Redeemer." God is known as both Rock and Redeemer. The same tradition of substituting "might" or "strength" appears in the Jewish Targum (the Aramaic version that was read in synagogue services) in most of these verses, but the KJV chose to keep the original sense instead.

Figuratively (Psa. 62:6, 7; 94:22; 2Sa. 23:3; the above references, etc.) God is often referred to as "rock, my Rock, Rock of Refuge, Rock of Israel, etc." It is easy to grasp why this metaphor became associated with Him. At the time of the Exodus some Israelites named their children accordingly: for example Zuriel ("my Rock is God") and Zurishaddai ("My rock is Shaddai" Num. 3:35, 1:16.)

Not only does this occur with the word rock, but we also find several other words, closely associated with Rock, used as names for God. For example, Table A.15.2 shows that the word refuge (Psa. 31:2; 62:7; 71:3; 94:22) is frequently used in these verses with rock as an appellation of God. This occurs commonly in most versions;

however, only a version comparison between the KJV and the NIV are shown in the table.

APPENDIX Chapter 15

Table A.15.2

Examples of the Combination of Rock and Refuge

	Psa. 31:2	**Psa. 62:7**	**Psa. 71:3**	**Psa. 94:22**
1 KJV	strong rock	salvation	strong habitation	defence (refuge)
2		my glory	rock and fortress	rock of my refuge
3		rock of my strength		
4		my refuge		
1 NIV	my rock of refuge	salvation	rock of refuge	fortress
2		my honor	my rock & fortress	rock take refuge
3		mighty rock		
4		my refuge		

The Table shows that the Psalmist (David) requests in Psa. 31:2 that Yahweh be his "strong rock" in the KJV. The NIV translates this request as, "my rock of refuge." Only this single metaphor is applied in Psa. 31:2. In Psalm 62:7 David characteristically applies a series of words to describe some of the attributes of his God. Again we find the expressions "rock of my strength," "mighty rock" and "my refuge" closely associated together. Psa. 71:3 uses rock and fortress to describe the place of refuge. A "strong habitation" in the KJV is referred to as a "rock of refuge" in the NIV.

Psa. 94:22 is even more explicit in connecting the ideas of rock and refuge. The KJV speaks of the LORD as his defence (a synonym for refuge)., The NIV translates defence as fortress.

From these facts it can be seen that rock and refuge are closely related metaphors; they were probably once used like adjectives describing attributes of God, but through the years these familiar words have become like names. Some versions (Beck) even treat them as names with proper name capitalization. Others do not, but they may be restricting proper name capitalization due to contemporary rules of capitalization.[200]

Particular Aspects Of God's Character Highlighted

The OT people of God were continually involved in the process of redemption because as a people they had the need for it. They understood that payment of a price was required for redemption, but it was God Himself who acted as the Go'el, the Redeemer, paying the price and providing redemption for His people. God, as close kinsman for these who were His very own people, carried out His role as Redeemer through His great might and love.

[200] The University of Chicago Press, Chicago, 14th Edition, 1993, Section 7.1, page 235. "Modern publishers of works in the English language, American perhaps more than British, usually discourage extensive use of capital letters in text. Proper nouns are still conventionally capitalized, but many words derived from or associated with them may be lower cased with no loss of clarity or significance."

Regarding Religious Names and Terms. Section 7.77, page 265.
"The editors of the University of Chicago Press urge a spare, down style in this field as in others: capitalize what are clearly proper nouns and adjectives, and lowercase everything else except to avoid ambiguity."

APPENDIX Chapter 15

The Special Need Of Men Met By The Revelation Of This Aspect Of His Character

The special need of man through all the ages relates closely to this title of God, the Redeemer. Man has always had the need, man continues to have the need and God, in His plan, meets this need.

An encyclopedia[201] presents comments excerpted here in conclusion of this discussion.

"The intermediary who secures the redemption is called the go'el or redeemer." "...The merciful provisions associated with the term in the ordinary life of Israel are here carried to the highest level in the relation of God to His people, and the kinsman's action in recovering possessions is likened to God's action in salvation." "...The Scriptural contexts are replete with references (1) to God's tender care for His heritage, (2) to the almighty power by which He has wrought salvation for them, and (3) to their security in Him in spite of all their adversaries." God's actions throughout the OT period validated the redemption relation. In all generations, man has had the need and at the right times God has acted to provide it. Messianic prophecy takes the

---

[201] *The International Standard Bible Encyclopedia,* Vol. 4, p. 62.

form of the promise that a Redeemer will ultimately come to Zion (Isa. 59:20); thus the coming salvation mentioned repeatedly in redemptive terms is conjoined with the coming of One whose specific role is that of Redeemer.

APPENDIX Chapter 15

15.6 Shield

In this portion of the study special consideration of the English phraseology is interesting. The use of the key word "shield" is most significant, since it provides a good opportunity to examine the English capitalization of this key word. The presence or absence of capitalization of key words can suggest to the reader whether a particular word is a name of deity. We have observed variations in capitalization between versions many times. It is appropriate to look closer at some of the variations that appear in the Text Table 15.3.

Table A.15.3

Scripture Version Comparisons for the Word Shield

Gen. 15:1	KJV NIV JER	I am your shield	Each phrase in the KJV, NIV and JER contains a possessive pronoun that inhibits capitalization of the word shield. All are considered titles.
	Beck	I am your Shield	The word shield is capitalized, asserting the title of deity in spite of the possessive pronoun
Deu. 33:29	KJV	shield of thy help	Implied: who is the shield of your help. This is a descriptive phrase. The word shield is not a title.
	NIV	He is your shield	Possessive pronoun inhibits capitalization of shield.
	JER	In Yahweh is the shield	A descriptive phrase. Word shield not a title.
	Beck	who is a shield	A descriptive phrase. Shield is not a title.

Table A.15.3 (Continued)

2Sa. 22:3	KJV	He is my shield	Poss. Pronoun inhibits capitalization of shield. (Title)
	NIV	God is my shield	God is implied, same poss. Pronoun inhibitor. (Title).
	JER	God is my shield	God is implied, same poss. Pronoun inhibitor. (Title)
	Beck	God is my Shield	Series of metaphors describing God. All treated as Titles.
Psa. 3:3	KJV	LORD art a shield	metaphorical use simply rendered (Title)
	NIV	you are a shield	metaphorical use with unusual application around him (Title)
	JER	Yahweh my...shield	possessive pronoun inhibitor substituted
	Beck	You are a Shield	describes an attribute of Yahweh; therefore a Title.
Psa. 28:7	KJV	LORD is my shield	possessive pronoun inhibitor. (Title)
	NIV	Lord is my shield	possessive pronoun inhibitor. (Title)
	JER	Yahweh my shield	possessive pronoun inhibitor. (Title)
	Beck	LORD is my shield	possessive pronoun inhibitor. (Title)
Psa. 33:20	KJV	LORD...our shield	same inhibitor. (Title)
	NIV	LORD...our shield	same inhibitor. (Title)
	JER	Yahweh...our shield	same inhibitor. (Title)
	Beck	who...shields us	total phrase an ascription. Word shield is not a title.

Table A.15.3 (Continued)

Psa. 59:11	KJV	O Lord our shield	same inhibitor. (Title)
	NIV	O Lord our shield	same inhibitor. (Title)
	JER	Lord, our shield	same inhibitor. (Title)
	Beck	O LORD, our Shield	pronoun inhibitor is ignored. (Title)
Psa. 84:9	KJV	O God our shield	Possessive pronoun inhibitor. (Title).
	NIV	Look upon our shield	in a couplet with anointed one. (Title)
	JER	God our shield	same inhibitor.
	Beck	Look at our ruler	ruler is not a title in this shield series.
Psa. 84:11	KJV	God is a...shield	descriptive statement with indefinite article. (title)
	NIV	God is a...shield	(same as the KJV reason.) (title)
	JER	God is battlement and shield	descriptive adjectives. (title)
	Beck	LORD is a...Shield	Capitalization may be simple word emphasis. (Title)
Psa. 91:4	KJV	truth shall be your shield	word shield not used as a title.
	NIV	faithfulness will be your shield	word shield not used as a title.
	JER	faithfulness for shield	word shield not used as a title.
	Beck	His arm is a shield.	Word shield not used as a title.
Psa. 115:9	KJV	LORD is...their...shield	possessive pro. inhibits title. (Title)
	NIV	the Lord is their shield	same inhibitor. (Title)
	JER	Yahweh...our...shield	same inhibitor. (Title)
	Beck	He...shields them.	(Not a title)

Table A.15.3 (Continued)

Psa. 115:10	KJV	LORD is...their shield	same inhibitor.	(Title)
	NIV	the Lord is their shield	same inhibitor.	(Title)
	JER	Yahweh...our shield	same inhibitor.	(Title)
	Beck	He...shields them.	(not a title)	
Psa. 115:11	KJV NIV JER Beck	application of the word shield similar in the four versions He is their help and shield		(Title)
Psa. 119:114	KJV	Thou art my...shield...	same inhibitor.	(Title)
	NIV	You, are my...shield	same inhibitor.	(Title)
	JER	You my...shield	same inhibitor.	(Title)
	Beck	You are my...shield	same inhibitor.	(Title)
Psa. 144:2	KJV	[the Lord]...my shield	same inhibitor.	(Title)
	NIV	He is...my shield	same inhibitor.	(Title)
	JER	Yahweh shelter...	my shield same.	(Title)
	Beck	Lord...is my shield	same inhibitor.	(Title)
Pro. 30:5	KJV	He is a shield	same inhibitor.	(Title)
	NIV	He is a shield	same inhibitor.	(Title)
	JER	He is the shield	same inhibitor.	(Title)
	Beck	He is a Shield	word shield is capped asserting deity.	(Title)

APPENDIX Chapter 15

Table A.15.3 Discussion

Examining the Gen. 15:1 quartet of versions will provide information that applies repeatedly in many of the other passages. For example, the word shield appears metaphorically in the phrase "I am your shield." This may be interpreted to mean "the LORD represents your shield" that is, that attribute of God that provides covering protection for an individual or for His people. Since protecting His people is characteristic of God, the word shield is a proper title of deity. However, the KJV, NIV and JER seem to limit capitalization of the word shield because of the presence of the possessive pronoun, which tends to inhibit capitalization of the noun.[202] Nevertheless, the Beck version does not apply this rule and capitalizes the word Shield, asserting the title of deity. The word Shield is considered a title of Yahweh.

The Deu. 33:29 quartet of versions offers some diversification. In the KJV the word shield appears in the first of two compound metaphors. The word is not a title of deity. But in the NIV the first compound metaphor is split apart, yielding the meaning "the LORD represents your shield." Shield would be capitalized except for the presence of the possessive pronoun. The word shield is considered a title of deity. This instance demonstrates the necessity of close attention to the version in use for the name or title study. In the JER case, the word shield is couched in an irregular,

---

[202] Do not capitalize proper nouns when a modifying possessive pronoun is present (Ref. text f.n. 127, p. 238).

grammatically strained descriptive phrase and is not a title. Beck also presents shield in a descriptive phrase, and the word is not considered a title of deity.

The Psa. 3:3 quartet of versions offers a unique series of variations. Here the pronoun is connected to a preposition with unusual results. In the KJV the phrase originally reads "thou, O LORD, art a shield for me." In the NIV the phrase reads, "You are a shield around me, O Lord." The JER substitutes an inhibiting possessive pronoun for the prepositional phrase, so there is no capitalization of the title word shield. However, the Beck translation uses the word Shield as an attribute of Yahweh, so the word is capitalized.

Finally then, consider a pair of verses as the last comparison examples. Psa. 59:11, in each of the four versions, contains very similar phraseology, "O Lord our shield. " Beck uses the form, O LORD and capitalizes the word shield. In Psa. 144:2 again the phraseology in the four versions is very similar. Comparison of the two verses shows that translations that include a possessive pronoun usually reject capitalization of the divine title, Shield.

One other point of interest; in Psa. 84:9 the Beck version elects to translate the verse with a substitute term, ruler, instead of the word shield. The word ruler is not a normal substitute for shield. Furthermore, it is not a term applied to God anywhere in Scripture with the sole exception of the description of the Messiah In Micah 5:2 (mashal, SRN 4910).

APPENDIX Chapter 15

Particular Aspects Of God's Character Highlighted

Application of the divine title shield makes vivid the protective covering or protection that God offers to His people or His nation. The Israelite was well-accustomed to the military shield and understood the purpose of this instrument. It provided protection from the attack of the enemy. It was easy for God's people to grasp the corresponding idea that God offered protection as a shield, but exercise of personal faith in Him was necessary for it to be effective.

What Is The Special Need Of Man Met By The Revelation Of This Aspect Of His Character?

Attack by Satan upon the people of God is fearful and troublesome. Man needs all the protection from these attacks possible. God offers protection, that is, God offers to shield His people from Satan, but man must believe this promise of God and actively trust in Him for protection.

APPENDIX Chapter 16

16.1 the Spirit of God
16.2 the Spirit of the LORD
16.3 the Spirit of the Lord GOD
16.4 the Spirit (including importance of capitalization)
16.8. Stronghold
16.12 Yahweh/Yah

Name Variations:

Variations in the first three compound names occur in the different Scripture versions and translations and even in various editions of the same version (i.e., KJV 1909/1917 versus the 1984 copy right editions). These variations, arranged in simple coding, are displayed in a combination of select Scripture versions in the following tables:

Table A.16.1

the Spirit of God

Verse Reference	KJV	NKJV	NIV	NEB	JER	NAS	RSV	BECK
Gen. 1:2	1	1	1	9	4	1	1	7
Gen. 41:38	1	1	2	8	2	10	1	7
Exo. 31:3	2	1	1	10	2	1	1	7
Exo. 35:31	2	1	1	10	2	1	1	7
Num. 24:2	2	1	1	2	2	1	1	7
1Sa. 10:10	1	1	1	2	2	1	2	7
1Sa. 11:6	1	1	1	2	5	1	2	7
1Sa. 19:20	1	1	1	2	2	1	1	7
1Sa. 19:23	1	1	1	2	2	1	1	7

Table A.16.1 (Continued)

2Ch. 15:1	1	1	1	2	2	1	1	7
2Ch. 24:20	1	1	1	2	2	1	1	7
Job 27:3	2	3	3	6	3	3	2	6
Job 33:4	1	1	1	2	6	1	2	7
Eze. 11:24	1	1	1	2	2	1	1	7

The compound names of deity, coded by number, are shown below:

Number 1 the Spirit of God

Number 2 the spirit of God

Number 3 the breath of God

Number 4 God's spirit

Number 5 the spirit of Yahweh

Number 6 God's breath

Number 7 God's Spirit

Number 8 Paraphrased out (the spirit of god)

Number 9 a mighty wind

Number 10 diving spirit or a divine spirit

APPENDIX Chapter 16

Table A.16.1 is read as follows:

"Horizontally:"

Example 1. In the eight versions Gen. 1:2 contains four different compound names of deity

Number 1 the Spirit of God　　Number 4 God's spirit

Number 9 a mighty wind　　Number 7 God's Spirit

Example 2. In the eight versions 1 Sa. 10:10 contains three different compound names of deity

Number 1 the Spirit of God

Number 2 the spirit of God

Number 7 God's Spirit

"Vertically:"

Example 3. In the 14 verses the KJV contains two different compound names

Number 1 the Spirit of God

Number 2 the spirit of God

Example 4. In the 14 verses the JER contains five different compound names

Number 2 the spirit of God　　Number 5 the spirit of Yahweh

Number 3 the breath of God　　Number 6 God's breath

Number 4 God's spirit

Notice that a change in capitalization can produce a variation in the compound names as shown in this Number Coding Table. For example, numbers 1 and 2 are the S̲pirit of God and the s̲pirit of God, and numbers 7 and 4 are God's S̲pirit and God's s̲pirit. It can easily be seen that nine combinations are acceptable as divine appellations (number 8 obviously is not a name). Now let us examine the compound name, "the Spirit of the LORD." Again consider variations among the select Scripture versions in Table A.16.2.

Table A.16.2

the Spirit of the LORD

Verse Reference	KJV	NKJV	NIV	NEB	JER	NAS	RSV	BECK
Jdg. 3:10	1	1	1	2	10	1	1	7
Jdg. 6:34	1	1	1	2	10	1	1	7
Jdg. 11:29	1	1	1	2	10	1	1	7
Jdg. 13:25	1	1	1	2	10	1	1	7
Jdg. 14:6	1	1	1	2	10	1	1	7
Jdg. 14:19	1	1	1	2	10	1	1	7
Jdg. 15:14	1	1	1	2	10	1	1	7
1Sa. 10:6	1	1	1	2	10	1	2	7
1Sa. 16:13	1	1	1	2	10	1	1	7
1Sa. 16:14	1	1	1	2	10	1	1	7
2Sa. 23:2	1	1	1	2	10	1	1	4
1Ki. 18:12	1	1	1	2	10	1	1	7
1Ki. 22:24	1	6	6	2	10	1	1	7
2Ki. 2:16	1	1	1	2	10	1	1	7

Table A.16.2 (Continued)

Verse Reference	KJV	NKJV	NIV	NEB	JER	NAS	RSV	BECK
2Ch. 18:23	1	6	6	2	10	1	1	14
2Ch. 20:14	1	1	1	2	10	1	1	7
Isa. 11:2	2	1	1	2	10	1	1	7
Isa. 40:7	2	3	3	3	11	3	3	15
Isa. 40:13	1	1	1	2	10	1	1	7
Isa. 59:19	1	1	3	2	11	13	13	3
Isa. 61:1	1	5	9	5	12	5	1	5
Isa. 63:14	1	1	1	2	10	1	1	7
Eze. 11:5	1	1	1	2	10	1	1	7
Eze. 37:1	2	1	1	14	10	1	1	16
Mic. 2:7	2	1	1	8	8	1	1	8
Mic. 3:8	2	1	1	8	11	1	1	7

The possible compound names of deity, coded by number, used in the above table are shown below:

Number 1 the Spirit of the LORD

Number 2 the spirit of the LORD

Number 3 the breath of the LORD

Number 4 the Spirit of the Lord

Number 9 the Spirit of the Sovereign LORD

Number 10 the Spirit of Yahweh

Number 11 the breath of Yahweh

Number 12 the spirit of the LORD Yahweh

APPENDIX Chapter 16

Number 5 the Spirit of the Lord GOD

Number 6 the Spirit from the LORD

Number 7 the LORD's Spirit

Number 8 Paraphrased out (patience/strength)

Number 13 the wind of the LORD

Number 14 his spirit

Number 15 the LORD's breath

Number 16 His Spirit

It can be seen from the appellation count view point that 15 compound combinations are acceptable.

Examining the "Spirit of the LORD" table shows some interesting variations. Looking first at the KJV column, we see that 21 of the passages contain the genitive phrase "the Spirit of the LORD." Spirit here is the Holy Spirit, and the phrase is properly capitalized as a compound name of God. Then, to continue in this column, there are five passages that contain the phrase, "the spirit of the LORD." From the works and attributes ascribed in the text to this word spirit, it can be easily accepted that both Spirit and spirit pertain to the Holy Spirit and that both phrases are compound names of Yahweh. It is assumed that the lack of capitalization is an editorial or stylistic difference and has little significance in this name selection process.

But pursuing the issue of capitalization of these two phrases, look across the columns at Isa. 11:2. We find that 6 of the 8 versions effectively do capitalize the phrase. In one version the name has been translated the Spirit of Yahweh, while in another the "s" genitive is used, giving the LORD's Spirit; this compound name is generally graced with capitals. Only in two of the versions is the word spirit not capitalized. This variation of capitalization in references to deity makes for more difficulty in identifying the names and titles of deity until it is recognized that the current style is to eliminate capitals in Scripture as much as possible.

Before we leave the subject, look across the columns at Isa. 40:7. Here an important variation in words occurs. The AV reads, "the spirit of the LORD." Instead, five of the other versions read, "the breath of the LORD." One version reads "the breath of Yahweh" and another substitutes the "s" genitive form to produce the phrase "the LORD's breath." All of these variations are considered names of deity, with or without capitalization of the opening terms of the compound, the variations occurring due to the editors' style preferences.

16.4 Spirit

Having examined the compound names, the Spirit of God and the Spirit of the LORD, attention is now turned to the use of the unembellished word Spirit as a name of deity. Preliminarily, we see that the word Spirit can be accepted as a divine reference, remembering that there are several verses that characterize this Spirit as God's very own Holy Spirit. For example, Psa. 51:11 reads, "Cast me not away from thy presence; take not thy holy spirit from me." And again, "They rebelled, and vexed his holy Spirit" (Isa. 63:10). With these highly significant applications of the word Spirit to guide us the other uses of the word spirit can more easily be examined. For example, in Gen. 6:3

we read, "and the LORD said, My spirit shall not always strive with man..." It is obvious that the LORD spoke here of His own Spirit.

But what of the other times the word spirit appears? Remember, as has already been stated, that the term can be found 222 times in the KJV OT.[203] Of these only 33 times is the word used to indicate deity. We will list these passages in Table A.16.3. Frequently comparison of several Scripture versions is in order when considering divine names or titles. But in this case study only the 1909/1917 KJV edition and subsequent 1984 copyright editions are compared.

Table A.16.3

Applications of the Word spirit to Deity

Ref. Verse	Verse Comments	1909/1917 Ed.	1984 Ed.
Gen. 6:3	My spirit (Yahweh speaking)	x	y
Num. 11:29	His (Yahweh's) spirit	x	-
Num. 14:24	another spirit (obscure)	0	-
Num. 27:18	is the spirit	x	-
Deu. 34:9	full of the spirit	x	-
1Ch. 12:18	the spirit came upon (clothed)	x	-
1Ch. 28:12	by the spirit	x	y
Neh. 9:20	thy good spirit	x	y

[203] KJV, 1909/1917 copyright edition

Table A.16.3 (Continued)

Ref. Verse	Verse Comments	1909/1917 Ed.	1984 Ed.
Neh. 9:30	by thy spirit	x	y
Psa. 51:11	thy holy spirit	x	y
Psa. 51:12	thy free spirit	x	y
Psa. 104:30	thy spirit	x	-
Psa. 139:7	thy spirit	x	-
Psa. 143:10	thy good spirit (my God)	x	y
Isa. 4:4	spirit of judgment	x	-
Isa. 4:4	spirit of burning	0	-
Isa. 30:1	my spirit	0	y
Isa. 34:16	his spirit	0	-
Isa. 42:1	my spirit	x	y
Isa. 44:3	my spirit	x	y
Isa. 48:16	his Spirit	z	y
Isa. 59:21	my spirit	x	y
Isa. 63:10	his holy Spirit	z	y
Isa. 63:11	his holy Spirit	z	y
Eze. 36:27	my spirit	x	y
Exe. 37:14	my spirit	x	y
Eze. 39:29	my spirit	x	y
Joe. 2:28	my spirit	x	y
Joe. 2:29	my spirit	0	y

Table A.16.3 (Continued)

Hag. 2:5	my spirit	0	-
Zec. 4:6	my spirit	x	y
Zec. 7:12	his spirit	0	y
Zec. 12:10	the spirit of grace and of supplication	x	-

Word Capitalization Randomness:

The 1909/1917 copyright edition of the KJV displays some interesting phenomena of word capitalization variance in relation to the word spirit. This has been seen before in relation to other names, such as Redeemer, Refuge and Rock, but perhaps not as easily identified. In order to understand this examine Table A.16.3. The References Passages of column 1 all contain the word spirit, predominantly relating to deity, as shown in the Comments Column. But in every referenced passage except 3 (Isa. 48:16; 63:10,11) that are marked with z the word spirit is spelled with a small "s." The 23 passages marked with an x in Column 3 make prominent this condition. But, more than this, in the Scripture Text each of these marked verses apply the word spirit to indicate the Holy Spirit. Therefore, as the word spirit normally speaks of the Holy Spirit in these passages, the word spirit is a candidate for acceptance as an appellation for deity.

Attention is now directed to the seven referenced passages marked with an "0" instead of an x. The 1909/1917 edition of the KJV does not identify these applications as related to the Holy Spirit. The reader must decide for himself which spirit is being discussed. This lack of uniform marking in the KJV is unfortunate, since the text in most of these seven (Num. 14:24 and Isa. 4:4 may be exceptions) cases clearly points out that the Holy Spirit is being indicated; the occurrence of word capitalization inconsistency is quite evident, and it tends to call into question any generalizations regarding divine reference when the word spirit appears.

Further consideration of this variation can be effected by comparing the same Scripture verses in the 1984 edition of the KJV. This is shown in Column 4 of Table A.16.3. Here the letter "y" indicates those passages where the word spirit is now spelled with a capital "S." It is obvious that not every occurrence of the word spirit in these verses in the newer KJV edition has been capitalized, but in 17 cases this has occurred (remember that three cases were already capitalized in 1909/1917). The texts of the remaining 13 passages not marked with a "y" often also speak of the Holy Spirit; however, this edition has not chosen to indicate this as in the case of the "y" verses. This inconsistency increases the difficulty of Divine Personage identification.

Capitalization in the KJV (as well as other versions) through the years has been largely a matter of taste or propriety on the part of the involved translator and editor. The tendency to decrease the employment of capital letters has progressed with time. This reduction has also been encouraged, in some cases, by the simple propagation of the earlier writings of our forefathers. This has brought some appropriate words with capitalization while other words that merit capitalization go begging. The simple copying process from generation to generation has also produced errors in Scripture Text that need correction. Certainly each case needs to be considered on its own merits.

But does it really matter? The word spirit already discussed demonstrates the point. Dr. F.H.A. Scrivener[204] of another generation, writes the following:

> "What in most instances is only a matter of taste or propriety, becomes of real importance where the Divine Persons are spoken of. The familiar rule that *Spirit* should have a capital when the Holy Ghost or Spirit Himself is indicated, while *spirit* ought to be used in other cases, even when His power or influence is referred to, may be as safe as any, yet in application it gives rise to occasional perplexity which the inconsistencies of the standard and other editions do little to remove. Thus in Gen. 41:38 the Bible of 1611 has *spirit* (changed as early as 1613, though *Spirit* was not finally adopted before 1762), while in the precise parallel (Exo. 31:3) it reads *Spirit*."

---

[204] F.H.A. Scrivener, Ma. D.C.L., LL.D. *The Authorized Edition of the English Bible (1611), Cambridge Press,* 1910, P. 115-116.

APPENDIX Chapter 16

Scrivener concludes his discussion with this comment:

> "Appellations derived from the Divine attributes should be indicated by capitals, whatever the variations of edition; and we ought to be more studious of uniformity in such matters than of following the inconsistencies of editors that have proceeded us. Thus, when relating to God, we adopt Father, the Most High, the Holy One, Maker, Mighty One, Redeemer and Saviour."

Particular Aspect of God's Character Highlighted:

Many of the characteristics of the Godhead are clearly presented in the passages relating to the personality, attributes and work of the Spirit, the Third Person of the Trinity. He is called the Holy Spirit, the Good Spirit, the Spirit of Judgment and Burning, the Spirit of Wisdom, Understanding, Knowledge, Might and Grace. The Spirit moves about as He wills, coming upon men to initiate, control and empower. The Spirit's action in the OT achieved much in the lives of specific individuals. The same is possible in every NT born again Christian, since the Spirit indwells on a permanent basis.

APPENDIX Chapter 16

16.8 Stronghold

Strong (adj.) means tough, durable, resistant to attack. The word hold (noun) means a citadel, fortress, fortified place; a man-made refuge or place of safety such as a castle or a natural strong hold or strong place.

Stronghold then means a place having strong defenses, a fortified place, a fortress or a place of safety. The single word "stronghold" and the two words "strong" and "hold" in combination mean the same thing; the single word form, stronghold is the standard term in more modern Scripture versions.

If the single word stronghold is being searched for and a Scripture version that divides the word is used, the correct results will not be obtained. Or, if the inverse approach occurs where strong hold is searched for, one should restrict the search to the traditional KJV. The terms strong hold and stronghold mean the same thing, but the search techniques are different.

So we must be careful to indicate which version of the Bible we are using as the lead Scripture in a computerized word search. We must also examine these versions in their various editions for their positive or negative evidence before we say whether a name or title of deity is or is not valid.

The comments about the various editions of the KJV show that there is some considerable possibility of confusion. The situation improves if one of the other versions is selected as the lead document. The KJV (1909-1917 edition) uses the term "strong hold" only eight times; the form "stronghold doesn't appear at all. But if we use the NIV (1984 copyright edition) as the lead search document there are 31 references to the word "stronghold," of which eight appear to be titles of God (see Table A.16.4). If the NAS version is the lead Scripture version there are at least 20 passages containing the word stronghold with five of these suggested as titles of God. Use of other versions of Scripture as the lead document will produce similar results.

Both the Webster's New World Dictionary (3rd College Edition, 1988) and the Webster's New Collegiate Dictionary (1949 edition) show the English word stronghold as a single word. However, expanded reference dictionaries suggest that the divided term strong hold is from 1375-1425 Middle English. This style was adopted by Early Modern English. Somewhere in the Early Modern English periods the words strong hold were joined together, making the single word recommended for use today.

Table A.16.4

The Word Stronghold or Strong hold

Reference	NIV (1984)	KJV (1909)	KJV (1984)	NAS (1975)
Jdg. 9:46	stronghold	hold	hold	inner chamber
Jdg. 9:49	stronghold	hold	hold	inner chamber
1Sa. 22:4	stronghold	hold	hold	stronghold
1Sa. 22:5	stronghold	hold	hold	stronghold
1Sa. 24:22	stronghold	hold	hold	stronghold
2Sa. 5:7	fortress	strong hold	strong hold	stronghold
2Sa. 5:17	stronghold	hold	hold	stronghold
2Sa. 22:3	stronghold*	high tower	high tower	stronghold
2Sa. 23:14	stronghold	hold	hold	stronghold
2Sa. 24:7	fortress	strong hold	stronghold	fortress
1Ch. 11:16	stronghold	hold	hold	stronghold
1Ch. 12:8	stronghold	hold	hold	stronghold
1Ch. 12:16	stronghold	hold	hold	stronghold
Job 39:28	stronghold	strong place	strong place	inaccessible
Psa. 9:9	stronghold*	refuge	refuge	stronghold
Psa. 18:2	stronghold*	high tower	high tower	stronghold
Psa. 27:1	stronghold*	strength	strength	defense
Psa. 37:39	stronghold*	strength	strength	strength
Psa. 43:2	stronghold*	strength	strength	strength
Psa. 52:7	stronghold	strength	strength	refuge
Psa. 144:2	stronghold*	high tower	high tower	stronghold

Table A.16.4 (Continued)

The Word Stronghold or Strong hold

Reference	NIV (1984)	KJV (1909)	KJV (1984)	NAS (1975)
Pro. 21:22	stronghold	strength	strength	stronghold
Isa. 25:2	stronghold	palace	palace	palace
Isa. 31:9	stronghold	strong hold	stronghold	rock
Jer. 48:1	stronghold	misgab	misgab	stronghold
Jer. 51:53	stronghold	strength	strength	stronghold
Eze. 24:21	stronghold	strength	strength	power
Eze. 24:25	stronghold	strength	strength	stronghold
Eze. 30:15	stronghold	strength	strength	stronghold
Joe. 3:16	stronghold*	strength	strength	refuge
Amo. 5:9	stronghold	strong	strong	strong
Mic. 4:8	stronghold	strong hold	strong hold	hill
Nah. 1:7	refuge	strong hold	stronghold	stronghold
Hab. 1:7	fortified city	strong Hold	stronghold	fortress
Zec. 9:3	stronghold	strong hold	stronghold	fortress
Zec. 9:12	fortress	strong hold	stronghold	stronghold

*See text discussion (p. 474).

Table A.16.4 presents a display of the words strong hold and stronghold as they appear in the NIV, the KJV (1909-1917), the KJV (1984 edition) and the NAS. The NIV and the KJV version data is supported by convenient SRN information which any student can validate. The NAS is added as an example from a third source. Of course, any version could be used for such an example with the expected variations.

APPENDIX Chapter 16

The Table shows the eight passages in the KJV (1909-1917 edition) that contain the words strong hold. The KJV (1984 edition) shows the same passages but with six verses using stronghold and two verses still using the Middle English style.

It is interesting in the comparison to note the increased number of occurrences of the word stronghold. This happens because the NIV is now applied as the control document, and all 31 of its uses of the term stronghold are listed. It can be seen that the NIV elects to apply the word stronghold in many passages where the KJV (either the 1909-1917 or the 1984 edition) uses another word. This becomes very important when seeking to identify a name of deity. For example, in 2Sa. 22:3, the word stronghold is a metaphor for God in the NIV, but in the KJV the words high tower are used instead. Since the word stronghold is in question here as a name of deity, the fact that the NIV contains a name of deity in this passage while the KJV does not is important. The eight verses where this happens in the NIV are marked in Table A.16.3 with an asterisk. The inverse of this contradiction can be seen in Nah. 1:7. Here the KJV (either edition) displays a name of God in the form of stronghold or strong hold while the NIV uses the term refuge, which is not sought after as a deity name.

Just a few words are necessary about the example when the NAS is used as the third alternative. Comparison of the NAS with the NIV or the KJV shows that if the NAS were being used to locate names of God, care would need to be exercised that some of the uses of alternates for the word stronghold do not produce search confusion.

APPENDIX Chapter 16

Particular Aspect of God's Character Highlighted

This study has already shown that the word strong hold can be translated from several Hebrew words. Furthermore, the English words strong hold can be synonymous with several other English terms. However, the possible conglomerate of the words stronghold can be reduced to simply mean a place having strong defenses, a place of protection from attackers. And that is beautiful, for therein is figuratively represented one of the great mercies of God, His protection, safety and comfort for those who trust in Him.

What Is The Special Need Of Man Met By The Revelation Of This Aspect Of His Character?

The physical and spiritual weaknesses of man have resulted in man's dispensational failures through all the testing periods of history. Man consistently has tried to manage alone without /God and without divine protection and safety. Man desperately needs God the Refuge, God the defense, God the Stronghold.

16.12 Yahweh/Yah

The Hebrew word Yah appears in 47 OT passages. In addition, the word appears twice in five of these verses.[205] So in total there are 52 appearances of this name. The application of the word Yah is most commonly found in Hebrew praise statements, particularly in the word halluyah (the English hallelujah), which means "praise ye the LORD." Twenty-four times the expression, "praise ye the LORD" is found in the OT AV. 22 of these passages used the Hebrew word yah, while two verses use the name Yahweh.[206] Indeed these cases demonstrate the intermingling of the name Yahweh and the shortened form Yah and the problem of separating them. Of course, there are other calls to praise not using the word hallelujah.[207]

NAME VARIATIONS:

Variations found among various Scripture versions will be examined now in this study, including the English word JAH and the intermingling of Yah (SRN 3050) and Yahweh (3068). The KJV will be used as the lead Bible or study standard.

---

[205] These multiple appearance passages are Psa. 104:35; Psa. 115:8; 118:5; 150:6; Isa. 38:11. It should also be noted that in Son. 8:6 the SRN 3050 word is translated into the English word vehement. This is of no interest in this study.

[206] See Jdg. 5:2 and Jer. 20:13.

[207] For examples, see II Chr. 20:21; Psa. 33:2; 67:3; Isa. 12:4. All of these verses use the Hebrew word yadah (SRN 3034), a synonym of hallelu.

APPENDIX Chapter 16

Name Variation Chart

Reference	YAH USAGE	KJV	NIV	NAS	JER	NEB
			.			
Psa. 68:4	Yah	JAH	the LORD	the LORD	Yahweh	out
Psa. 77:11	Yah	the LORD	the LORD	the LORD	Yahweh	O LORD
Psa. 89:8	Yah *	O LORD	O LORD	O LORD	Yahweh	O LORD
Psa. 94:7	Yah	the LORD	the LORD	the LORD	Yahweh	the LORD
Psa. 94:12	Yah	O LORD	O LORD	O LORD	Yahweh	O LORD
Psa. 102:18	Yah	the LORD	the LORD	the LORD	Yah	the LORD
Psa. 104:35	Yah 1*	the LORD	the LORD	the LORD	Yahweh	the LORD
Psa. 105:1	Yah	the LORD	the LORD	the LORD	Yahweh	the LORD
Psa. 105:3	Yah	the LORD	the LORD	the LORD	Yahweh	the LORD
Psa. 105:4	Yah	the LORD	the LORD	the LORD	Yahweh	the LORD
Psa. 105:7	Yah	the LORD	the LORD	the LORD	Yahweh	the LORD
Psa. 105:19	Yah	the LORD	the LORD	the LORD's	Yahweh's	the LORD
Psa. 105:21	Yah	lord	master	lord	in charge	master
Psa. 105:45	Yah 1	the LORD	the LORD	the LORD	Yah	the LORD
Psa. 106:1	Yah 1*	the LORD	the LORD	the LORD	Yahweh	the LORD
Psa. 106:48	Yah 1*	the LORD	the LORD	the LORD	Yah	the LORD
Psa. 111:1	Yah 1*	the LORD	the LORD	the LORD	Yah	the LORD
Psa. 112:1	Yah 1*	the LORD	the LORD	the LORD	Yah	the LORD
Psa. 113:1	Yah 1*	the LORD	the LORD	the LORD	Yah	the LORD
Psa. 113:9	Yah 1	the LORD	the LORD	the LORD	Yah	out
Psa. 115:17	Yah	the LORD	the LORD	the LORD	Yahweh	the LORD

Name Variation Chart (Continued)

Reference	YAH	KJV	NIV	NAS	JER	NEB
	USAGE					
Psa. 115:18	Yah 1*2	the LORD	the LORD	the LORD	Yah	the LORD
Psa. 117:2	Yah 1*	the LORD	the LORD	the LORD	Yahweh	the LORD
Psa. 118:5	Yah *2	the LORD	the LORD	the LORD	Yahweh	the LORD
Psa. 118:14	Yah	the LORD	the LORD	the LORD	Yahweh	the LORD
Psa. 118:17	Yah	the LORD	the LORD	the LORD	Yahweh	the LORD
Psa. 118:18	Yah	the LORD	the LORD	the LORD	Yahweh	the LORD
Psa. 118:19	Yah	the LORD	the LORD	the LORD	Yahweh	the LORD
Psa. 122:4	Yah 1*	the LORD	the LORD	the LORD	Yahweh	the LORD
Psa. 130:3	Yah *	the LORD	O LORD	LORD	Yahweh	LORD
Psa. 135:1	Yah 1*	the LORD	the LORD	the LORD	Yah	the LORD
Psa. 135:3	Yah 1*	the LORD	the LORD	the LORD	Yahweh	the LORD
Psa. 135:4	Yah	the LORD	the LORD	the LORD	Yahweh	the LORD
Psa. 135:21	Yah 1*	the LORD	the LORD	the LORD	Yah	the LORD
Psa. 146:1	Yah 1*	the LORD	the LORD	the LORD	Yahweh	the LORD
Psa. 146:10	Yah 1*	the LORD	the LORD	the LORD	Yah	the LORD
Psa. 147:1	Yah 1*	the LORD	the LORD	the LORD	Yahweh	the LORD
Psa. 147:20	Yah 1	the LORD	the LORD	the LORD	Yah	the LORD
Psa. 148:1	Yah 1*	the LORD	the LORD	the LORD	Yahweh	the LORD
Psa. 148:14	Yah 1	the LORD	the LORD	the LORD	Yah	the LORD

Name Variation Chart (Continued)

Reference	YAH	KJV	NIV	NAS	JER	NEB
	USAGE					
Psa. 149:1	Yah 1*	the LORD	the LORD	the LORD	Yahweh	the LORD
Psa. 149:9	Yah 1	the LORD	the LORD	the LORD	Yah	the LORD
Psa. 150:1	Yah 1*	the LORD	the LORD	the LORD	Yahweh	the LORD
Psa. 150:6	Yah 1*2	the LORD	the LORD	the LORD	Yah	the LORD
Isa. 12:2	Yah *	the LORD	the LORD	the LORD	Yahweh	the LORD
Isa. 26:4	Yah *	the LORD	the LORD	GOD	Yahweh	the LORD
Isa. 38:11	Yah *2	the LORD	the LORD	the LORD	Yahweh	the LORD

APPENDIX Chapter 16

Coding and Comments for The Name Variations Chart

Column 1 references the 47 passages containing the contraction Yah. In four of these verses there are also multiple applications of Yah. In addition, certain passages also contain both names Yah and Yahweh (Column 2).

Column 2 The Hebrew contraction of Yahweh (SRN 3068) is Yah (SRN 3050). Even though the full name Yahweh and the contraction Yah are popularly translated into the English as the LORD, the two words coexist and can be separated by their SRN identifiers. Yahweh is regularly transliterated Yahweh and Yah is translated as JAH once in the KJV[208] and as Yah elsewhere. The contraction Yah appears almost exclusively in Hebrew poetry, and it is particularly useful when the word Yahweh appears more than once in a verse; it is a means of producing variety of expression.

Notice in column 2 that certain information is coded either with an asterisk or with a combination of numbers and an asterisk. It is the intent to display by this method the location of the two words Yahweh and the contraction Yah as they relate to each other in given verses. Sometimes a passage will contain both Yahweh and Yah. This is identified with an asterisk. Consider two examples, Psa. 89:8 and 104:35. Both contain the two words and are therefore marked with an asterisk. But Psa. 104:35 is also marked with a number 1 to indicate that this verse contains both words and also

[208] Yah (SRN 3050) is translated JAH in Psa. 68:4.

that the contraction is in the expression Hallelujah. It is to be noticed that many relationships of this type exist in the 47 passages. One other important point...in Psa. 115:18 the Yah is in the expression Hallelujah (coded with a 1) and, further, the name Yah occurs twice in the passage and so the reference is also marked with a 2 (therefore, full coding is 1*2. See verse 150:6).

3. Column 3 Presents the KJV English translation of the name Yah.

4. Columns 4 through 7 present the NIV, NAS, JER and NEB translations.

Regarding "alleluia" especially as found in the JER version (see column 6):

Hebrew usually located the hall^{e}lluya at the end of a Psalm; however, it is common in the JER to find the hall^{e}lluya assigned to the succeeding psalm instead. The initial passage where this happens is preceding PSA 105:1, where the word hallelujah is taken away from the last verse of Psa. 104. There are 17 passages in the Jerusalem Bible in which "alleluia" opens a psalm as listed below.

Psa. 105:1	Psa. 113:1	Psa. 135:1	Psa. 149:1
106:1	114:1	136:1	150:1
107:1	116:1	146:1	
111:1	117:1	147:1	
112:1	118:1	148:1	

Column 2 coding Summary:

An asterisk (*) indicates repetition of the word LORD, translated either from Yah or Yahweh.

A 1 signifies the presence of the expression Hallelujah or in English, "Praise the LORD."

*2 indicates two occurrences of the name Yah in a single passage.

These codings allow in-depth observations about the 47 passages containing the name Yah, yielding more detailed information about the Hebrew text than is possible when an English Bible reads both Yah and Yahweh as LORD.

Remember that as the various translations and editions are compared the purpose of the comparison is to secure Biblical truth first. But the comparison also allows one version to shed light on others, yielding additional meaning and greater clarity through variations in word form—sometimes in the very presence of a divine name. Special idioms and phraseology may be identified by means of such comparisons.

Then, turning attention again to selected examples in the Name Variation Chart, first consider Psa. 68:4. The name Yah is uniquely presented in this passage as JAH in the KJV. The NIV characteristically translates the name Jah to the LORD. The NAS version also applies the well-accepted translation the LORD. The NEB paraphrases the name JAH out of the verse. The JER version sometimes expands JAH to the long form Yahweh. It is obvious that a name search for Yah relying on such information would be hindered, yet Yah is a valid name of deity.

Consider Psa. 77:11. The KJV, NIV, NAS and NEB translate the name Yah by the LORD. Once again the JER replaces Yah with the long form Yahweh.

The problem of identification of the name Yah has a complicating factor in Psa. 89:8. For example, the KJV reads, “O LORD God of hosts, who is a strong LORD like unto thee? Or to thy faithfulness round about thee?” The first phrase contains the address Yahweh Elohim (LORD God). The second phrase contains the question, who is a strong LORD (Yahweh, actually Yah) like unto thee? If the name Yah is the object of the search, then remember that Yah is a shortened form of Yahweh and that it will usually be translated the same as the longer form, Yahweh. Look for Yahweh and check the Hebrew spelling as to the form of the word. It is Yah or Yahweh? Although their presence in the same passage may be indistinguishable in English the Hebrew original is unmistakably clear. In this verse the two specific words Yah and Yahweh appear. So again, the search for the contracted form Yah requires additional effort rather than simple dependence on the English translation. The name Yah occurs most frequently especially in the poetic materials of Psalms and Isaiah.

APPENDIX Chapter 16

In the KJV Psalm 104:35 exhibits a state similar to that in Psa. 89:8. The name LORD in the next to the last sentence, "Bless thou the LORD, O my soul." is translated from the Hebrew Yahweh. The second occurrence of the word LORD in the phrase, "Praise ye the LORD" is translated from the Hebrew Yah. Both Hebrew words are treated as the full form Yahweh, but they are written in Hebrew as two different words. This general circumstance occurs in many OT verses but with slightly different phraseology. For example, in Psa. 106:1 the name the LORD in the phrase "Praise ye the LORD" is translated from the Hebrew Yah. The name LORD in the next phrase, "O give thanks unto the LORD," is translated from the Hebrew Yahweh. This is somewhat confusing, especially when searching for the name Yah, using an English concordance. Usually, however, the Hallelujah phrase occurs alone, without any other supporting phrase or name present. Psa. 105:45; 113:9 and 147:20 are examples.

The phrase "Praise ye the LORD" merits some attention. This Hebrew phrase, transliterated halelluyah, becomes the well-known English "imperative" calling for giving glory to God.

The praise passages involving the name Yah are predominantly in the book of Psalms. However, there are three verses in Isaiah that resort to the name Yah. Isa. 12:2 contains the emphatic expression Yah Yahweh. This occurs again in Isa. 26:4, a double application of the name Yahweh wherein the contraction is used in conjunction with the full form Yahweh to intensify the expression. In Isa. 38:11 a unique double expression is formed, using the contraction Yah twice.

Consideration of columns 3, 4, 5 and 7 clearly illustrate the difficulty of searching for the name Yah in an English concordance. The name is not disguised, as it were. If the English translation is the LORD one must still inquire which name is present in Hebrew. The JER version, shown in Column 6, confounds the Yah/Yahweh usage in the OT. The Hebrew name Yahweh is regularly transliterated as Yahweh. The contraction Yah also is presented as Yahweh. The separation of the two names Yah and Yahweh becomes a problem for the student who uses that version to resolve.

Particular Aspects Highlighted:

It has been the custom in these studies to consider the aspects of God highlighted by His names, but in this final chapter it is realized that the significance of Yahweh and Yah have been under consideration from the very opening of Chapter 1. A thorough review will only begin to highlight the marvelous aspects of God's character. He is, all in all, manifesting His character through His works to all mankind. He is God whether we address Him as Elohim or God, Yahweh, or Yah, the Lord or the LORD. The puny efforts of man to describe the aspects of His character or His attributes go wanting—but we can praise Him. How appropriate are the Hallelujahs we sing to Him!

The Old Testament Names of God

A Perspective

Chapter 17

Contents

Summary:

With the completion of Chapter 16 we come to the end of our studies of the Names of God in the Old Testament. The original plan to list the many names of God in the OT has been achieved and the results entered in this unique Perspective. The first concept of this effort envisioned only a very limited listing of names of deity, perhaps including just the 8 names now entered in Chapter 3. However, that project grew, developing a manuscript that not only lists the names of God in the OT but also includes arguments as to the whys of the acceptance (or rejection) of the candidate, the purpose of the particular name application and a statement as to the identity of the Person of the Godhead being addressed.

The original plan has developed into a study covering 208 names and reflects the blessings of a name study extending over 11 years.

In this Perspective, the 208 candidate names are arranged in alphabetical order and contain 202 authenticated appellations as well as 6 examples of names removed from the smooth information flow because of faulty or questionable accreditation.

For example, consider in Chapter 8, the proposed stand alone term "Great." This word can be used in either a qualitative or quantitative relationship. The word used in a quantitative sense is not applied as a name of God in the OT. But in qualitative applications such as "great is the LORD" or "thou are great O LORD" there is a possibility that the word "great" describes an attribute of God and therefore qualifies as a name of deity. However, for this word to formulate a metaphor the word Great has to be a noun, but it is always an adjective. Because of the existing controversy over the application of this word, in this manuscript the word "great" is not accepted as a name of God. However, it certainly is worth thinking about, illustrating the point that the detail of invalidated candidates are not to be forgotten.

Another interesting example of variation in the appellation argument is also in Chapter 8 where the compound phrase "Hope of Israel" is proposed as a Scripturally supported compound name. In this case the variation has to do with capitalization of proper nouns especially in the basic KJV version. The fact that the KJV fails to support the compound with capital letter tends to weaken the argument that the phrase is an appellation of God. However, there is sufficient support material in other Scripture versions to encourage the acceptance of the phrase "Hope of Israel" in this manuscript. This argument is shown to demonstrate the study detail applied even on a proposed non-KJV candidate.

Consider another anomalous condition. In Chapter 5 the word "crown" in the form Crown of Glory or Glorious Crown is proposed as an appellation. But in the argument presentation of this word, we observe some differences of opinion in Scripture version applications. We also have found that some current presenters differ in accepting the word as an appellation. But in spite of some arguments that the word might not be a name, this manuscript accepts the word crown as a name with further investigation left to the reader.

There is a different name identification problem demonstrated in the Sixteenth Chapter. The word stronghold as the more modern versions present this word is compared to the older spelling strong hold. It is easy to see that the KJV version used as the basic study version would have yielded quite different results in the location of the proposed appellation. If the term is spelled stronghold in place of strong hold. Indeed, the word, and possible name, may not be found at all when applying current state-of-the-art computer methods in the search techniques.

Then, in Chapter 13, the term "Mighty" is considered. It became clear early in the consideration that the word "Mighty" is always an adjective and never a stand alone noun or name of God.

Finally, let us consider the candidate appellation "shepherd." Although this term is used in many places in the OT in a manner clearly applying it as a name of God, there seems to be some confusion accepting the word "shepherd" as a name of deity. We first encounter the term speaking of God as the "Shepherd", the stone of Israel (Gen. 49:24). The same word for shepherd appears in Psa. 23:1—the LORD is my Shepherd. In Psa. 80:1 the LORD is addressed as the Shepherd of Israel again applying the same Hebrew word <u>ro'eh</u> for Shepherd. In Isaiah 40:11 we find the shepherd feeding His flock, speaking figuratively of the LORD caring for His own people. So with these examples speaking figuratively of the LORD acting as the Shepherd in mind, we examine the Ezekiel 34:11-15 verses where the LORD is clearly described as the Shepherd concluding with "...I will feed my flock saith...the Lord God." Perhaps a more meaningful rendered is "...I will Shepherd my flock..." for Yahweh is called "the Shepherd" that is His name. Not only is He referred to as Shepherd in the Ezekiel verses but the same word ro'eh is applied in the other verses referenced above in a manner that allows the meaning shepherd to be transferred to the Ezekiel verses.

The entries in the Tabulation Contents contain 202 validated appellations. However the possibilities that still other names should be added to this list is real. It is a reasonable assumption that additional 'el compounds will yet be located. Additional "of—(genitive)" names may also be added to other perspectives. It is strongly recommended that the reader continue the study achieving some of the greatest of blessings studying His Name...

TABULATION CONTENTS

Finally consider the summary list of the observed titles and appellations. The entries can be tabulated in several ways that affect the count. Overall there is a total of 208 entries. This quantity includes both the El and the Elohim near duplicate names (20 pair). For example, "Living God" can be translated from either el chay, elohim chay or eloah chay. However, if we allow only a single name count regardless of whether the name is compounded with either El or Elohim, then the total observed members of this list is 198. Removing the unaccredited names (6 in number) remakes the 198 sum to 192.

Now turn particular attention to the observed collection of titles and appellations called the Tabulation Contents. Here is displayed the names, titles or appellations of God observed during the preparation of this Perspective. The collection also indicates the alphabetically arranged contents showing the manuscript page location of the name of interest as well as the Scripture reference. A running summary of the quantity of names and titles is also supplied for convenience.

The Godhead names are displayed in both English and Hebrew. This means that the term God may be identified merely as the English word God. However, the various Hebrew names from which the English word God is translated, is also shown. For example, there is God(Elohim, SRN 430); God(El, SRN 410) and God (Eloah, SRN 426). Then there is lord(Adon, SRN 113); Lord(Adonay, SRN 136) and LORD(Yahweh,

SRN 3068). It will be observed that some compound names are formed with an epithet being attached to one or more of the basic names of God. Living God may be written Living God(El) or Living God(Elohim) or Living God (Eloah). These occurrences are indicated in names tabulation with the marking (+).

TABULATION CONTENTS (Continued)

TABULATION CONTENTS (Continued)

025	Psa. 2:4	God(Adonay) (6; 29)	
026	Gen. 31:13	God(El) of Bethel (356)	
027	Gen. 14:18	God(El) (3; 29)	
028	Psa. 114:7	God(Eloah) (3; 29)	
029	Gen. 1:1	God(Elohim) (29)	
030	1sa. 17:45	God(Elohim) of Armies of Israel (356)	
031	Psa. 86:15	God(El Full of Compassion (306)	
032	Dan. 6:26	God(Eloah) of Daniel (342)	
033	2Ki. 20:5	God(Elohim) of David (342)	
034	Isa. 54:5	God(Elohim) of the whole Earth (24)	
035	Gen. 24:3	God(Elohim of the earth (356)	
036	2Ki. 2:14	God(Elohim) of Elijah(342)	
037	Gen. 46:1	God(Elohim) of his Father (346)	
038	Gen. 31:53	God(Elohim) of my Father (346)	
039	Deu. 26:7	God(Elohim) of our Father (346)	
040	Gen. 31:53	God(Elohim) of their Father (346)	
041	Gen. 46:3	God(El) of thy Father (346)	
042	Exo. 3:13	God(Elohim) of your Father (346)	
043	Psa. 89:7	God(El) to be Feared (306)	
044	Jer. 32:27	God(Elohim) of All Flesh (346; 24)	
045	Psa. 99:8	God(El) that forgives (30b)	
046	Isa. 45:18	God(Elohim) former of the earth (24)	
047	Dan. 11:36	God(El) of gods(El) (306)	+
048	Deu. 10:17	God(Elohim) of gods(elohims) (306)	+

TABULATION CONTENTS (Continued)

TABULATION CONTENTS (Contents)

TABULATION CONTENTS (Continued)

TABULATION CONTENTS (Contents)

TABULATION CONTENTS (Continued)

TABULATION CONTENTS (Continued)

TABULATION CONTENTS (Continued)